School of American Research
Advanced Seminar Series

DOUGLAS W. SCHWARTZ, GENERAL EDITOR

SCHOOL OF AMERICAN RESEARCH BOOKS

The Pottery of Santo Domingo Pueblo
KENNETH CHAPMAN

The Pottery of San Ildefonso Pueblo
KENNETH CHAPMAN

A Colony on the Move:
Gaspar Castaño de Sosa's Journal,
1590-1591
ALBERT H. SCHROEDER AND DAN S. MATSON

Reconstructing Prehistoric Pueblo Societies
EDITED BY WILLIAM A. LONGACRE

Reconstructing Prehistoric
Pueblo Societies

Reconstructing Prehistoric Pueblo Societies

EDITED BY
WILLIAM A. LONGACRE

A SCHOOL OF AMERICAN RESEARCH BOOK

UNIVERSITY OF NEW MEXICO PRESS · Albuquerque

Preface

The second in a series of advanced seminars, sponsored by the School of American Research, was held April 9-13, 1968 in Santa Fe, New Mexico. The topic was prehistoric Pueblo social organization.

Nine scholars from the United States and Canada participated: William A. Longacre (Department of Anthropology, University of Arizona); David F. Aberle (Department of Sociology and Anthropology, University of British Columbia); Jeffrey S. Dean (Laboratory of Tree-Ring Research, University of Arizona); Edward P. Dozier (Department of Anthropology, University of Arizona); James N. Hill (Department of Anthropology, University of California at Los Angeles); William Lipe (Department of Anthropology, State University of New York at Binghamton); Paul S. Martin (Department of Anthropology, Chicago Natural History Museum); R. Gwinn Vivian (Arizona State Museum, University of Arizona); and Douglas W. Schwartz (School of American Research, Santa Fe).

Six papers were prepared in advance of the seminar, forming the basis for discussion during the five-day seminar. The revised papers and statements from the discussants form the basis for this volume.

The focus of the seminar was on the methodology and theory for achieving strong inferences about the nature of social organization in extinct

Puebloan societies. Prehistorians, of course, have long been concerned with organizational and behavorial aspects of past peoples. Only in recent years, however, have systematic attempts to test hypotheses about prehistoric social organization been carried out using appropriate data recovered from archaeological sites.

The concern with social organization here reflects a larger trend in archaeology, stressing the recovery of pertinent data for the testing of hypotheses about many aspects of extinct cultural systems. This recent tend is the result of a shift from a basically inductive approach to prehistory to a more explicitly deductive approach. This requires a great deal of attention to research design and the development of test implications for the alternative hypotheses that an investigator may be interested in testing. The approach is healthy, scientifically, and we feel it will ultimately lead to stronger inferences about the past. Perhaps most important, the inferences resulting from this approach will be testable upon independent archaeological data, giving us an objective way to evaluate our conclusions.

The topic of our advanced seminar revives an earlier explicit interest in prehistoric Puebloan social organization by archaeologists and merges with a long-standing interest by cultural anthropologists. The lack of archaeological research into the nature of social organization in the Southwest seems to be the result of an a priori decision by the prehistorians working in the Southwest that such a nonobservable phenomenon as social organization cannot be recovered from an archaeological site. The seminar contradicts that decision.

The results of recent research designed to explore the nature of social organization in the prehistoric Southwest are indeed encouraging. At the same time they are not earth-shaking and are clearly rather crude. We recognize both the smallness of our success to date and the great potential that such research has for the future. The participants in the advanced seminar hope that these papers and the discussion will reflect some of that potential and will stimulate increased research into the behavorial and organizational aspects of extinct societies in the Southwest and elsewhere as well.

The participants in the seminar are grateful to Douglas W. Schwartz, director, and the members of the board of directors of the School of American Research. They provided the opportunity for us to take part in a most rewarding and stimulating seminar. In addition, their hospitality made our stay in Santa Fe a most enjoyable experience. We are also grateful to Mrs. Ella Schroeder and Mrs. Douglas Schwartz for their helpful assistance and extreme patience with us during our five days in Santa Fe.

William A. Longacre

University of Arizona

Contents

Preface   vii

Illustrations   xi

1. A Historical Review   1
   WILLIAM A. LONGACRE

2. Prehistoric Social Organization in the American Southwest:
   Theory and Method   11
   JAMES N. HILL

3. An Inquiry into Prehistoric Social Organization in
   Chaco Canyon, New Mexico   59
   R. GWINN VIVIAN

4. Anasazi Communities in the Red Rock Plateau,
   Southeastern Utah   84
   WILLIAM D. LIPE

5. Aspects of Tsegi Phase Social Organization:
   A Trial Reconstruction   140
   JEFFREY S. DEAN

6. The Postmigration Culture:
   A Base for Archaeological Inference   175
   DOUGLAS W. SCHWARTZ

7. Explanation as an Afterthought and as a Goal   194
   PAUL S. MARTIN

8. Making Inferences from the Present to the Past   202
   EDWARD P. DOZIER

9. Comments   214
   DAVID F. ABERLE

References   225

Index   245

Illustrations

1. Pueblo del Arroyo, a Chaco town   63
2. Chaco town sites   70
3. Pueblo Alto Water Control System   71
4. Glen Canyon area   89
5. Topography of Red Rock Plateau   90
6. Distribution of White Dog phase components   96
7. Distribution of Klethla phase components   105
8. Distribution of Horsefly Hollow phase components   106
9. Characteristics of Klethla and Horsefly Hollow phase sites
    (a) Lake Canyon and Wilson Canyon areas   107
    (b) Moqui Canyon and Lake Canyon areas   108
    (c) Upper Glen Canyon, Upper Castle Wash, and
       Forgotten Canyon areas   109
10. Summary of site characteristics by area   110
11. Tree-ring indices from Mesa Verde   113
12. Tsegi phase room clusters   156
13. Betatakin floor plan   158
14. Kiet Siel ground plans
    (a) A.D. 1271   160
    (b) A.D. 1275   160
    (c) A.D. 1282   162
    (d) A.D. 1286   162

A Historical Review

WILLIAM A. LONGACRE

Department of Anthropology,
University of Arizona

My purpose in this brief essay is not to present a history of South-western archaeology. Rather, the focus is upon attempts over the past 100 years or so at reconstructing social organization in the prehistoric Pueblo area. I have tried to identify research trends at various periods during the past century in an effort to place modern research directed toward the reconstruction of prehistoric Pueblo society into perspective.

To do this, I have adopted the periods proposed by Taylor (1954). The beginnings of systematic investigations in the Southwest go back to the latter portion of the nineteenth century. Taylor describes this period as the "Cushing-Fewkes" era, and it brackets the third of a century roughly from 1880-1915. Prior to this time, there was little systematic research in the Southwest. Before 1820, ruins were noted and described intermit-tently, but it was not until the 40 years before the Civil War that the rich archaeological resources of the area became well known (Brandes 1960).

Following the Civil War, a variety of factors combined to set the stage for the beginnings of rigorous anthropological investigations in the Southwest. Some of these include the advent of rail transportation in the area, the subduing of hostile tribal groups such as the Navajo and Apache, and the presence in the East of individuals trained in the youthful science of anthropology, along with the initial appearance of institutions devoted to the study of man and his cultures.

Taylor has labeled the beginning of scientific investigations in the Southwest the "Cushing-Fewkes Period," and he characterizes it as reflecting a basic concern with connecting living Pueblo peoples to the prehistoric past (1954: 561). He also notes (ibid.) that during this era there was considerable confusion about the complexity of Southwest prehistory and a lack of concern with temporal placement of archaeological sites. Equally important, I feel, is that the investigators tended to be general anthropologists, equally concerned with ethnology, linguistics, and archaeology. Cushing viewed archaeology as simply ethnology projected back into the past (1890: 160).

The living Pueblos were seen as surviving examples of a broad single culture that enjoyed great antiquity. The idea of a homogeneous culture in the Southwest was widely held (Hewett 1905: 586); Cushing referred to it as Original Pueblo or "Shiwian" (1890: 157) and suggested that this broad cultural pattern could be extended to Mexico, Central America, and even to Peru (1890: 190-93). Since the prehistoric cultures were broadly similar to the modern Pueblos, one could interpret prehistoric societies by direct analogy to the living peoples.

Given these assumptions, it was logical to turn to the living societies themselves to understand their history. Oral history and especially migration legends were viewed as important, basic data for the scholar interested in interpreting the prehistoric ruins of the Southwest. Intensive collecting of myths and legends was carried out by Fewkes at Hopi and Cushing at Zuni.

But mythology was not to be the solution to the interpretation of prehistoric ruins. It quickly became obvious that there were inconsistencies and vagueness in the oral accounts of tribal history which had to be resolved. The directions of wandering in the migration legends were vague, as were all points of geographic reference. Each clan had a slightly varying version of their own movements. Even so, anthropologists viewed these data as significant historical clues which could be clarified and verified through archaeology.

A Historical Review

In a major publication of Hopi migration texts, Fewkes suggested that, "It is published as an aid to the archaeologist who may need traditions to guide him in the identification of the ruins of northern Arizona . . ." (1900: 578). He argued that archaeology holds the key to solving the problems that the inconsistencies in the myths raised (1896: 152). Perhaps the most systematic attempt to correlate mythological evidence and archaeology was Fewkes' survey of the Verde Valley and the area near the Hopi villages (Fewkes 1898).

Other workers in the Southwest during this period were also convinced that mythology could be combined with archaeological research to reveal a reasonably accurate history of the living Pueblos. Cosmos and Victor Mindeleff used myths and ethnographic analogy to interpret archaeological sites (cf. Mindeleff 1891: 15; 1898: 120; 1900: 645). Cushing used information in Zuni myths to present a series of hypotheses regarding the prehistoric background of the Zuni people (1896: 343, 361-73). Bandelier, too, attempted to tie prehistory to the historic groups through myth and tradition (cf. Lange and Riley 1966: 3).

Concern with the history of Pueblo peoples such as the Zuni and Hopi, along with the assumptions regarding the direct descent of these groups from the inhabitants of prehistoric Pueblo ruins and the homogeneity of Pueblo culture, permitted speculation about organization of the extinct societies of the area. At least the outlines of Pueblo social organization were becoming clear, and the ethnologists could begin asking historical questions about the development of Pueblo society in the Southwest. Direct analogy to the Zuni and Hopi could readily be invoked to interpret Pueblo ruins.

One of the important problems facing investigators during this era was the need to explain the apparent shift from small scattered settlements to fewer, larger towns. Mindeleff (1900) argued that defense from Athabaskan raiders forced the amalgamation of smaller villages into larger towns. He speculated that descent units such as clans were originally localized residence groups within these larger villages (ibid.). Fewkes noted the same pattern (1911a: 12; 1919: 70-75) and argued that the small settlements were occupied by basic social units such as a clan and that the fusion into larger towns created a number of changes in social organization:

Clans or social units at first isolated later joined each other, intermarriage always tending to make the population more homogeneous.

3

. . . The inevitable outcome would be a breaking down of clan priesthoods or clan religions and the formation of fraternities of priesthoods recruited from several clans (1919: 75-76).

Thus, Fewkes argued that the sodalities were a later development in the Puebloan Southwest and appeared with the amalgamation of several clans; he suggested that a decreasing proportion of kivas to rooms through time would support this suggestion (1911b: 79-80; 1919: 76).

Matrilocal postmarital residence rules were inferred to be present in the prehistoric past from analogy with the Zuni and Hopi. Matrilocality was used to explain the irregular ground plan in many ruins (Mindeleff 1898: 120-21). Hewett (1908: 99) presented two models based on analogy to explain ruins with a regular ground plan in contrast to those with irregular outlines. He argued that the arrival of a social group and the construction of a large block of rooms adjoining an existing pueblo could be spotted in the ruins with regular plans. In contrast, ruins with irregular plans that seemed to have been enlarged gradually through the construction of additional rooms with no apparent plan revealed normal population expansion and the effects of matrilocal residence patterns (ibid.).

The basic unit of social organization of the living Pueblos was seen to be the "clan" (Cushing 1896: 368). It was logical, therefore, to assume that such was the case in prehistoric times as well (Cummings 1910: 30). It was of great concern to identify these basic social units in the prehistoric ruins to understand the development of the historic clans (Bandelier 1881: 126-27; Mindeleff 1891: 104). Kivas were viewed as important indicators of localized clans as well as reflecting relatively permanent residence (Mindeleff 1897: 197-98; Fewkes 1917: 469, 1911a: 24; Cummings 1910: 24). Morgan had suggested that an analysis of the patterns of doorways and partition walls in Southwestern ruins might also be used to identify groups of related families (1965: 207-08).

Some of the questions being asked during this era have a fairly modern tone. It was an interesting period, characterized by great concern over the reconstruction of extinct Pueblo societies and the history of living Pueblo peoples. Research was made relatively uncomplicated by the adoption of assumptions such as the homogeneous nature of Pueblo culture, past and present. Subsequent archaeological work rejected many of the basic assumptions held during this period and dismissed as "useless speculation" ideas of early workers about the nature of prehistoric Pueblo societies.

From the point of view of the 1960s, this rejection seems unfortunate indeed. Many interesting ideas were put forth regarding changes in residence composition, mechanisms of social integration, and other facets of sociocultural change. Had research continued through subsequent decades, perhaps means for testing some of these interesting hypotheses might have been developed. But a revolution occurred in Southwestern archaeology in the second decade of the twentieth century that was to preclude such interests.

Taylor (1954: 563) refers to the great change in Southwestern archaeology around 1915 as the "Time-Space Revolution." The concern was for facts. Basic research quickly demolished the uncomplicated view of prehistoric Pueblo culture, and concern about chronology quickly developed. Speculation was rejected as unscientific and was replaced with the careful gathering of factual data. Workers such as Kidder, Nelson, Morris, Colton, and Spier dominate this era. Basic chronological techniques such as seriation, stratigraphy, and cross-dating were applied.

Culture history, strongly influenced by culture-area theory, and the view of culture as a thing of "shreds and patches" dominated the archaeology of this period. Prehistoric cultures were described and defined on the basis of trait lists. But the traits, to be usable, had to be objectively and scientifically observable. Aspects of prehistoric cultures that were not directly observable in the archaeological record could not be included. I feel this is an extremely important period in the history of Southwestern archaeology as it set the tone of essentially all of the work for the next several decades and even into the present period.

The identification of prehistoric "cultures" as constellations of culture traits that were primarily defined stylistically and the placement of these "cultures" in time and space became the mainstay of Southwestern archaeology. Taylor has called this development the "fill-in-the-gaps" attitude (1954: 566). The period from roughly 1915 to 1950 was a most productive one in the Southwest. Great amounts of research were conducted, and the complex outlines of Southwestern prehistory gradually emerged. The details of these developments are relatively well known, and I will not repeat them here.

Let me simply emphasize what appear to me to be important trends. As I have noted, sociological reconstruction was relegated to the domain of speculation and, as such, did not belong to scientific studies. The anthropological theory that guided archaeological research from 1915 on was culture-area and trait inventory theory of the culture historical "school"

5

(Greenberg 1968: 310-11). Even though great changes were wrought in cultural anthropology during the 30s and 40s, resulting from the impact of structural-functional, cultural ecological, and cultural evolutionary theory, no great changes are observable in the archaeological research during this period in the Southwest.

During this time, mythology as an aid to the archaeologist was largely abandoned. Various workers were able to demonstrate the inaccuracy of legend as a tool for culture history (Roberts 1931: 9; Hargrave 1931; Kidder 1962: 160). Only occasionally during this period is mythology invoked to support archaeological inference (Colton 1932a: 23, 1933, 1936; Reagan 1920: 387-88). There is virtually no concern on the part of the archaeologists with reconstructing Pueblo social organization during this period.

But concern with the development of Pueblo societies did not entirely disappear from Southwestern studies. It was the cultural anthropologists who continued to speculate about the development of social institutions and other nonmaterial aspects of Pueblo culture. Hypotheses were presented that might have been tested, but they seem to have been largely ignored. Strong (1927: 54) presented a series of propositions regarding the development of lineages and clans in the Pueblo area.

The most explicit statement on the evolution of Pueblo society was formulated by Steward (1937) in a series of hypotheses involving the ecological aspects of the development of culture in the Southwest. But that same year, the anthropological world was warned that, "At best, reconstruction of prehistory is dangerous, in that consideration of every item of culture make-up is necessary for valid conclusions, and yet our only data on ancient social organization and its history must come from modern peoples" (Hawley 1937a: 506).

Southwestern archaeologists continued to ignore, for the most part, the suggestions by cultural anthropologists regarding the nature of societal development in the Southwest (Haury 1956: 3). But the publication of Taylor's monograph, A Study of Archaeology, in 1948 along with Kluckhohn's earlier constructive criticism (1940) dramatically changed the direction of developments in Southwestern archaeology. Taylor's scathing review, highlighting the lack of concern for nonmaterial cultural developments, produced almost instant reaction.

For the first time in more than 40 years, we see a chapter of an archaeological monograph devoted to the reconstruction of social organization (Martin and Rinaldo 1950: 556-69). Arguing from changes in settlement

A Historical Review

patterns, house sizes, numbers of metates per house, and other data, Martin and Rinaldo (ibid.) were able to present inferences on the development of social organization in the Mogollon area. Their efforts led them to conclude their argument with a philosophical observation. "Some may say that it is too soon to make such reconstructions, that enough data are not yet collected. If one doesn't start to collect such data, one may overlook material or information which may subsequently assume a greater importance and no longer be available for study" (ibid.: 569).

In my opinion, this is an astute observation, and it points out another important trend in Southwestern archaeology prior to 1950. The overriding concern with objective scientific investigations, I feel, was based in the assumption that one could excavate a site and, through careful record keeping, recover all the facts in an unbiased manner. The view seems to have been held that one collected one's data essentially in a theoretical "vacuum," and the facts, once assembled, would "speak for themselves" (cf. Kluckhohn 1940). The attempt by Martin and Rinaldo (1950) to ask questions of their data that were not in their minds when these data were collected underscored the fallacy of the assumption that "the facts would speak for themselves."

The year 1950 was important in Southwestern studies. A number of papers were published that attempted to reconstruct the culture history of various Puebloan societies, with emphasis upon nonmaterial organizational developments (Hawley 1950a; Reed 1950; Eggan 1950; Martin and Rinaldo 1950). Eggan's monograph (1950: 123-33) is perhaps the most explicit and presents a refinement of Steward's hypotheses (1937) involving the evolution of western Pueblo society. Eggan's statement is important because it not only presents rather detailed hypotheses of the development of Puebloan society, but it also hints at generalizations about the nature of social organization in a cultural system adapting to its total environment. Clearly, it was for the archaeologists to take these hypotheses to the field and to design research to test their validity.

But this was not to be the case. Eggan's reconstruction was received by Southwesterners as a positive contribution with little suggested revision (for example, Ellis 1951). Eggan argued that the potential for the archaeologist to make strong inferences regarding the development of social institutions through field research was great (1952: 38). But the hypotheses he presented (1950: 123-33) quickly became the framework by which prehistorians interpreted their data.

7

During this period, the concept of "settlement pattern" had been adopted by Southwestern archaeologists as a tool for sociological inference. But changing settlement patterns in the Puebloan area were interpreted in terms of the hypotheses presented by such workers as Steward and Eggan (cf. Haury 1956: 9). Statements of culture history began to appear that sound strangely like those made by Fewkes and others in an earlier era: "There is no evidence as to whether the lineages evident in the earlier unit pueblos survived the consolidation into larger communities and hence became clans, as among the Chaco Anasazi, unless the multiple Great Kivas can be inferred to represent such a social organization" (Wendorf 1956: 25).

Archaeological contributions to the reconstruction of social organization during the 1950s included comprehensive and cautious studies of various kinds of data that led to refinements of Steward's and Eggan's hypotheses (for example, Bluhm 1957: 151-71). Relatively uncautious statements also appeared, reporting the nature of societal developments and the possibility of diffusion of such forms of organization as the "lineage system" (Wendorf 1956: 24). Cultural anthropologists were pleased with the interest expressed by archaeologists in reconstructing social organization, but they urged caution and testing hypotheses in the field (for example, Dozier 1965). But perhaps one of the most important developments of the 1950s was the conviction on the part of Southwestern archaeologists that "inference as to the non-material aspects of archaeological groups must be as much a part of our reports as is the description of architecture and pottery" (Haury 1956: 10).

Perhaps it is too early to attempt a discussion of trends in research devoted to the reconstruction of social organization of the present decade. But I believe such trends are discernible and reflect a major shift in the nature of such research in the Southwest.

On the one hand, interest continues in the current period in the culture history of Puebloan societies. Some workers continue to feel that the most important data for getting at the nature of culture and social organization of the "distant past" will come from a careful analysis of present-day social systems (Ellis 1964: 9). It is argued that uncovering the basic structure of modern Pueblo society will provide indications of the more stable and, therefore, more ancient aspects of social institutions. These data, in combination with the findings of archaeology, linguistics, physical anthropology, and the traditions of verbal history, are seen as the key for unraveling the complexities of culture history and the development of social organization (ibid.).

On the other hand, a trend seems to be developing that emphasizes the discovery of generalizations regarding the evolution of cultural systems, using the Southwest as an optimum laboratory for such research. Culture history is not viewed as the ultimate end of such research but more as a by-product. Testable hypotheses are taken to the field and structure basic research. The aim of such studies is to control the nature of cultural systems within their environmental context and the processes of cultural stability and change that operated in the past.

The basic goal of such research, then, is to contribute to our understanding of the nature of culture and of culture processes. Culture is viewed as the means by which human populations adapt to their total environment, both natural surroundings and other human populations. As such, it is explicitly cultural evolutionary in emphasis. Since one of the most basic adaptive mechanisms in a cultural system is the social organization, great emphasis has been placed on research leading to the elucidation of social institutions. This research trend in the Southwest has been largely spearheaded by Martin and his colleagues, reflected in recent work conducted in east-central Arizona.

One of the primary emphases has been upon the demonstration of organizational and behavioral aspects of extinct societies. These research efforts have been conducted within a context of archaeological theory developed by Binford and his colleagues, the details of which are presented by Hill in this volume and will not be repeated here. Thus far, the results of such research have been encouraging. Such aspects of extinct Puebloan societies as the presence of villages made up of residence groups practicing matrilocal residence patterns in the Southwest by A.D. 1100 have been indicated (Longacre 1963, 1964a, 1968; Hill 1966, 1970; Martin, Longacre, and Hill 1967). Changing patterns of social integration mechanisms have been explored (Longacre 1966). Functional variability in pueblo rooms has been tested (Freeman and Brown 1964; Hill 1968, 1970). It seems clear that at least some of the assumptions about the nature of societies that occupied the Pueblo ruins in the Southwest which are based upon analogy with the modern Pueblo societies can now be tested (Eggan 1966: 136; Martin 1967).

The 1960s appear to reflect a continuation in trends established in the previous decades, as well as the appearance of new directions of research.

9

The concern with reconstructing social organization which typifies the 1950s continues into the present period. This is reflected in the work of Martin and his colleagues in the Vernon area as well as in the research of many others. For example, Rohn (1965) has attempted to define socioeconomic groups in the Mesa Verde area. Speculation on the nature of social organization is not uncommon in site reports (for example, Dittert, Hester, and Eddy 1961: 234). Ethnologists continue to present reconstructions of social organization both in historical (Ellis 1964) and processual (McFeat 1960; Dozier 1960) terms.

The appearance of new trends of research in the 1960s represents a marked departure from the method and theory that characterize Southwestern archaeology after 1915. This is not to say that the new directions of research are totally divorced from past work. Obviously, the new kinds of questions that are being asked are being generated within the context of relatively good chronological controls and a fairly complete knowledge of the style zones of the prehistoric Southwest.

The departure from the method and theory of traditional Southwestern archaeology is not inconsistent with the fact that great use is being made of the results of earlier research. But major differences should be made explicit. The new research directions are not "building" on past work in the sense of refining it or carrying it to a new climax.

Perhaps the most important differences in method and theory are (1) the great concern with testing and a desire to approach demonstration and (2) the importance of ecology for explanation in contrast to diffusion. Along with these would be included the major shift in theory from a "normative" point of view to a systemic approach to the study of culture.

Recent studies would seem to indicate that reconstruction of social organization, especially in a context of processual-explanatory theory, will continue to be an important trend in Southwestern studies. Such a prediction may be made even though a major synthesis of Southwestern prehistory recently published fails to mention social organization (McGregor 1965). The papers that follow would appear to support such a prognosis.

Prehistoric Social Organization in the American Southwest: Theory and Method

JAMES N. HILL

Department of Anthropology,
University of California
at Los Angeles

INTRODUCTION

For a number of years archaeologists have been educated to believe that very little can be learned about prehistoric social organization. We are taught that the structural or organizational aspects of extinct societies are, unlike material remains, "intangible" and hence unrecoverable. Because the organizations themselves no longer exist, it is assumed that to make inferences about them is to indulge in speculation (which is unscientific). Most students are imbued with this viewpoint long before they become professional anthropologists, and they come to believe it as an axiom. A number of formal expositions have been published on this point of view, with the suggestion that it is possible to set fairly clear limits on the kinds of inferences that archaeologists can reasonably make (cf. Rouse 1953; Smith 1955; Thompson 1956; MacWhite 1956; Ascher 1961; Hole and Heizer 1965: 225).

While there are some variations in this general argument, the basic tenet is that many aspects of prehistoric behavior do not leave material remains; and even if such remains are left, they are subject to the vagaries of preservation. M. A. Smith (1955: 6-7) puts it this way:

It has to be acknowledged that there is no logical relation between human activity in some of its aspects and the evidence left for the archaeologist. Accordingly there are real and insuperable limits to what can legitimately be inferred from archaeological material. . . . Since historical events and the essential social divisions of prehistoric peoples don't find an adequate expression in material remains, it cannot be right to try to arrive at a knowledge of them in archaeological interpretation. A recognition that archaeological evidence, when it is confined to material remains, demonstrably supports only a limited range of conclusions about human activity is incompatible with too ambitious a programme for archaeology.

In short, the kinds of inferences we may make are limited by the nature of the data recovered—the kinds and numbers of materials that are preserved. It is thus "dangerous" to make inferences beyond the artifacts themselves. Some statements are so pessimistic as to suggest that "our only data on ancient social organization . . . must come from modern peoples" (Hawley 1937a: 506; see also Ascher 1961; Chang 1967).

Largely because of the perpetuation of these points of view, it has been difficult to develop a theoretical and methodological framework that will permit the satisfactory elucidation of prehistoric organizations. At the same time, archaeologists have been interested in making sociological inferences, and a number of scholars have decried the paucity of such efforts (Taylor 1948; Haury 1956; Willey and Phillips 1958; Sears 1961). The problem is that we have not known how to go about it. There have, of course, been some notable contributions along these lines, although most of them have been restricted to examination of the gross outlines of settlement pattern, ceremonial organization, mortuary practices, craft specialization, and social status (Sears 1961).

In the American Southwest (as elsewhere), many of the inferences about prehistoric social organization have been made by ethnologists (Haury 1956; see especially Hawley 1937a; Steward 1937, 1938; Titiev 1944; Eggan 1950; Dozier 1965). While archaeologists have also contributed, their inferences have usually been based on these statements. Nonetheless, it is evident that Southwestern archaeologists have shown an increasing interest in the organizational aspects of prehistoric societies, and this is reflected in a number of inferential and programmatic statements in the literature (for example, Hawley 1937a, 1950; Ellis 1951; Martin and Rinaldo 1950; Haury 1956; Jennings 1956; Reed 1956; Wendorf 1956; DiPeso 1958; Bluhm 1960; Martin et al. 1962).

In the last few years (since about 1960), with the increasing acceptance of "systems archaeology,"[1] there have been a number of even more fruitful and exciting contributions to the study of prehistoric social organization in the Southwest. Freeman and Brown (1964) and Hill (1966, 1968, 1970), for example, have demonstrated functional (use) variability among rooms in pueblo sites; Longacre (1963, 1964a, 1964b), Hill (1966, 1970) and Martin, Longacre, and Hill (1967) have tentatively demonstrated the existence of uxorilocal residence in the Southwest by at least A.D. 1100, as well as certain changes in social-unit composition of pueblo villages through time. Rohn (1965) has found good evidence to suggest the locations of social units at Mug House on Wetherill Mesa. And Longacre (1966) may even have demonstrated the existence of intrasite exchange (reciprocity). A number of other contributions, though outside the Southwest, include those by Deetz (1960, 1965), Binford and Binford (1966, 1968), and others. Longacre's paper (this volume) presents a more thorough consideration of past efforts toward elucidating prehistoric social organization in the Southwest.

I should point out, however, that almost all of the inferences made with regard to prehistoric social organization (and other inferences as well) have shortcomings in the nature and degree of demonstration. Most of our inferences, as a matter of fact, are not demonstrations at all; they are hypotheses or propositions that are often presented as fact, but are left untested. This is a situation that is applicable to most of the social sciences, of course, and the problem has been succinctly stated by a noted philosopher of science (Wilson 1952: 26-27):

> The most important feature about a hypothesis or proposition is that it is a mere trial idea. . . . Unfortunately, in many fields, especially on the border lines of science, hypotheses are often accepted without adequate tests. Plausibility is not a substitute for evidence, however great may be the emotional wish to believe.
> The difficulty of testing hypotheses in the social sciences has led to an abbreviation of the scientific method in which this step is simply omitted. Plausible hypotheses are merely set down as facts without further ado.

Obvious examples from Southwestern archaeology include such commonly stated inferences as "This room is probably a storage room," "That room is a ceremonial room involving predominately male activities," "These three-room blocks may represent the locations of separate social units," or "Arroyo-cutting caused widespread abandonments in the Southwest" (the latter being an *explanatory* hypothesis). The list could be expanded almost indefinitely; propositions are generated (usually on the basis of archaeological or ethnographic evidence), but there is little or no effort to find independent data to support or refute such ideas (Binford 1967a; Hill 1968). Are we to evaluate archaeological inferences solely by reference to the experience and education of the investigators involved (Thompson 1956, 1958)? Or can we test our propositions so that the tests are not only understandable and reproducible by others but also provide objective measures of the degree to which the inferences have been confirmed or refuted?

There is already good evidence that the latter alternative is correct, and one of the primary purposes of this paper is to illustrate some of the ways in which general scientific methods can be useful in describing prehistoric social organization in the Southwest. This paper is thus intended primarily as a statement of method—a discussion of *how* one might go about elucidating certain aspects of prehistoric social organization.

In doing this, it is necessary to consider in some detail the theoretical underpinnings believed to be crucial to the task; it is evident that the methods and techniques currently being developed cannot be understood or appreciated in the absence of appropriate theory.

After considering the crucial theoretical background and providing a brief illustration of the applicability of general scientific methods to the pursuit of prehistoric social organization in the Southwest, I propose to examine several different aspects of historic Puebloan social organization (and archaeological data as well) to suggest some of the testable propositions that we might deal with. Following this, I will consider possible limitations in the kinds of inferences that can be made with respect to prehistoric social organization.

It would be an impossible task, of course, to try to cover *all* social organizational features that may be considered important. Pueblo social organization is extremely variable even today (Hawley 1937a; Eggan 1950; Dozier 1965), so that the numbers of different forms of residence units, task units, sodalities, and statuses is very large. An effort is made, however, to present a representative sample of the *kinds* of questions that may presently be asked and the general nature of their solutions. There will be very little consideration of intersite variability in terms of activity differences, seasonality, and so forth.

I will, for the most part, restrict the discussion to prehistoric *Pueblo* communities (*circa* A.D. 900 on) and to the Colorado Plateau. While most of the propositions are based on Hopi and Zuni ethnographic data, some consideration is also given to the Rio Grande data (with which I am less familiar).

The paper is not intended as a guide or "cookbook" for the demonstration of specific aspects of prehistoric social organization; it is rather an attempt to present some theoretical and methodological ideas that may be found useful in dealing with any aspect of prehistoric social organization. The methodology itself (general scientific methods), of course, is not limited in applicability to the American Southwest nor to problems of social organization; it is applicable to any archaeological pursuits involving the testing and confirmation of inferences.

Before proceeding, it is necessary to briefly define "social organization." I will follow Service's general definition (1962: 19-25) and consider social organization to include all organizational or structural aspects of a society and their relationships to one another. I depart somewhat from the details of Service's definition, however, and will include four major organizational categories, as follows:

1. *Residence Units:* Localized aggregations of people living together for various purposes (for example, nuclear family households, extended family households, localized lineage segments, and so on. Clans, phratries, moieties, and so forth may also be localized residence units, although this is presumably infrequent.

2. *Task Units:* Organizations serving in the performance of specific tasks or sets of tasks. The task unit is composed of one or more individuals who may be members of the same or a different residence unit. The task involved may be performed within the localized residence unit or outside of it.

3. *Sodalities:* Nonresidential associations having corporate functions or purposes that serve to integrate two or more residence units. The unit is not generally localized or is localized for brief periods only; and membership crosscuts residence units. While sodalities may perform various tasks (point 2), they are thought of primarily as formal integrative institutions (for example, ceremonial societies, warrior societies, and so forth).

4. *Statuses:* Different categories of individuals, residence units, or sodalities that serve in the organization of interpersonal and inter-institutional behavior. They may be divided into achieved and ascribed statuses. Statuses may be distinguished on the basis of age, sex, group membership, specialization, and so forth.

It should be emphasized that these organizational categories are not mutually exclusive; they can crosscut one another in a variety of ways. I will consider them separately in this paper, however.

THEORETICAL CONSIDERATIONS

While it may be correct to say that anthropology has little *theory*, in the strict sense (*cf.* Hempel 1966; Suppes 1967), no doubt all of us are guided in our research by certain premises or assumptions. These, in turn, guide the selection of our *problems*, and our problems then lead us to the selection of methods and techniques appropriate to their solution. I can think of no case in which an archaeologist has carried out a piece of research without being guided by certain assumptions and problems—although in a great many instances these things are simply assumed rather than explicitly stated. It is manifestly impossible to collect "all the data," and an investigator will emphasize the collection of those data that are relevant to his problems. In short, theory, problem, method, and technique cannot be separated.

> Every theory serves, in part, as a research directive; theory guides the collection of data and their subsequent analysis, by showing us beforehand where the data are to be fitted, and what we are to make of them when we get them. The word "data," it cannot too often be emphasized, is an incomplete term, like "later than"; there are only data *for* some hypothesis or other. Without theory, however provisional or loosely formulated, there is only a miscellany of observations, having no significance either in themselves or over against the plenum of fact from which they have been arbitrarily or accidentally selected (Kaplan 1964: 268).

Problems involving the description and explanation of prehistoric social organization are derived from a different set of theories or premises than are problems involving chronology and the historical "relationships" among culture traits.

The effects of theory on problem orientation and methodology can be illustrated by examining some of the effects of what is perhaps the most widely held theoretical framework in current archaeological research. This is the theory or premise that culture is a collection of shared ideas, norms, values, beliefs, mental templates, and so forth. It follows from this premise that since people within a community share their culture, they usually participate equally in it. Culture is considered a relatively *homogeneous* thing, and the individuals who "share" it are striving to behave in accordance with the accepted ideas and norms (cf. White 1954; Aberle 1960).

This, then, leads to the implicit idea that to *describe* a culture (living or extinct), the major *problem* must be to isolate the norms. These norms are believed to be manifested in the empirical data as "typical" behaviour ("typical" artifacts in the case of the archaeologist). The researcher's problem becomes one of trying to find out what is typical of a particular region, society, or archaeological site. He attempts to identify the typical (or "diagnostic") ax, the typical projectile point, the typical kiva, and so forth. Variability within the community is ignored in the pursuit of norms, and once the norms are considered discovered, they are used as *indices* of the culture; the cultural description becomes a list of diagnostics. So, there can be little doubt that our problem (describing norms) derives directly from the theoretical view that culture is shared and homogeneous.[2]

Given this presumed homogeneity within site components (and even regions), it follows that there is little point in studying variability *within* them! The next step, then, is to compare site components with one another in terms of the typical artifacts. The problem becomes one of culture comparison (often for "historical" purposes). Since the individual "cultures" are described as aggregates of diagnostic traits, the methodology used in comparing them must make use of these same traits. The traits are counted and compared, and the different site components or regions are considered to *share* the same culture in direct proportion to the numbers of traits they have in common.

The techniques of excavation and reporting also follow. If cultures, and thus sites, are generally homogeneous, then one clearly does not need to have a sample that is representative of an entire community; a few pits or block excavations should be sufficient to obtain a good collection of diagnostics; there may be no recognized need for any form of probability sampling, for example. In terms of reporting, one would expect to find no need for listing artifact counts by room or area within a site, since there is little concern with variability within site components. The interest is primarily in variability between components (between sites or levels). Thus, the data are usually recorded by site and level only.

These statements should be sufficient to illustrate the relationships among theory, problem, method, and technique, and they suggest one of the major reasons why there has been so little success in elucidating prehistoric social organization. Analyses of social organization require attention to intrasite and intraregion variability, and a concern for this does not follow from the premise that culture consists of shared ideas and behavior. This kind of "normative" view simply obscures the fact that there are a large number of *different* groups and statuses within a society, and the people involved in them are often *not* participating in the same kinds of behavior.[3] For example, men, women, and children frequently participate in very different kinds of tasks; priests and warriors may be involved in activities not shared by other members of a society; certain residence units may carry out specific sets of activities that are not carried out by other residence units, and so forth. Each of these social segments may be expected to make and use specific kinds of material items suited to their particular activities, and these activities may be performed in spatially different locations within the community. So, it is incorrect to assume that the inhabitants of a prehistoric village were behaving in the same ways and attempting to make the same kinds of artifacts. Artifacts do not necessarily represent norms or shared ideas; they represent functional contexts in society—activities and social segments (Binford 1965, 1968).

Even within a certain general class of artifacts (for example, projectile points), different forms and styles are associated with different activities and segments of society. If a site yields three different styles of projectile points, there is no need to assume that one of them represents the "norm," while the others are in some sense deviant; they may have been used in hunting different animal species, or their differences might even represent symbols of status or ownership among social units. In addition, a specific kind of artifact may be found in different behavioral contexts at different *times*. A pot, for example, may serve as a water storage vessel for a number of years and then serve as a symbol of status in a burial. As a matter of fact, a single artifact may function in several different contexts at the *same time*. A ceramic vessel, for example, may be designed primarily as a cooking vessel; yet it may possess certain design elements that serve to identify it as belonging to a certain lineage (status symbols; cf. Binford 1965).

This leads us to the major theoretical tenet of this paper—namely, that cultures are complex behavioral *systems*. A cultural system is internally heterogeneous; it is made up of a large number of internal divisions or subsystems (groups, statuses, activities, and so forth). These internal divisions are interconnected and crosscut one another in a variety of ways, but not such that they cannot be identified as separate subsystems. Thus, within any given community there may be several localized residence units (households, extended households, lineages, and so on); specific rooms or areas within a village may be used in the performance of specific kinds of activities. Certain of these activities may be performed by individuals or groups of different status (for example, men, women, children, hunters, priests, and chiefs).

In short, the structure of a community is neither homogeneous nor random. This is true of all communities about which we know anything at all—modern, primitive, and extinct.

It follows, then, that where different kinds of activities are carried out within a community, one would expect to find different kinds of artifacts; and the presence of different artifacts in particular rooms or areas within an archaeological site should be usable as evidence in inferring the activities of these rooms and areas—assuming that one can identify the uses of the artifacts involved. In areas where food processing and cooking was done, for example, one might expect to find such items as mealing bins, metates, manos, firepits, fire-blackened pottery, charred bone remains, and a number of other things as well. Where ceremonies were carried out, one might find very different kinds of features and artifacts. Butchering locations might be expected to have such materials as choppers, thin used flakes, fragments of bone exhibiting butchering marks, and so forth. It should be possible to determine whether men or women were involved in certain activities by the nature of the materials recovered in particular locations. The locations of residential units might be characterized by non-random clusters of style elements that were peculiar to the different units.

This view may be succinctly stated as follows (from Hill 1966: 10):

The spatial distributions of cultural materials are patterned or structured (non-random), and will be so within an archaeological site.

A. These patterns reflect the loci of *patterned behavior* that existed in prehistoric times.

B. The kind of behavior represented in these loci depends on the nature or "behavioral meaning" of the item or set of items, the distribution of which is being studied.

C. These "behavioral meanings" can be determined with the aid of specific ethnographic evidence or general world-wide comparative evidence. There is a great variety of such "meanings" with which items (or style elements) can be associated:

1. Some items or style elements have direct "activity" meanings (i.e., they are associated with certain economic, sociological, or religious activities).

2. Some of these functional classes of items may reflect the composition of *social segments* (e.g., specific classes of items may be used by men, women, hunters, priests, etc.).

3. Within any given class of items there may be stylistic differences associated with the various social segments (e.g., men, women, hunters, priests, households, lineages, clans, etc.).

These statements are derived from the previously stated theory that cultures are systemic. It is thus evident that a great deal can be learned about prehistoric social organization, in the Southwest and elsewhere, by studying the spatial distributions of artifacts and style elements (cf. Longacre 1963, 1964a, 1964b; Freeman and Brown 1964; Hill 1966, 1968, 1970; Martin, Longacre, and Hill 1967).

In addition to the idea that cultures are systems, a second theoretical statement is also important—namely, that cultural systems (including social organization) are *adaptive*. Cultural variability and change are not adequately explained by invoking such presumed forces as norms, motivations, cultural tendencies, and the like; nor are they completely explained as resulting from diffusion, contact, influences, and migrations. While the latter explanations are sometimes appropriate, they are only partial explanations. This viewpoint need not be elaborated here, however, since this paper is concerned primarily with the *description* of prehistoric social organizations rather than with the explanation of variability and change (see White 1949; Service 1962; Binford 1962, 1968; Sahlins 1964).

GENERAL METHODOLOGICAL CONSIDERATIONS

It would be impossible, in this paper, to present all of the aspects of general scientific methodology that are applicable to the elucidation of prehistoric social organization. I am not competent to do so in any event (*cf.* Nagel 1961; Platt 1964; Chamberlin 1965; Hempel 1966). Nevertheless, some important points concerning the nature of scientific demonstration must be made prior to considering specific methods for dealing with particular prehistoric social organizational features in the Southwest. As was pointed out in the introduction, we frequently make guesses or conjectures concerning prehistoric organization, but these are usually left untested. Such inferences are often presented as fact (or as the closest approximation to fact considered possible at the moment). One may feel inclined to *believe* the inferences or not, depending in part on his evaluation of the investigator's competence. Actually, this need be only the *beginning* of scientific research. The investigator has presented a proposition or hypothesis, but he does not know the degree to which he may have confidence in it. While such inferences are correct as far as they go, they add nothing to the store of knowledge. The inference that a particular prehistoric room represents a kiva, for example, may lead us to the conclusion that it was used in the same ways as a modern Hopi kiva. But in addition to not having any verification of this, we also have not learned anything new. We have simply accepted what is *already* known about the functions of modern kivas and *applied* it to the past. This constitutes a tacit admission that nearly all of what we can learn about the past is already known! We can simply consult the ethnographic literature and ignore the archaeological data.

It will be useful to continue with the case of the inferred kiva at this point, since it provides an excellent example of the methodology being proposed here. The inference that a particular Pueblo room was used in the same ways as a modern kiva is a *proposition*. Although this proposition may have been generated on the basis of ethnographic evidence, it really matters little how it was generated or from what evidence. A proposition can be generated on the basis of ideas provided by direct ethnographic evidence, by worldwide comparative evidence, by intuition, or even by a bad dream.[4] There are no specific rules for the development of propositions or hypotheses, and this step in scientific methodology can be an extremely imaginative and creative one; it is also where most of the experience and expertise come in. Philosophers of science sometimes refer to this phase of research as the *context of discovery* (Hempel 1966).

A hypothesis is usually considered to be an *explanatory* statement; it proposes an explanation for an observation or set of observations, and the explanation is in terms of both general laws and specific conditions (Hempel 1966). In this paper, however, I am using the term "proposition" loosely, to refer to any testable statement. In the case of our kiva-like room, for example, no explanation is being called for; the proposition is simply that the room was used in the same kinds of activities that are carried out in present-day kivas.

In almost all situations, more than one proposition must be considered and tested—and this is exceedingly important. In the present instance, the alternative propositions might be as follows:

1. The room was used for the same activities as are carried out in a modern *living* room.
2. The room was used for the same activities as are carried out in a modern *storage* room.
3. The room was used for the same activities as are carried out in a modern *clanhouse* (Eggan 1950: 104; Dozier 1965: 45).
4. The room was used for the same activities as are carried out in a modern *moiety chief's house* (Dozier 1965).

And there might be others. The point is that all conceivably relevant propositions should be considered (Chamberlin 1965). These propositions are then tested, one by one, beginning with the least likely one. Some of them may be discarded immediately, on logical grounds; others may be rejected on the basis of an easily performed test. The investigator may then be left with two or more propositions which cannot, on the basis of presently available evidence, be rejected. In any event, the most efficient procedure is to devise tests that are designed to *refute* each proposition rather than confirm it (Platt 1964). A major reason for this is that very few propositions can actually be unequivocally confirmed. While we can increase the probability that a particular proposition is better than others, we can rarely reach certainty. It is often much easier to demonstrate that a proposition is *not* valid (Platt 1964; Hempel 1966).

But how does one actually *test* any of these propositions? We have now reached what may be called the *context validation* (Nagel 1961; Hempel 1966). It is one thing to generate a proposition (context of discovery) and quite another to test it adequately. While there are no strict rules for thinking up a proposition (unless it is deductively drawn), such rules *do* exist in the context of validation.

First of all, the proposition must be stated so that it is testable—by reference to empirical data. This clearly eliminates all *ad hoc* explanatory propositions, such as ideas, norms, motivations, cultural tendencies, and so forth, for which there are no empirical data available for testing. In short, a good proposition must have what are called "test implications" in terms of measurable data (Hempel 1966), and these test implications are derived from the proposition itself. The test implications for a given proposition actually amount to a listing of all of the evidence one would expect to find in the empirical data *if* in fact the proposition is correct (and conversely, a listing of the kinds of evidence which, if found, would demonstrate it to be false).

Test implications, then, can be considered as synonymous with "expectations" in the data. They usually take the form of "If. . . then. . ." statements (Hempel 1966). *If* the proposition is correct, *then* one would expect certain data in support of it. In the example above, the statement might read as follows:

Proposition: This room was used for the same activities as are carried out in a modern Hopi kiva.

Test Implications: (derived in this case from ethnographic data— Titiev 1944; Eggan 1950; and others).

If the proposition is correct, *then* one would expect to find the following evidence:

1. The room should contain certain features that are different from those in other rooms—for example, fireplace, bench, ventilator, wall niches, and so forth.
2. It should contain evidence of ritual activities—for example, idols, fetishes, and so forth.
3. It should contain special types or styles of pottery (not burned on the bottoms).
4. It should contain large quantities of corn and squash pollen (and seeds).
5. It should contain evidence of manufacturing activities (for example, weaving and the manufacture of chert hunting implements).
6. It should contain some evidence that eating was done in the rooms (but not cooking). This would be indicated by the presence of food remains and perhaps bowls suitable for serving.
7. It should contain artifacts that were most likely used by males and relatively few that one would expect females to have used.

A closer examination of the modern Hopi data, in terms of the specific activities and material items that are involved in kiva usage, would suggest many more test implications than are included here. And it would certainly be possible to devise a long list of things that one would *not* expect to find in such a room if it was used in the same manner as a Hopi kiva. One would not expect to find large quantities of metates, manos, mortars, pestles, fire-blackened pottery, burned bones, charred corn cobs, worked sherds, and so forth. Again, the list could be enlarged, primarily by reference to the kinds of materials found in Hopi living rooms, storage rooms, and other areas (but not in Hopi kivas).

In any event, a list of test implications for each of the alternative propositions should also be made. After this is done, the investigator examines the data relevant to each of the test implications in an effort to either affirm or deny each of these expectations. He then may tabulate the numbers of test implications that were borne out (affirmed), and not borne out (denied), for each of the propositions.[5] He then has an objective basis by which to compare the validity of all the propositions with one another; he can presumably reject certain propositions as no longer feasible, and he can assess the *degree* to which the remaining propositions are likely to be correct.

It may be, of course, that a simple tabulation of the test results will not be sufficient. Certain of the test implications may be adjudged more important than others, and these may receive greater weight in the analysis of the results. For example, the presence in our kiva-like room of large quantities of charred food remains and fire-blackened pottery would weigh heavily against the idea that it can be considered as equivalent in use to a modern Hopi kiva.

A crucial point in all of this—one that is usually ignored—is that propositions of any nature should be tested with data that are *independent* of the data used in generating them in the first place (Binford 1968). It would be neither logical nor useful, for example, to generate the proposition that a certain room is equivalent to a present-day kiva on the basis of its size and internal features, and then employ these same data (size and features) in testing it. Similarly, it would not be useful to propose that a room is a storage room on the basis of the fact that it is small, dark, and contains no firepit—and then proceed to state that because it has these features it is in *fact* a storage room. These are clearly examples of circular reasoning—and yet such reasoning is remarkably common.

In the above example, one would most likely generate the proposition on the basis of certain formal similarities to present-day kivas—that is, that the room is subterranean, has a certain size, and contains some peculiar features. He would then examine the ethnographic evidence, generate the test implications, and proceed to collect the test data.

In summary, a proposition (of any nature) might be developed and tested as follows (Hill 1968):

1. An observation (or set of observations) is made that is considered to require an explanation or validation.

2. A consideration of the observed data itself may suggest an explanation (perhaps several of them). One might argue, for example, that a bench, ventilator, wall niches, and so forth, are indicative of ceremonial uses.

3. Analogies with ethnographic or other data might then serve to strengthen the probability that the initial proposition is correct (for example, one might find that present-day kivas have similar features).

4. A formal statement of the proposition might then be made, together with a list of test implications—including those that would demonstrate that the proposition is *false*. (In the above example, these implications were based on ethnographic evidence, but they could derive from other evidence as well.)

5. The data that are relevant to these test implications are then examined (or collected in the field).

6. The results are tabulated, evaluated, and compared with the test results of the alternative propositions.

While I have stressed the importance of using *independent* data in testing a proposition, it is important to recognize that this may not always be possible. Such a situation might be encountered, for example, if a proposition has already been so adequately tested that one simply runs out of ideas for additional test implications. By way of illustration, we might suppose that an investigator has tested the proposition that a particular class of rooms had been used in cooking activities. The investigator might have generated a long list of test implications and found nearly all of them confirmed in his data—thus supporting his proposition. The next time this same proposition is put forth (say with data from another site), the investigator may actually generate it with data that had served as test implications of the *original* proposition. The question is, is it then necessary for him to develop a new and different (independent) set of test implications for use in testing it the second time (and other times)?

Probably not. Once a proposition has been satisfactorily confirmed, it should not be necessary to develop additional test implications. It would be too much to ask of an investigator that he continue to gather additional test data indefinitely!

At the same time, there is a very real danger that once a proposition has been tested, and given some credence, the result will simply be applied blindly in another context. In the above illustration (cooking activities), for example, one of the test implications might be the presence of a firepit. It would not be satisfactory to say that all rooms having firepits (for example, in another site) were used in cooking activities. One would want to test this idea by at least looking for the test implications that were used in the original test.

It is important to note, in this connection, that the investigator will want to generate as many specific propositions (and test implications) as possible *before* going into the field! The reason for this should be clear. If one generates a series of propositions ahead of time, he will be aware of the kinds of data that must be collected to test them. If he does not do this, he will fail to collect the relevant test data (and collect a great deal of "data" that are not relevant to anything in particular). This amounts to wasted time and money and is inefficient from a scientific point of view. Once field work has been completed, it is unlikely that the investigator will be able to gather the additional data that may be required to test newly generated propositions.

One way to lessen this difficulty, of course, is to carry on a running analysis while the field work is still in progress. Concurrent analysis may require that previously generated propositions be modified or replaced, and it may lead to new propositions. The investigator may then modify his research design with the aim of collecting data that were not formerly considered relevant.

A final methodological point requiring emphasis is that in testing any proposition the test implications that do *not* test in the affirmative are just as important as the ones that are confirmed. They are perhaps even more important, since they provide new information. They may provide evidence of culture-change, and they may suggest new propositions for testing (that are by no means dependent on ethnographic information).

This can be illustrated by reference to my recent study of the uses of prehistoric pueblo rooms, in *New Perspectives in Archaeology* (Binford and Binford 1968). I demonstrated, in that paper, that certain rooms at

Broken K Pueblo (Martin, Longacre, and Hill 1967) that were thought to be kivas were, in fact, used in a very similar manner to modern western Pueblo ceremonial rooms. One of the test implications was clearly not confirmed, however. I expected that if the four excavated kiva-like rooms were used in the same ways as modern kivas, there ought to be large quantities of the pollen or seeds of corn and squash on their floors. Not only was there significantly *less* corn and squash in these rooms than other rooms at the site, but there was also a great deal *more* "weed" pollen than expected (especially chenopods and amaranths). This suggested that the pollen and seeds of these domesticates were *not* used frequently in the Broken K kivas, and it indicated the possibility that a minor change in kiva activities occurred sometime between A.D. 1300 and the present (Hill 1968; Hill and Hevly 1968).[6]

A series of new propositions may be generated on the basis of this evidence. Without listing the alternative propositions, the following hypotheses may be listed:

1. A shift in the physical or biological environment occurred during or before the thirteenth century A.D. in this area.

2. This environmental shift created conditions inimical to agriculture, promoting reduced crop yields.

3. Reduced crop yields forced the inhabitants of the site to rely heavily on wild foods, both in terms of subsistence and ritual.

Each of these propositions yields a number of subpropositions and test implications, and they can be tested in the manner suggested above. As a matter of fact, they have already been tested with remarkable success (Hill 1970).

In short, when propositions are properly tested, an expansion of knowledge is inevitable. The number of testable propositions that can be generated and tested is almost infinite, and it should be possible to expand our knowledge of prehistoric social organization almost indefinitely. This expansion of knowledge will not depend on ethnographic information, even though such information is the most immediate and useful source of ideas for generating propositions (Binford 1967a, 1968). It is evident that we must use the *archaeological* data to a much fuller degree if we are to elucidate prehistoric social organization successfully. Those methodological approaches regarding ethnographic analogies as answers should be abandoned (cf. Ascher 1961; Hole and Heizer 1965: 211; Chang 1967).

ASPECTS OF PREHISTORIC SOCIAL
ORGANIZATION: SOME EXAMPLES

The theoretical and methodological approaches crucial to describing prehistoric social organization have been discussed, but it will be useful to provide some additional specific examples of their use. This really amounts to considering the procedural steps that an archaeologist might make in generating and testing specific kinds of propositions, including some brief (and tentative) listings of appropriate test implications. It should be emphasized, however, that I do not pretend to present all possible test implications for any of the propositions, nor is it possible to present many of the alternative propositions that might be considered in each case. The following discussions should be considered as *examples* illustrating the application of a methodology and nothing more.

One of the most significant problems confronting an effort of this nature is that we know remarkably little about the material correlates of historic Pueblo social organizations. The ethnographies do not tell us very much, for example, about the specific kinds of activities that are carried out in different kinds of rooms in a pueblo, nor do they say very much about the particular kinds of artifacts and other materials that one might expect to be associated with these activities. The material correlates of residence units and statuses are even more difficult to find in the literature. This means, of course, that it is often difficult to determine specific test implications for these organizational units in the archaeological situation—where physical remains constitute our data. Ethnographers have clearly been more interested in norms and kinship systems than in describing the kinds of material items and style elements associated with particular kinds of activities. A great deal can be done in spite of this drawback, but it is hoped that future Pueblo ethnographers will devote more attention to the material correlates of cultural behavior.

Task Units

In describing the organization of tasks or activities within a prehistoric pueblo, one may take at least two different approaches. The first is to begin by describing the variability in room types, plazas, and other areas within the site and then ask the question, "What kinds of activities were being performed in these rooms and areas?" The other approach is to begin with a specific list of *activities* that are of interest to the archaeologist and ask the question, "Where were these activities being performed?" Both of these are reasonable and can lead to comparable results, of course—although the methodologies involved differ somewhat.

In the former approach (see, for example, Hill 1968) the investigator might proceed initially, as suggested, by making a careful and quantitative analysis of formal variability among rooms and other areas. The aim would be to discover discrete, essentially nonoverlapping, room and area "types." Each type would consist of a cluster of associated attributes generally not found in the other types.[7] Most pueblos will contain at least three formal types of rooms, although these are occasionally difficult to isolate. There may be, for example, a category of large rooms containing such features as mealing bins, firepits, and ventilators (perhaps living rooms); a category of small, generally featureless rooms (perhaps storage rooms); and a somewhat smaller number of rooms having features similar to those in modern ceremonial rooms. There may also be a plaza, a midden area, and other reasonably discrete spatial divisions that can be isolated. This is merely an example, of course, since pueblos are known to vary greatly in the formal attributes of their internal structure. One can presume, however, that nonrandom structural variability will be found in all pueblo sites.

After describing this variability, the next step might be to generate some tentative explanations that would account for it. It is evident that variability, among rooms at least, must have resulted from the fact that they were built for different purposes. An examination of the attributes of the various room and area types should lead the investigator to develop a series of reasonable arguments concerning the kinds of activities that might require such types.

In this example, we might infer that the "large" rooms were built to be occupied by relatively large groups of people—or because several different activities were to be performed in them simultaneously. The presence of firepits in these rooms would suggest that the activities required heat or light or both; the presence of mealing bins would indicate food processing; the ventilators would suggest a need for fresh air, draft, or light. It may be inferred that all of these attributes would be expected primarily in living rooms.

The small rooms, on the other hand, would not be presumed to be living rooms. They must have been used in activities that did not require heat, light, food-processing equipment, or even a large amount of space.

These attributes suggest that the rooms may have been storage rooms. It could be inferred that the kiva-like rooms had been designed for somewhat special uses, simply on the basis of the fact that they are very different. Even without ethnographic evidence, the investigator would very likely consider the possibility that they were ceremonial rooms.

The next step, as indicated above, would be to search for analogies in the ethnographic literature. Are there similar kinds of rooms (and other areas), containing similar clusters of features, in the modern pueblos? In this case the answer is clearly yes. The analogies will be strengthened, if it can be shown that both the historic and prehistoric room types occur in roughly the same proportions and have a similar patterning in terms of spatial distribution.

At this point, of course, the investigator would state the formal proposition that the prehistoric rooms and areas were used in the same activities as are the historic ones.[8] An examination of the activities performed in the modern room types would then yield a series of test implications for each (in terms of artifacts and their relative frequencies and spatial distributions), and the investigator would turn to the archaeological evidence to determine the degree to which his expectations are met (cf. pp. 20-27).

My own examination of the western Pueblo ethnographic literature has yielded a wide range of specific activities that occur in different locations within modern pueblos (Hill 1968); and while I cannot review the nature of these activities here, it may be worthwhile to list a few likely test implications:

1. The large rooms (presumed living rooms) might be expected to contain the following:
   a. Significantly higher densities of most artifacts and other materials than are found in small rooms or kiva-like rooms.
   b. A wider variety of cultural materials than is found in other rooms.
   c. Evidence of food processing prior to cooking (metates, manos, and certain other artifacts; remains of processed food, including seeds and pollen in the basins of mealing bins, and animal bones).
   d. Evidence of cooking, in addition to the firepits (charred food remains, large numbers of unpainted "utility" vessels that had been burned on the bottom).
   e. Evidence of eating (charred food remains, bowls that might be usable in serving food—especially those with smudged interiors).

    f. Evidence of water storage (large, narrow-necked, painted jars).

    g. Evidence of manufacturing activities (raw materials, blanks, debris).

2. The small rooms (presumed storage rooms) might be expected to contain the following:

    a. Lower densities of cultural remains than in other rooms or areas (including manufacturing debris).

    b. Smaller variety of cultural remains than in other rooms or areas.

    c. Larger quantities of the remains of food crops than found elsewhere (including the seeds and pollen of corn and squash).

    d. Evidence of ethnographically recorded storage techniques (for example, more large, open-mouthed, unpainted jars than in other areas).

    e. Evidence of other stored materials in addition to food crops (for example, ceremonial paraphernalia, tools, nondietary plant remains, and so forth).

    f. Very little evidence of manufacturing activities (represented by lithic debris and other by-products of manufacturing).

3. The kiva-like rooms: test implications already presented (p. 23).

4. Plaza (or areas between room-blocks) might contain the following:

    a. Small slab-lined box (or its equivalent) in the center. It might contain seeds or pollen of spruce, corn, and squash.

    b. Manufacturing debris (perhaps somewhat different kinds of debris than in the rooms).

    c. Evidence of activities that would reasonably be performed outdoors, or are known to be performed outdoors (for example, pottery manufacturing and firing equipment, heavy butchering activities, and so forth).

These test implications can be expanded, of course, by a more thorough examination of the ethnographic evidence.

It should be noted, too, that there are other kinds of rooms and areas in modern pueblos than have been considered here, and the activities involved in them would yield different sets of test implications. There are, for example, a number of rooms that archaeologists might consider kiva-like, but that, in fact, served somewhat different purposes. With the development of appropriate test implications, the archaeologist should be able to identify prehistoric rooms that were similar in use to Hopi clan-houses (Eggan 1950: 298; Dozier 1965: 45), eastern Pueblo moiety houses

(Hawley 1950a; Dozier 1965), and various ceremonial association rooms such as those used by present-day curing, warfare, hunting, and clowning societies among the eastern Pueblos (Dozier 1965). While it may be that many of the same kinds of artifacts are used in these different kinds of rooms (Dozier 1965), it seems likely that careful examination would reveal some distinguishing attributes that could serve as usable test implications.

It is important to recognize, of course, that any room or area will almost certainly have been multifunctional. Most Pueblo ceremonial rooms, for example, are involved in kachina society activities at one time or another, in addition to other activities; storage rooms may be involved in cooking activities, and so on. Nevertheless, it should be possible to develop a series of test implications relevant to isolating the primary uses of rooms and other areas within a pueblo, as well as those useful in demonstrating the existence of secondary activities of various kinds.

An additional problem facing the investigator is the possibility that certain kinds of activities that are expected to have occurred in particular areas within a site may actually have been carried out in other locations. In this event, of course, a number of the test implications for a given room or area type would not be met in the archaeological record. This might lead the investigator to the unwarranted conclusion that the activities in question were not performed at all by the occupants of his site. It is entirely possible for an investigator to focus his attention so firmly on a particular type of room or area that he overlooks the possibility that he might find evidence of his "missing activities" in other locations.

This situation may be avoided by focusing less attention on the test implications of rooms and areas and more attention on the test implications of individual activities. In this approach, the investigator would first consider the kinds or clusters of cultural remains that are expected to have been associated with particular activities and then study the spatial distributions of these clusters within the site.

As a final consideration here, it is important to be constantly aware that in describing the organization of activities in any society, one must go beyond the site itself. No society carries on all of its activities within a single village, and we may presume that prehistoric Puebloan peoples performed many activities in the vicinity of their agricultural fields, hunting grounds, water sources, shrines, and so forth.[9] In each of these locations, their activities were undoubtedly somewhat different, and it should

be possible to employ the same general methods presented here in elucidating them.

Residence Units

On initial consideration, prehistoric residential units seem difficult to
deal with, in terms of both locating the rooms occupied by different units
and understanding the nature of the postmarital residence pattern that
existed in a prehistoric village. While I do not want to imply that these
are easy tasks, many of the problems involved are more apparent than real.
The major problem appears to stem from the theoretical view that I have
termed the "normative approach." The implication is that since prehistoric peoples themselves are extinct, we cannot find out what they regarded as discrete residence units or what they considered to be the
normal residence rules. In essence, this view implies that if we cannot discover what the people thought regarding their behavior, we cannot make
well-founded inferences about the behavior itself. And since most of us
do not really believe that prehistoric thoughts can be discovered adequately, we are somewhat hesitant to make inferences about past
behavior.

Actually, there is no need to be concerned with what people thought at
all; we are really interested in what they actually did (real behavior). It
does not seem likely that we, as archaeologists, can deal adequately with
such concepts as kinship systems, lineages, clans, and so forth—at least insofar as they are abstractions in the minds of people. It does seem likely,
however, that inferences can be made about such things to the extent that
they represent nonlinguistic and nonmental behavior. We can certainly
learn a great deal about prehistoric residence units, since residence units
are observable, measurable behavioral entities that leave observable remains in the archaeological record. Some reasonably successful research in
this regard has already been carried out in the Southwest (Longacre 1963,
1964a; Hill 1966, 1970; Martin, Longacre, and Hill 1967).

The general methodology for describing prehistoric residence units is
the same as that for describing activity areas or task units. Certain observations or information lead to the generation of hypotheses, and these may
then be tested with independent data.

As with task units, at least two different approaches can demonstrate
the existence and nature of prehistoric residence units. The investigator

may begin by describing various spatial divisions within a pueblo that appear to represent the locations of different residence units and then ask the question, "Are these the locations of discrete residence units?" Or, he can begin with a list of particular *kinds* of residence units that he hopes to isolate (for example, households, extended family households, and so forth) and ask the question, "What room-blocks or areas were occupied by each of these units?" Again, both approaches may be useful; the latter approach is the one that has received most attention so far in the Southwest (see Longacre 1963, 1964a; Hill 1966, 1970).

In the first approach, the investigator might initially proceed by making a careful study of any architectural divisions within the pueblo that might indicate residence units of various kinds. The idea that village layout, for example, may reflect the locations of such units is commonplace (see Eggan 1950: 3; Reed 1956; Rohn 1965). Different residence units might be indicated by the presence of discrete room-blocks or by individual blocks of rooms that appear to be associated with particular kivas (Bullard 1962: 101); they may be indicated by an obvious dual division, such as is seen at Pueblo Bonito (Judd 1964). They may even be suggested by certain groups of rooms connected by doorways in a distinctive fashion (Rohn 1965).

On the basis of this evidence, the investigator might develop various reasonable arguments concerning the particular kinds of residence units that might have occupied the various internal divisions of the pueblo. It might be argued, for example, that groups of two or three rooms (including a living room and storage room) were probably occupied by nuclear family units. Groups of fifteen to twenty-five rooms might have housed large extended families or lineage-sized units; larger divisions might be indicative of clan-sized units, phratry-sized units, or even large dual divisions.

The next steps in the analysis would be, of course, the establishment of positive analogies with modern pueblo room groupings, the statement of formal propositions of equivalence, the generation of test implications, and the testing of the propositions against the archaeological data.

I have attempted below to list a few of the test implications that might be relevant to the demonstration of various kinds of residence units. I present, by way of illustration, only certain test implications that may be useful with respect to nuclear family households, extended family households or lineage-like units, and dual divisions of the type found among many of the present-day eastern Pueblos.

1. Nuclear Family Household Units:[10]
   a. The group of rooms should number between about two and five (Titiev 1944; Eggan 1950; Dozier 1965).
   b. The unit may be partitioned off from other such units by a wall (Dozier 1965).
   c. Each room should be different in terms of usage (and perhaps size). Some functional differentiation is expected in any household. Each unit should contain approximately the same combination of room types (Dozier 1965: 38; Rohn 1965: 66).
   d. There should be a large room containing the main firepit, mealing facilities, and ventilator. The smaller rooms should contain different types of features or none at all (Mindeleff 1891; Titiev 1944; Eggan 1950).
   e. Doorways should be arranged to afford entrance to each room within the unit but not frequently to other units (Dozier 1965: 39).
   f. Each unit should possess style peculiarities not shared by adjacent units. The styles of doorway construction, wall construction, and so forth, may differ between units (Rohn 1965: 66). There may also be minute differences in pottery styles and manufacturing techniques, as well as possible small differences in the styles of other artifacts and features.

2. Extended Family Household Units or Lineage-like Units:[11]
   a. The group of rooms should be larger than that composing a nuclear family household. It might contain fifteen to twenty-five rooms (as an estimate), although it is not possible to be precise here.
   b. The unit may be partitioned off from other such units, by a wall; or it may be spatially separated from other such units.
   c. The unit should be composed of two or more household units (as discussed above).
   d. Each such unit may contain an extra large room or kiva-like structure, such as a kiva, clanhouse, and so forth. While "unit-type" pueblos may each have one of these, the later and larger pueblos may exhibit evidence of one such room shared by several residence units of the nature considered here (cf. Steward 1937).
   e. Each unit should possess style peculiarities not shared by other such units. There may be differences in the styles of artifacts, features, and architecture. (These style differences should be of a less refined or "sensitive" nature than those restricted in distribution to individual household units.)[12]

35

3. *Dual Divisions (as among eastern Pueblos):*[13]

a. The dual divisions may be separated by a wall or completely separated spatially (as at Taos; see also Rohn 1965: 69).

b. There may be two large kivas, one for each half of the village—although there may be only one large kiva (Dozier 1965: 44-45). These might contain somewhat different features and artifacts if, for example, one kiva belonged to the summer moiety and the other to the winter moiety. At Hano, somewhat different ceremonies are performed in the two large kivas (Dozier 1966a: 79).

c. Each half may contain a chief's house or meeting house. It would be somewhat larger and different from other houses and may contain evidence of the storage of ceremonial paraphernalia, etc. (Dozier 1965). Closer examination of the ethnographic situation may indicate the particular kinds of features and materials to be expected in such houses.

d. There may be evidence of other communal rooms or kivas, an approximately equal number in both halves of the pueblo. There may be functionally equivalent units in both halves.

e. Each half may possess style peculiarities not shared by the other. These would be even less refined style differences than those restricted to room-blocks occupied by either households or larger groups. This is suggested by the fact that many eastern Pueblos have nonexogamous moiety divisions and should thus contain certain style differences (see also Rohn 1965: 69).

In conjunction with the kinds of test implications already listed for the demonstration of residence units, certain implications must be met when clusters of *style* elements are used in differentiating the units:

1. Nonrandom distributions of style elements should delineate localized areas of the pueblo as being different from one another. (These style elements may be ceramic design elements, architectural design elements, and so forth.)

2. It should be found that these elements can be associated (at least logically) with the construction or maintenance of a *residential* unit. (This would indicate that the style elements were actually relevant to isolating residence units and not something else.)

3. Temporal continuity should be found for these style elements within each of the areas of the pueblo which represent different residence units. (This would indicate that the residence units were "permanent" or stable.)

In addition to these expectations, of course, it must be demonstrated that the observed spatial clusterings of style elements are not better explained by some alternative explanation—such as the possibility that they represent different activity areas. Large, localized clusters of style elements within a pueblo are not likely to represent such areas, however; primary activity differences can usually be correlated with different room types, and these room types are generally scattered throughout the spatial extent of the pueblo.

Another explanation that might be proposed for differences in clustering of style elements is that the different clusters represent different time periods. This, however, is irrelevant to the isolation of residence units, since time itself is not a cause of anything. The discovery that two or more localized clusters of style elements within a site date to different time periods would simply indicate that the residential units involved were not contemporaneous—the time differential cannot be used to negate the existence of the residence units themselves.

The test implications presented above are not as exhaustive or precise as one might wish, and it is important that we examine particular ethnographic situations that are applicable to our propositions much more carefully than has been done here. Almost certainly, more specific material attributes can be expected to characterize residence units of various types and sizes.

Residence Patterns

While some of the specific methodology relevant to isolating residence units is also relevant to determining the nature of prehistoric Puebloan residence patterns (postmarital residence), the demonstration of the two can be logically separated. Regardless of the numbers and sizes of residence units within a pueblo, it should be possible to learn at least the general outlines of postmarital residence pattern.

Longacre (1963, 1964a) first demonstrated that residence patterns can be inferred from prehistoric Puebloan data (see also Hill 1966, 1970; Martin, Longacre, and Hill 1967). Basing his study on data from Carter Ranch Site, in east-central Arizona (Martin et al. 1964), Longacre was able to tentatively demonstrate the existence of uxorilocal residence by at least A.D. 1100.[14] His initial proposition was based on ethnographic data. He observed that among the modern western Pueblos the art of pottery making is transmitted from mother to daughter through time and always *within* the localized matrilineal framework (*cf.* Bunzel 1929: 51-54). Knowing this, he formulated the proposition that there should be more similarities in ceramic design elements through time, *within* the uxorilocal group, than there would be *between* such groups at any given point in time (1963: 59-62). Presumably, mothers would teach their daughters certain subtle peculiarities of design technique which would not be shared by women who learned how to make pottery within a different uxorilocal unit. On this basis, Longacre proposed that *if* uxorilocal (matrilocal) residence had existed at Carter Ranch Site, *then* it ought to be found that certain localized areas of the pueblo contain somewhat different clusters of ceramic design elements—and this proved to be the case.

Longacre made use of only one test implication, however—ceramic design elements. We now know that similar localized clusters may be isolated by examining the distributions of pottery types, firepit shapes, storage pit characteristics, and other things (Hill 1966, 1970). It is evident that virtually *anything* that was made and used primarily by *females* is usable in this regard. Male-associated stylistic elements, on the other hand, apparently do *not* cluster in this way (although this has not yet been conclusively demonstrated). We would not expect them to, of course, since in an uxorilocal situation it is only the women who remain localized; the men move out of their natal residence units at marriage (Table 1).

There is more to demonstrating the prehistoric existence of uxorilocal residence pattern (or any other residence pattern) than simply plotting the spatial distributions of style elements, however. Other test implications must be met, the most important being that the style element clusters discovered must be made up of elements that can be associated with *female* residence activities. A summary of the most crucial test implications is given below; the reader will notice that it is similar in many respects to those required in the demonstration of residence *units.*

1. Nonrandom distributions of items (or style elements within classes of items) should delineate localized areas of the pueblo as being different from one another.

2. It should be found that these elements can be associated (at least logically) with *female* activities primarily and not with male activities. (This would suggest that different aggregates of females were performing tasks.)

3. It should be found that these female-associated items or style elements were used (or usable) in maintaining a residential unit. (This would indicate that the items or style elements were actually relevant to isolating *residence* units and not something else.)

4. Temporal continuity should be found for those items or elements within each of the areas of the pueblo which represent different aggregates of female activity. (This would indicate that the residence units were permanent or stable.)

In addition to these expectations, of course, it must also be demonstrated that the spatial clusterings of style elements do not represent

Table 1

RESIDENCE PATTERNS AND THEIR HYPOTHETICAL
DISTRIBUTION CORRELATES

Residence Pattern	Definition	Distribution of Female Stylistic Items	Distribution of Male Stylistic Items
Uxorilocal	Husband and wife live in vicinity of wife's maternal relatives	Nonrandom	Random
Matrilocal	Husband and wife live in vicinity of wife's mother	Nonrandom	Random
Matrilocal, with resident male head	Same, but a mother's brother and his family reside within the group	Nonrandom	Random
Virilocal	Husband and wife live in vicinity of husband's relatives—patrilineal or matrilineal	Random	Nonrandom
Patrilocal	Husband and wife live in vicinity of husband's father	Random	Nonrandom
Avunculocal	Husband and wife live in vicinity of husband's maternal uncle	Random	Nonrandom
Neolocal	Husband and wife live separate from either mate's relatives	Random	Random
Bilocal	Husband and wife live either in vicinity of husband's or wife's relatives	Random	Random
Duolocal	Husband and wife live separately, with own relatives	Nonrandom	Nonrandom

39

different activity areas within the pueblo. This would be accomplished by citing the evidence suggested previously on p. 37.

It should be emphasized that this method for the isolation of prehistoric residence patterns is applicable to other kinds of residence patterns as well. Suppose that in analyzing data from a particular site we consider the alternative proposition of virilocal residence. The test implications for this situation would be exactly the same as those just listed, except that whenever the world "female" occurs it would be replaced by "male," and vice versa. In this case, we would expect to find localized (nonrandom) clusters of male-associated items or style elements and a more random distribution of female-associated elements (Table 1). Items associated with residential units, and also manufactured by males, particularly include the elements of house construction. One might expect to find nonrandom distributions of such style elements as numbers of doorways, height of doorsill, shape of doorway, numbers of ventilators, style of ventilators, thickness of walls, size and shape of wall stones, and so forth.

A further alternative proposition might be that a particular site had a bilocal residence pattern. This is apparently the case among many of the present-day Rio Grande pueblos (Dozier 1965), and archaeologists interested in residence patterns in that area would certainly want to test this proposition. In this residence situation, husband and wife live (upon marriage) in the vicinity of either the husband's relatives or the wife's relatives (Table 1). In this case, as in the neolocal situation, we would not expect to find localized clusters of either male- or female-associated style elements.

In any event, this discussion should be sufficient to illustrate some of the methods involved in isolating residence patterns. One of the complications is that it is difficult to be sure that certain artifacts can be associated with one sex or another. At the same time, we can rarely reach certainty in any of our inferences, and there are a great many cultural elements that most of us would agree were probably manufactured or used by either men or women. Further, exactness here is not of crucial importance since in demonstrating residence patterns we are using not just one class of artifacts or style elements but a long list of them. A single test implication is generally insufficient.

It cannot be overemphasized that in isolating residence patterns the distribution of both male- and female-associated items must be examined (cf. p. 38, no. 2). We cannot assume, for example, that localized clusters of female-associated style elements alone are indicative of uxorilocal residence—it must also be found that male-associated elements were not localized. The recent tentative demonstrations of uxorilocality at Carter Ranch Site and Broken K Pueblo (Longacre 1963, 1964a; Hill 1966, 1970; Martin, Longacre, and Hill 1967) have fallen short in this respect, since there has been no systematic attempt to trace the distributions of male-associated style elements.

A final problem regarding discovery of prehistoric residence patterns is a most interesting and crucial one, and it involves us in a consideration of learning theory (Aberle, personal communication). The problem can be illustrated by an example. Suppose we have a *virilocal* residence situation in which the women who are "marrying in" alter their pottery-making and other styles to conform to those of their mothers-in-law and sisters-in-law! The question is, will a woman in this situation abandon the kinds of style elements she learned in her natal household and adopt new ones to conform to those used in her new household? If so, then we would not only expect to find localized clusters of male-associated style elements, but we would also expect clusterings of female-associated elements. This would be contrary to the expectations for virilocal residence given in Table 1. The resulting localized clusters of female-associated elements might even lead the investigator to infer an uxorilocal residence pattern when in fact it was virilocal! The obverse of this situation would be a case in which *uxorilocal* residence is obscured when in-marrying men alter the style peculiarities of their manufactured materials to conform to those of their fathers-in-law and brothers-in-law. We would be on much surer footing if we knew to what degree (if any) people will learn new style elements after marriage. To find out, we must examine learning situations in a number of present-day societies more closely.

There are, however, at least two other approaches to the solution of this problem. In the first place, it would be particularly useful to examine the spatial distributions of both male- and female-associated stylistic elements in present-day societies having different residence patterns. If the proposed associations among residence patterns and style clusters (Table 1) are confirmed ethnographically, our confidence is increased that this was the case in prehistoric times as well.

Secondly, it would be useful to know whether or not there are differences in the clustering of male- and female-associated elements among archaeological sites. In short, do some sites exhibit localized clusters of male-associated elements, but not female-associated elements? Are there some sites having clusters of both or neither? If, for example, prehistoric sites in the western Pueblo area usually have localized clusters of female-associated elements, while those in the eastern Pueblo area have no localized clusters at all (or clusters of male-associated elements only), we are in a firmer position for believing that style-element distributions are indicative of residence patterns. The reason for this, of course, is that we would expect such differences in style-element distribution, given that the present-day western Pueblos are uxorilocal, while the eastern Pueblos are bilocal (perhaps formerly virilocal).

These problems aside, whenever we are attempting to isolate residence patterns it is important to test *alternative* propositions. We cannot simply assume that the prehistoric residence patterns in a given area were the same as the modern ones for that area. By testing *several* propositions, we will have some assurance that one of them is more likely to be correct than the others.

Sodalities

The general method presented earlier for hypothesis testing is also useful for learning about prehistoric sodalities of various kinds. A sodality, it will be recalled (p. 15), is a nonresidential and generally non-localized association that serves to integrate residence units with one another. Most of the sodalities among present-day Pueblo groups are ceremonial sodalities (that is, their apparent purposes involve performing ritual). There is a great variety of such sodalities among Pueblo peoples, including kachina societies, initiation societies, warrior societies, curing societies, hunting societies, clowning societies, and so on (cf. Eggan 1950; Dozier 1965). Kachina societies are found in almost all of the Pueblos (Hawley 1950a: 296; Dozier 1965: 43-44). The western Pueblos tend to emphasize ceremonial organizations connected with the kachina cult and tribal initiation, while many of the eastern Pueblos emphasize curing, clowning, hunting, and warfare (Eggan 1950; Dozier 1965).

Membership in these sodalities crosscuts residence units, in the sense that the members are usually recruited from a number of different residence units. Only among the Hopi is there any tendency to recruit members from particular residence or kinship groups (Eggan 1950: 90-91).[15] Because of this nonlocalization of membership, it might appear that the discovery of such associations should be very difficult for the archaeologist.

42

This need not be the case, however, since all of these sodalities are localized on occasion. Each association has a kiva or room where it meets periodically to carry out its particular activities and where it keeps its fetishes and other ceremonial paraphernalia (Dozier 1965: 45-46). It should be possible to identify these rooms or kivas in the archaeological record. Some of the attributes or test implications of a prehistoric ceremonial room have already been considered (p. 23), and Dozier (1965; 45-46) has listed several more including the following:

1. Small size
2. Location near back of pueblo (where light is restricted)
3. Mural paintings on walls or floors
4. Slat altars
5. Stone figurines of animals
6. Obsidian blades
7. Odd-shaped stones and similar items
8. Anthropomorphic wooden figurines
9. Feather-wrapped corn ear

Thus, if an archaeologist discovered a room possessing all or some of these attributes, he could be reasonably certain that it was a ceremonial room—the meeting place of one or more sodalities.

Given the likelihood that such rooms can be discovered, we would also like to have some reasonably precise idea of what kinds of sodalities performed their activities in these rooms. In short, what were some of the specific kinds of ceremonial or other activities performed in a given prehistoric room? If it could be presumed that such a room had served as the locus of activity for a single ceremonial organization (for example, the kachina cult), then the answer to this question might not be difficult. The procedure in this case would not differ from that previously described:

1. Statement of the proposition that the room was used by the kachina cult (or any other sodality that might be suspected).
2. Statement of alternative propositions (that it was used by the hunting society, and so on).
3. Determination of the test implications for each of the propositions (that is, the kinds of evidence each sodality might be expected to leave in the archaeological record).
4. Testing of each proposition (That is, determining how many of the test implications of each alternative proposition are met in the data from the room in question).

5. Comparison of the test results, and evaluation of the relative merits of the propositions.

Having done this, and assuming that all of the relevant alternative propositions had been tested, it seems likely that we would be able to discover which one or two of the different sodalities had occupied the rooms. This procedure may be suitable, but at least two significant complications must be considered. First of all, Dozier (1965: 46) implies that the artifacts and other materials used by different sodalities might be very similar. If this is correct, it may be very difficult to demonstrate that a particular prehistoric room was used by one sodality and not another—the test implications would all be the same! Actually, I suspect that there are minor differences in the artifact kits of the different associations and that a careful examination of ethnographic data would bear this out. They might be very fine differences, such as the relative numbers of different kinds of material, the spatial characteristics of placement of these materials, or even certain style peculiarities of which we are not presently aware. Any *behavioral* differences among the sodalities stand some chance of being reflected in the archaeological record.

The second complication is more bothersome, though probably not insurmountable. It is raised because among present-day Pueblo groups, there is generally no one-to-one correlation between ceremonial room and sodality. While a single association might be responsible for a particular room, other groups may also use it from time to time (Eggan 1950: 105). This suggests that in any given prehistoric ceremonial room we can expect to find evidence of more than one kind of ritual or other activity and thus evidence of more than one sodality. This situation should not discourage our efforts, however; it seems likely that we will be able to identify such multiple usage.

Regardless of the outcome of our testing in any given case, we should be able to learn a great deal more than we do now about the kinds of uses of such kiva-like rooms. It may even be discovered that certain rituals that are performed in such rooms today were probably not performed in the past, and vice versa. In any event, the attempt should be made, and we have the methodological means for doing it.

There were probably other kinds of sodalities besides strictly ceremonial ones, of course. In a precise sense, modern Pueblo clans and dual divisions are sodalities; they meet the qualifications of being nonlocalized organizations with certain corporate functions (Service 1962: 21). They also are known to make use of particular rooms in carrying out their rituals, meetings, and other activities. It seems likely that these kinds of rooms, too, can be identified in prehistoric pueblos—assuming that we can find out what the appropriate test implications for them might be.

In addition, it may even be possible to determine that certain of the rooms associated with these sodalities were more frequently used by particular residence units than by others. It may be found, for example, that certain style elements (ceramics, architecture, and so forth) characteristic of a particular residence unit are found in certain ceremonial rooms—and that other ceremonial rooms possess style similarities to *different* residence units. Such a finding has been made at Broken K Pueblo, in east-central Arizona (Hill 1970). At present, however, it is difficult to be sure that style similarities alone can be used in inferring the association of kivas with particular residence units. It would be interesting to know whether or not Hopi kivas (and their contents) share elements of style with the lineages and clans that own them, or whose members may frequent them most often.

It seems most likely that among the later pueblos, at least, one might expect to find style elements representative of two or more different residence units in any given ceremonial room. One would expect this because present-day sodalities are integrative organizations, with membership drawn from more than one residence unit. If this were the case in prehistoric times, it may be possible to determine which residence units a given ceremonial room was associated with.

In addition to formal sodality organizations, there were undoubtedly a number of other social organizational features in prehistoric Pueblo communities that served (among other things) to integrate different residence units with one another. One such feature might have been economic reciprocity; certain groups may, for example, have exchanged particular kinds of manufactured goods, raw materials, and so forth (Eggan 1950: 60). Longacre (1966) has found some suggestive, though tenuous, evidence of this at Broken K Pueblo.

Statuses

Puebloan societies are often thought of as somewhat devoid of status differences, and this may be true in the sense that in wealth or political power there are no marked differences. There are a number of status differences, however, in terms of both ascribed and achieved status. Men, for example, are different in status from women—and they are treated differently (both while they are living and upon death). Children are of a different status from adults; lineage heads and village chiefs are not always of the same status as others; there is a small degree of status differentiation on the basis of specialization (see Kroeber 1917; Titiev 1944; Eggan 1950; and others). There are even slight status differences among residence units and sodalities. In the Hopi villages, for example, the bear clan usually provides the village chief and is largely responsible for the important winter solstice ceremony (the Soyal) (Titiev 1944; Eggan 1950: 106-07). All such status differences should be observable in the archaeological record, to the degree that the behavior associated with them has material correlates.

There is no need, at this point, to review the procedural steps for generating and testing hypotheses. It will be sufficient to simply list some of the kinds of evidence that might be useful as test implications for some of the major status differences that might be discovered archaeologically. Many of the material evidences of status differences will be found in burial data and involve differences in mortuary treatment, as follows:

1. Sex Differences (differences in treatment):
   a. Location
   b. Variations in burial pits
   c. Burial position
   d. Numbers of accompanying grave goods
   e. Kinds of accompanying grave goods (including contents of ceramic vessels)
   f. Style differences on ceramics and other goods
   g. Spatial placement of grave goods

2. Age Differences (infants, juveniles, adults, aged):
   Same kinds of test implications as for sex differences

3. Differences in Specialization:
   Same kinds of test implications (as above) may be involved, but there may also be other differences in treatment:
   a. Large quantities of accompanying artifacts of a single type (including blanks and manufacturing tools perhaps)
   b. Interment adjacent to other specialists in cemetery

4. Differences in Political-Economic Status:
   Same kinds of test implications (as above), but there may also be other differences in treatment. It is very likely that high status individuals will exhibit differences in numbers and types of grave goods.[16]

Prehistoric Social Organization in the American Southwest

While it is likely that achieved statuses were more important than ascribed statuses (other than age and sex) in prehistoric Pueblo societies, it may be possible to demonstrate ascription in some cases—at least tentatively. Such status differences might be reflected in mortuary data if a small number of skeletons are associated with very different kinds of grave goods. We would expect more "fancy" or "exotic" goods with such individuals—goods that would not be suited to "practical" or subsistence usage. Some artifacts may even have been manufactured for interment only.

Ascribed status might also be observed in infant burials. Since infants are too young to have achieved status, we might expect that most infant burials would not be accompanied by quantities of fancy or exotic items; they would not possess any of the attributes of mortuary treatment associated with presumed high-status individuals. If, however, a small number of infants are associated with such attributes, while most others are not, there is justification for at least generating the proposition that ascribed status had existed.

Also with regard to mortuary data, it may be possible to determine the particular residence unit to which an individual or group of individuals belonged while they were alive. Longacre (1963, 1964a) found that at Carter Ranch Site certain localized groups of burials could be associated with one or the other of the uxorilocal residence units he had identified, simply because similar ceramic design elements occurred on the burial pottery. This is certainly enough evidence upon which to propose that certain individuals had belonged to particular residence units, although it would be useful to have additional data with which to test the proposition. It might be, for example, that other kinds of style associations could be found or that the different burial groups would exhibit certain minor osteological differences (teeth patterns, and so forth) that would indicate different biological backgrounds.[17]

Evidence of status differences may also be found in areas other than burial grounds, of course. Status differences based on sex should be indicated, for example, by the presence of certain female- or male-associated artifacts in different locations within a pueblo. We can at least expect to find that kivas or ceremonial rooms will not contain many female-associated items (Hill 1968, 1970).

Evidence of specialization might stem from certain rooms in a pueblo that contain features, tools, blanks, manufacturing debris, and so forth, that were all usable in the manufacture of a particular kind of item. We

47

would particularly expect to find large quantities of finished and partially finished items, much as Charles DiPeso has discovered at Casas Grandes (personal communication). If ceramics or other composite tools were manufactured by a specialist, it should be possible to establish that fact through refined studies of style elements on the items (including evidence of homogeneity in motor habits). If the manufacturing location for such materials can be discovered, it should be possible to trace the "routes" of distribution of the product within (and between) sites.

I have discovered some reasonably good evidence of specialization at Broken K Pueblo, where it appears that particular residence units were specializing to some degree in the kinds of game they were hunting (Hill 1970).

Differences in political-economic status might also be discovered. A village chief might be expected to have a somewhat larger house than others, and it might be centrally located (although this seems doubtful for most Pueblo communities). One might also expect to find evidence of centralized storage facilities and hence evidence of a redistributive economy. At Acoma, where political power is somewhat centralized, it is known that the cacique (who is a member of the antelope clan) has certain agricultural fields tilled for him by the entire community, and the produce is stored in a central location (in the war chief's house) for redistribution at kachina ceremonies (Eggan 1950: 247).

This should be sufficient to at least suggest the kind of reasoning that must be involved in generating test implications for demonstrating status differences.

LIMITATIONS OF INFERENCE

It would appear, from the preceding discussion, that virtually all aspects of prehistoric behavior are amenable to discovery—given appropriate methods and techniques. While I have attempted to argue this and have presented a methodological approach that should be useful in this regard, I am by no means prepared to argue that there are no limits at all! On the other hand, it would be presumptuous to attempt to state with any degree of precision what the limitations actually are; we simply do not know. It is clear, however, that some of the commonly *believed* limitations are not as limiting as they have been thought to be. I will attempt, at this point, to discuss some of these presumed limitations, together with the arguments against them. I will then consider the general nature of what some of our real limitations might be and make some suggestions concerning the kinds of results we can expect in the future.

It was suggested, in the introduction, that one of the major presumed limitations to the elucidation of prehistoric social organization is that most of the behavioral aspects of culture are "intangible" and thus unrecoverable (see especially Smith 1955; MacWhite 1956). This seems to be a direct result of the theoretical view that cultures are really systems of norms, ideas, beliefs, values, and so forth (which are indeed intangible). It is argued that once the people are gone, there is no way to find out what their "real" or "nonmaterial" culture actually was. For some reason, social organization is regarded as part of this nonmaterial culture. While I would not deny that norms, and so forth, exist, I have argued that they are not aspects of real, observable behavior; and for this reason we need not be disturbed because we cannot discover them archaeologically.

On the other hand, elements of *behavior* involve real people and real things. They take place in particular locations and frequently leave observable remains that may be used in inferring the nature of the behavior involved. Certain significant kinds of behavior may leave no evidence, but most of the things the archaeologist is interested in *do* leave such remains —the problem is in knowing what kinds of evidence a particular item of behavior might be *expected* to leave in the archaeological remains (test implications), and what kinds of methods and techniques can be used to discover this evidence. The evidence is only "intangible" in the sense that we may not yet have developed techniques for observing it. As a matter of fact, the term "intangible" is inadequate, since the evidence is either there or it is not; it is not in some gray area between presence and absence.

A second widely held assumption is that we are inescapably limited because so much of the data available to the ethnographer is not available to the archaeologist. This has been termed the problem of "hidden data" or "missing data" (Binford 1968). Data may be missing for a variety of reasons—they may not be preserved; the archaeologist may not record them; the site being analyzed may be in a region in which particular kinds of data are considered difficult or impossible to recover; the cultural level of complexity involved may be such that certain kinds of data are believed unrecoverable.

It is true, of course, that most of the material correlates of behavior are *not* preserved. But this has led us to the unwarranted conclusion that the particular behaviors themselves can no longer be inferred. Actually, we do not need all, or even most, of these material correlates. There are even instances in which quite significant and complex elements of behavior can be described on the basis of a single item of evidence. One can, for example, infer the presence of centralized economic authority solely because a site contains a large central granary and few individual household storage facilities.

In short, most elements of behavior have more than one or two material correlates, and relatively few of them may be needed to demonstrate the prehistoric existence of the behavior. If we begin thinking less about the significance of individual artifacts and more about the *sets* (or clusters) of data that might be associated with a particular element of behavior, we can begin to make (and test) inferences that are presently not believed possible. The presence of baskets might be inferred from the presence of basket-making artifacts or even fire-cracked rock (stone boiling); the presence of residence units can be discovered from the nonrandom distributions of many different kinds of style elements. It may not be of crucial importance that all of the remains have been preserved.

Another point is also important in this connection. Since many prehistoric activities leave *clusters* of artifacts and other materials in the archaeological record, it is often possible to infer the uses of *particular* artifacts simply because they are associated with artifacts of *known* use. In a modern kitchen, for example, we could infer something about the uses of spoons (assuming we did not know them), simply because they are found associated with forks, knives, plates, and glasses—all of which are known to be used in food preparation and serving. By the same token, we might find that a certain "problematical" artifact is usually associated with particular kinds of materials, the uses of which are already reasonably well known. We have been limited in the past by the notion that *individual* artifacts are the primary units of observation—that they should each tell us something in themselves (without consideration of their association with other materials).

Another frequently cited, although related, limitation is that we must depend solely on ethnographic evidence in making inferences about prehistoric social organization. Since there are so many "missing data," we must rely on observations in the ethno-historic present (Hawley 1937a; Ascher 1961; Willey 1966: 3; Chang 1967). As I have pointed out (p. 21), this view implies that we really cannot use archaeological data at all in dealing with prehistoric social organization. This idea must be abandoned if we are to learn very much that is new about the past.

. . . So long as we insist that our knowledge of the past is limited by our knowledge of the present, we are painting ourselves into a methodological corner. The archaeologist must make use of his data as documents of past conditions, proceed to formulate propositions about the past, and devise means for testing them against archaeological remains (Binford 1968).

Actually, ethnographic information is very helpful, and it is important that it be used to a much greater extent than it has been in the past, but I have argued here that it is most fruitfully used in generating propositions and test implications—not in testing them (cf. Binford 1967a, 1967b; Hill 1968). The mere *testing* of a proposition presents us with information that was not previously known, and it provides evidence from which further propositions can be generated. It is particularly important that we take advantage of the test implications that are *not* confirmed, since these open the door to new problems—especially those of culture-change.

A final argument that is sometimes made is that our inferences about the past are frequently unverifiable and that we must rely on the expertise of the archaeologist in evaluating the validity of an inference (Thompson 1956). The methodology proposed here, however, obviates this problem, since once a proposition has been *tested*, any archaeologist can examine the methods by which the test was carried out, as well as its results, and judge for himself the acceptability of the inferences that are made. The problem of smoothing communication and understanding among colleagues is not solely a matter of reaching agreement on terminology; it is much more a matter of providing our colleagues with inferences based on test results that can be objectively evaluated (and sometimes even repeated). This is not meant to suggest, of course, that untested propositions, conjectures, and guesses should never reach the printed page; such inferences may be of great help to others. At the same time, however, they should be clearly labeled as such, and an effort should be made to suggest the kinds of data that would be needed in testing them.

But what are some of the limitations of archaeological inference? Perhaps most important is that we are always limited by our theory. I have previously pointed out that the most influential current theoretical view (the "normative approach") has limited our thinking to certain kinds of problems (pp. 16-18). The implicit idea that cultures are homogeneous has led us to ignore variability *within* archaeological sites and regions and has encouraged a research goal involving the elucidation of what was in men's minds (norms, and so forth). It has followed from this, then, that one of the major problems is the comparison of norms (represented by "diagnostic" traits) in space and time and the explanation of culture-change in terms of influences or idea transmission. This view has also guided our research with regard to prehistoric social organization, in the sense that it has encouraged us to look for evidence of prehistoric abstractions (conceptions of kinship, and so forth).

The theoretical view presented here may also be found limiting in terms of the kinds of questions it permits us to ask about the past. For the present, however, the theory (unformalized) that cultures are internally heterogeneous systems is a productive one. The kinds of questions that have been considered in this paper stem directly from this theoretical view. It no longer seems adequate to describe and compare cultures as if they were "normative wholes." Indeed, the concept of culture itself may be losing much of its former usefulness. It is becoming increasingly clear that we cannot describe whole cultures and that overall indices of culture (such as diagnostics and norms) simply cover up significant variability that exists in a society. It seems likely that we will become less and less interested in cultures (and social organization) as *wholes* and more and more concerned with describing (and explaining) individual aspects of cultural systems, such as residence patterns, status differentials, and the many individual aspects of task organization. We can then begin comparing these things—within sites, within regions, and cross-culturally—and generating testable propositions to explain them.

In short, I feel that our most serious limitation is *theory*. It governs the questions we ask (problems), and these in turn govern the kinds of methods and techniques that are useful in answering them. As was pointed out earlier, our theory and problems, whether they are explicit or implicit, affect us even to the point of influencing the kinds of data we collect and the manner in which they are reported.

Finally, another major limitation is that we are restricted in the kinds of propositions we can test by the *techniques* that are currently available for gathering and analyzing data. Some of our test implications are unusable, simply because they cannot yet be examined or measured in the archaeological record. For example, to discover the former contents of pits or ceramic vessels, sophisticated chemical analyses that are as yet undeveloped or impractical may be required. Techniques for objectively measuring fine differences in ceramic design have not yet been developed, nor have we discovered a way to identify many pollen grains to the level of species differences. The list could continue indefinitely, of course. In this connection, it is apparent that techniques of dating are in need of refinement. A concern with prehistoric social organization leads directly to the need to be able to date rooms and areas in a pueblo relative to one another; otherwise we will not know whether we are describing contemporaneous social organizations or organizations that are separated in time to some extent.

The specific methods and techniques that are required in dealing with the kinds of problems considered in this volume are, in some respects, quite different from those that are most useful in collecting, describing, and comparing lists of culture traits. It may be worthwhile to mention a few of these differences. One of them is that we are becoming much more dependent on ethnographic and social anthropological information than we have been in the past—although this information is used in a different way (to generate hypotheses and test implications). If we are ignorant of the variability in specific social organizations in the Southwest (and in the world), we will not know what the alternative propositions are that might be tested, nor will we know what test implications are appropriate.

A second notable difference is that the theory of classification is different. Instead of viewing "types" as inherent entities to be described and "canonized" (such as the standard Southwestern pottery types), it has become important to view types as ever changing and as dependent on the particular problems which they will help elucidate (cf. Brew 1946). For example, if the interest is in discovering the activities carried out in pueblo rooms, we will want to know what particular kinds of ceramic vessels were used for; and to determine this, the attributes of vessel form become important. In this case, one relevant typology will be based on differences in form. If the interest is in isolating residence units, then minute differences in design elements (including those reflecting differences in motor habits) become important; and design differences serve as the basis of typological divisions. While the standard Southwestern pottery types do serve their present purposes, they are inadequate for other purposes. In short, the current "theory" of typology has limited us, and it appears to be in need of review again.

Problems of prehistoric social organization also require that improved sampling techniques be developed, and there has been a recent interest in this. It has become important that we obtain as close to a representative sample as we can; otherwise much of the internal variability within a community cannot be understood. While test pits, trenches, and block excavations may yield trait lists that are suitable for dating purposes and some degree of comparison, they do not permit adequate analysis of social organization.

The increasing interest in statistics is also, in part, a result of an interest in different kinds of problems. While it is useful to use statistics in comparing trait lists, they are indispensable for analysis of prehistoric social organization. It is important to be able to compare numbers of items among rooms and sites and to be able to objectively evaluate the significance of observed differences. Statistical analyses provide these measures.

It is again important to emphasize that the theory and general methodology described in this paper are applicable to more than prehistoric pueblos; they are presumably applicable to all sites, areas, and time periods. It is not necessary to have rooms bounded by walls to test propositions about prehistoric social organization. Convincing evidence in support of this assertion has been found at a prepithouse site in eastern Arizona (P. S. Martin and J. M. Fritz, personal communication) and at a small site that I am currently excavating in California.

The same theory and method are also applicable to the description and explanation of cultural variability and change, although it has not been possible in this paper to consider these things. A number of propositions have already been generated to describe and explain various aspects of Puebloan (and pre-Puebloan) social organizational changes, and many of them have been proposed by ethnographers (see especially Strong 1927; Kroeber 1928; Steward 1937; Eggan 1950). Some of them are clearly testable, since they yield test implications that can be observed in the archaeological record.

An example of one of these is the proposition that at some point there was a shift from bilocal or virilocal residence to uxorilocal residence in the Southwest (Steward 1937; Eggan 1950). A discussion of some of the test implications of different residence patterns has already been given (pp. 37-42; Table 1). It should be possible to test for this shift and to isolate the period in which it occurred, by describing the residence patterns existing at a number of villages from all time periods. The inference of such a shift is logical, and it seems likely, to me at least, that it occurred in the vicinity of A.D. 500-800 (when agriculture became highly productive). This proposition can be tested by describing the residence patterns that existed both before and after this period. By the same token, one could also test the proposition that the Rio Grande Pueblos had an uxorilocal residence pattern at some time prior to contact with the Spanish (Eggan 1950).

Another such proposition is that suggested by Eggan (1950: 213), to the effect that the Zuni had a dual division form of organization prior to about A.D. 1700. Some of the test implications of dual division have been given (p. 36), and the testing of Eggan's proposition should be relatively easy.[18]

An example of a testable *explanatory* proposition is the suggestion that the aggregation into larger villages in the 13th and 14th centuries was brought about because of changes in the physical environment that reduced crop yields and created a need for more dependable water supplies. While it is not feasible to discuss all of the pertinent test implications here, it would be necessary to generate test implications for at least three subpropositions (cf. Hill 1970).

1. That there was a shift in the physical environment.
2. That crop yields were reduced at this time.
3. That the large sites occur predominantly in areas that had permanent water supplies (that is, major drainageways and springs).

The alternative propositions would also have to be tested, of course.

It should be clear, at this point, that it is only by proceeding *deductively* that we will be able to learn very much about prehistoric social organization. It is only through the statement of problems and hypotheses that data become *relevant*. Otherwise our observations on the archaeological record are usually wasted. If we *begin* our research with hypotheses or propositions, however, we are guided (indeed required) to seek the observations that they imply—and many, or even most, of these observations will neither be observed nor thought of as relevant prior to having the hypotheses in mind.

Hempel (1966) makes the interesting and important point that even the presence of a *problem* is insufficient in deciding what data may be relevant. Problems do not of themselves yield test implications; one must generate *hypotheses*.

All of this is not meant to imply that a certain amount of unstructured data collection must necessarily be condemned. At the same time, I suspect that such a situation rarely if ever exists. Most archaeologists choose to collect data that are relevant to something, whether or not that something is explicitly stated, and whether or not the data are considered to be immediately useful—otherwise they would have no reason to collect the data at all! Nonetheless, there is a great need for considerably more hypothesis testing. Excellent discussions of archaeological epistemology, involving detailed comparison of the deductive and inductive approaches for acquiring information, are found in Fritz (1968), Plog (1968), and Fritz and Plog (1968).

In conclusion, it seems likely that the theory and method presented here will permit much more refined analyses of prehistoric social organization than have been possible so far—in terms of both description and explanation—and the results of these analyses will be susceptible to objective evaluation. It should be possible to compare specific kinds of social organizational features in space and time and even arrive at significant cross-cultural explanatory hypotheses. The important limitations are not in the data themselves; they lie rather in our abilities to ask questions that are testable. These abilities are heavily influenced by the theories under which we carry out our research. I have attempted to explicate a theoretical approach and method that have so far been both successful and promising.

NOTES

1. "Systems archaeology" is one of several terms (including "new archaeology," "structural-functional archaeology," and so on) that have been used to label recent theoretical and methodological developments stimulated largely by Lewis R. Binford, his students, and his colleagues.

2. I should point out that modern normative theorists in social anthropology do not regard cultures as homogeneous (lacking in internal variability). My use of the terms "normative" and "normative approach" is not precisely equivalent to current anthropological usage.

3. In addition to obscuring variability, the normative approach implies a primary concern with the study of abstractions—norms, ideas, beliefs, and so forth. These are not measurable, and thus not subject to scientific manipulation or verification (Binford 1965, 1968).

4. Propositions may be generated inductively or deductively. Inductively drawn propositions usually develop from observations on the data themselves (observations of what is being explained). Deductive propositions are drawn from theoretical statements or laws, and they follow from these generalizations. Deductively drawn propositions are more forceful and have a more general significance, but we are frequently frustrated by

not yet having suitable laws or theories from which to generate such propositions (cf. Hempel 1966).

5. It is not solely a matter of presence or absence of these data, of course. If, for example, an investigator finds four kiva-like rooms in a site, and one of them contains a mano, this need not suggest that the room was not used as a kiva—or that kivas are in fact associated with manos. This is where statistics (significance tests, and so on) come in, of course. It may be that certain other kinds of rooms are much more strongly associated with manos and that the single mano in the kiva is statistically insignificant.

6. An attempt to measure the relative amounts of pollen types in modern Hopi room types (including kivas) was unsuccessful, since permission to take samples was not granted. The accomplishment of that study would have made an evaluation of this inference more secure. It is well known, however, that large quantities of corn and squash pollen are regularly introduced into Hopi kivas (Forde 1931; Parsons 1936; Titiev 1944).

7. The quantitative techniques that may be used in isolating types cannot be considered here (see Spaulding 1953; Siegel 1956; Hill 1970; Sackett 1966).

8. It may be, of course, that strong positive analogies cannot be discovered, as would almost certainly be the case if the prehistoric site were a prepueblo site, or if it were a very different pueblo than the historic examples. In this event, one might propose that the uses were *not* equivalent in all respects. This would lead to a series of propositions relevant to describing the differences in use, and one might have to consult worldwide comparative ethnographic evidence in an attempt to find better analogies (which would then be used in generating both additional propositions and test implications).

9. Some Pueblo groups perform kachina dances in special locations two to three miles from the pueblo (Dozier, personal communication).

10. "The nuclear family is characteristically a unit comprising a husband, wife, and children, with perhaps an unattached relative, such as a widowed grandfather or grandmother or an unmarried brother, sister, nephew, or niece" (Dozier 1965: 38). It usually occupies no more than two or three rooms (Dozier 1965: 39).

11. This unit is the basic economic and social unit in most Pueblo societies. It can be matrilocal, patrilocal, bilocal, or ambilocal (Dozier 1965), and it is usually composed of several related nuclear family households occupying adjacent groups of rooms; it is generally an extended family or lineage segment grouping (Titiev 1944; Eggan 1950: 29-30, 188-89).

12. The precise style elements that might characterize these units as opposed to the smaller household units cannot be suggested, since such data have not been examined by ethnographers. It has been shown, however, (using archaeological data), that room groups of twenty or so rooms may be distinguished by somewhat different style elements than distinguish much larger divisions of a pueblo (Hill 1966, 1970).

13. These dual divisions are frequently endogamous, loosely patrilineal groups. Each division is responsible for the major political, social, and ceremonial events that occur during its period in power (summer and winter moieties) (Dozier 1965).

14. An uxorilocal (or matrilocal) residence unit consists of an adult woman with her husband and unmarried children, including married daughters and their husbands and children. This residence pattern is characteristic of the Hopi, Hopi-Tewa, and Zuni; it may have been present in the past at Acoma, Laguna, and the eastern Keresan pueblos (Eggan 1950: 29-30; Dozier 1954: 312). Eggan (1950) has even suggested the pos-

57

sibility that *all* of the eastern Pueblos originally had uxorilocal residence patterns (see also Ellis 1951: 149).

15. It seems likely that in the earlier "unit-type" pueblos (which often had a single ceremonial room) membership in ceremonial organizations was drawn from the local residence unit only. The kiva may have been owned and utilized by a single lineage, for example (cf. Eggan 1950).

16. Among the eastern Pueblos, society members are accorded special burial treatment that is not accorded nonsociety members (Dozier, personal communication).

17. Tanoan Pueblo cemeteries are known to contain individual family burial plots. It should be possible to distinguish bilateral extended family burial plots and perhaps even nuclear family plots within them (Dozier, personal communication).

18. It is interesting to note that this proposition was generated on the basis of Zuni myth; it illustrates that the inspiration for a proposition can come from any source.

An Inquiry into Prehistoric Social
Organization in Chaco Canyon,
New Mexico[1]

R. GWINN VIVIAN

Arizona State Museum,
University of Arizona

A review of archaeological reports on the prehistoric Pueblo Southwest, published within the past 25 years, reveals that prehistoric Pueblo social organization has not been of overriding concern to Southwestern archaeologists. When interpretations of social organization from archaeological data have been considered, they have frequently been based on analogy to historic Pueblo social organization, and the archaeological data are inserted into the framework of the recent system. Even such reconstructions are not often attempted, and the aim of much work in the Southwest continues in accumulating archaeological fact for elaboration of regional sequences.

It is not always a lack of archaeological data that prevents investigation of prehistoric social organization, but a reluctance on the part of archaeologists to go a step beyond the establishment of regional sequences. Certainly the methods employed by the Field Museum of Natural History (Hill 1966; Hill and Hevly 1968; Longacre 1964a, 1966; Martin et al. 1962,

1964; Martin, Longacre, and Hill 1967) should be applicable to other areas of the Southwest. Despite the lack of research directed toward the recovery of information reflecting social structure in the Chaco area, published studies combined with new information on water control systems provide a basis for making inferences regarding the organization of prehistoric social units in Chaco Canyon.

At approximately A.D. 1050, there were three rather well-defined types of communities in Chaco Canyon: large "classic" sites, such as Pueblo Bonito (Judd 1964); small pueblos, such as Bc 50 and 51 (Kluckhohn and Reiter 1939); and McElmo Phase sites, such as Kin Kletso (Vivian and Mathews 1966). The first two types appear to have a long history of development in the canyon; the third was probably brought into the Chaco sometime after A.D. 1000. Differences are most evident in community plan and architectural style, although other dissimilarities have been noted and will be discussed below. Only the two long established types will be considered in this paper. This choice was made because of the extended *in situ* development of these types and because very few sites of the third community type have been excavated in Chaco Canyon.

Archaeologists working in Chaco have recognized the differences between the large classic sites and the smaller pueblos since the 1930s, when excavations by the University of New Mexico established, through dendrochronology and ceramic studies, that these sites were contemporaneous and not representative of two temporal stages in Chaco Canyon prehistory. The explanations offered for these rather marked dissimilarities were very general, however. Hawley (1937b: 116-17) considered all Chacoans to be one homogeneous group whose members varied in their selection of habitation. Dutton's (1938: 79-80) explanation paralleled that of Hawley, and she noted that, "Possibly, in the Great Houses of Chaco Canyon, there were some who elected to make their homes away from the larger pueblos." Kluckhohn (Kluckhohn and Reiter 1939: 151-62) felt that village dwellers might have represented culturally similar but conservative members of a single group, but he preferred to view the inhabitants of villages as migrants from another region, "representatives of a related but somewhat less advanced cultural heritage drawn to the Chaco by the prosperity of its inhabitants." Vivian (1959) and Vivian and Mathews (1966) noted the village-town dichotomy and suggested that there was evidence for different phases of Anasazi development and tradition.

I believe the differences between these community types indicate something more than the architectural proclivities of several thousand prehistoric inhabitants of Chaco Canyon. I suggest that the two contrasting community types in Chaco reflect the operation of two different systems of social organization. To provide a background for my arguments, a brief review of Chaco prehistory is given below.

PREHISTORY OF CHACO CANYON

The Chaco Wash, beginning near Star Lake, New Mexico, flows west from the Continental Divide for approximately 70 miles where it turns north, and some 80 miles later it joins the San Juan River near Shiprock. The Chaco Wash and its tributaries drain an area of approximately 4,500 square miles; the area drained is often referred to as the Chaco Basin.

The Chaco Canyon is 20 miles long and is almost at the head of the Chaco Wash and its tributary system. "Within this drainage Chaco Canyon is unique; it is the only canyon of any extent, and it is the only large confined area, a strip from a half to three-quarters of a mile wide and 20 miles long, where the aggrading alluvium was held within an area suitable for flood water irrigation" (Vivian and Mathews 1966: 1). Water and alluvium are derived from the headwaters of the Chaco Wash to the east, through two breaks in the Chacra Mesa bordering the canyon on the south, and through small but important tributaries on the north.

In addition to these vital natural resources, Chaco Canyon provided other attractions to early farmers. An abundance of sandstone, especially a dense variety occurring in uniform layers with good natural cleavage, was available for building, and the architectural results are one of the hallmarks of Chaco culture. A belt of pine stretched from the Continental Divide along the higher elevations through at least the canyon area, providing construction materials and fuel. No good faunal study has been made for the Chaco, but it is probable that animal life was plentiful.

Given the above conditions, Chaco Canyon probably represented an oasis of sorts in the Chaco Basin and attracted early farming peoples. It is possible that more than a single cultural tradition might have been brought into the Chaco by early migrants. Instances of groups with diverse cultural traditions inhabiting the same locality are known from several areas in the Southwest. The information available indicates that pithouse settlements were common on the mesa tops above the canyon and in the rolling hill area south of the canyon by at least A.D. 700.

A shift to aboveground structures was apparently coeval with a major shift to the canyon bottomlands and may have occurred no earlier than A.D. 750. Population centered in the canyon and again in an area to the south, although population density was higher in the canyon than in the more open southern area. The important period between A.D. 750 and 850 is practically undocumented archaeologically. At approximately A.D. 850, however, the first evidence for two community types in Chaco is present. The first developmental stages of these types have not been demonstrated through excavation, nor has it been determined whether these two patterns represent the parallel development of two distinct cultural traditions or the evolution of two variants of a single tradition.

The community types appearing at approximately A.D. 850 and continuing until the abandonment of Chaco sometime after 1130 are referred to here as "village" and "town" sites. These terms are used to reflect the formal planning of towns as opposed to the amorphous nature of villages, the greater architectural sophistication present in towns, and the larger size of towns. Some of these differences are made more graphically evident in Fig. 1.

The Three-C site (Vivian 1965), considered as representative of early villages, was occupied from approximately A.D. 870 to 950. It consisted of a nine-room, one-story pueblo, arranged in a double tier with two kivas on one side. Wall construction included horizontal slab masonry, adobe turtlebacks with stone spalls, and vertical-slab-based walls which might have supported horizontal slab masonry. The kivas represented early manifestations of two divergent styles, the Chaco and the San Juan or Mesa Verde.

Vestiges of other early villages have been found beneath the sites of Bc 50 and 51 (Hibben 1937: 82-84) and Bc 59 (Vivian 1965: 43). Some of an additional ten excavated, but unreported, villages may also date in the ninth century. Although no complete site survey has been undertaken in Chaco Canyon, several hundred villages are known within the canyon, and a rough sampling of surface sherds indicates that at least half are representative of a period between A.D. 850 and 1030. Most village sites are located on the south side of the canyon.

Coincident with the development of village sites, Chaco towns were evolving on the opposite or north side of the canyon. At the time that the inhabitants of the Three-C site were constructing and residing in their nine-room pueblo, building was underway in at least four of the classic

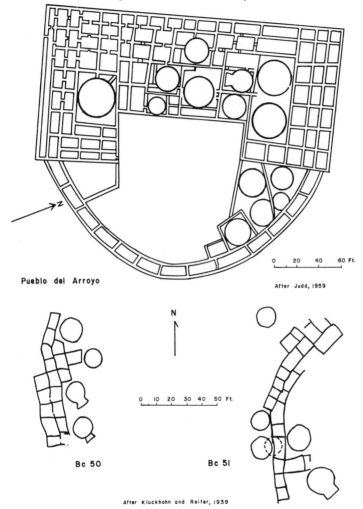

FIGURE 1. PUEBLO DEL ARROYO, A CHACO TOWN, has tree-ring dates from
A.D. 1052 to 1117. The northern unit of the town and the arced front row of rooms
have not been excavated. Bc 50 and Bc 51, Chaco villages, have tree-ring dates from
A.D. 922 to 1077. The nearby village site of Bc 59 has several tree-ring specimens dated
at 1110.

towns—Pueblo Bonito, Una Vida, Peñasco Blanco, and Kin Bineola. Tree-ring dates from these sites include a range from A.D. 825-935 at Pueblo Bonito, 847-950 at Una Vida, 898-934 at Peñasco Blanco, and 941-943 at Kin Bineola (Bannister 1966: 178). All of the logs with these dates were used with an unfaced slab type of masonry described by Hawley (1934: 13) as Masonry Type I. This masonry was composed of rough and irregularly shaped sandstone slabs laid in an abundance of mortar from the two sides of the wall so that their inner ends roughly interlocked. It contrasted with later styles in that it was not cored and the surfaces, while relatively smooth, were not veneered.

Of these sites, only Pueblo Bonito has been totally excavated, and inferences regarding the early towns must be based almost entirely on this one example. During its early period, Pueblo Bonito was composed of more than 75 ground-floor rooms arranged in "a crescentic assemblage of living rooms each with paired storerooms at the rear, subterranean kivas out in front and a community trash pile beyond the kivas" (Judd 1964: 61). There is some indication that a great kiva was constructed at the early Bonito townsite. Judd (1964: 211) reported a great kiva (not designated by number or letter) 53 feet in diameter in a 69-foot pit, 10 feet below the surface of the West Court. Although he believed that it postdated the earlier portion of the site, he stated, "In the portion we exposed, practically every facing stone had been removed; hence we had but little on which to judge the age of that ruin" (Judd 1964: 211). In addition, he remarked that a previously undisturbed "Old Bonitan" (Judd's designation for the original crescentic town dwellers) rubbish pile was found outside the south wall of the great kiva. Much of the "Old Bonitan" refuse excavated by Judd was disturbed by building postdating the early townsite. There is evidence for at least two-story construction at early Pueblo Bonito, and the kivas are of Chaco style (Judd 1964: Fig. 23). Judd (1964: 61) also notes, and it is evident from Fig. 3 in his 1964 report that a transverse block of small rooms divides this early structure into two fairly equal parts, a division that appears to have been maintained throughout the building history of Pueblo Bonito.

Architectural details from other early towns are not well known, but Bannister (1966: 178) remarks that a three-story pueblo was constructed by the builders of Peñasco Blanco. The original plan of Peñasco Blanco apparently was also crescentic.

It should be noted that there is evidence in the form of dated logs, but no structures, of early building at the sites of Chetro Ketl and Hungo Pavi. Early dates from Chetro Ketl range from A.D. 945 to 995, and two dates from Hungo Pavi are 942 and 943. The presence of these timbers, associated with other timbers cut at a later date and employed in construction of later rooms, has been explained as reuse of logs in later structures. There was a surge of building in many of the towns at approximately 1030, and excavation at Pueblo Bonito revealed that remodeling and razing of much of the old unfaced slab masonry section of Pueblo Bonito was carried out after 1030. Portions of similar old style structures known from Kin Bineola, Una Vida, and Peñasco Blanco may represent only remnants of formerly more extensive buildings. Since large-scale razing of structures and planned construction of new large units characterize the later history of building in the towns, it is possible that early dated logs in later rooms are materials salvaged from leveled living units.

The early village and town sites are more similar ceramically than they are architecturally, and the introduction of new ceramic types appears to be contemporaneous in both. The only ceramic data available for early towns are from the excavation at Pueblo Bonito and the sectioning of the Peñasco Blanco refuse mound by Frank H. H. Roberts. In both instances, pottery similar to that recovered from the Three-C site is in the lowest levels. Ceramics located in tests at Una Vida have not been reported, and no excavation has been done in the ruin of Kin Bineola.

The above discussion has dealt primarily with village and town sites as they appeared from 850 to approximately 1030. The date 1030 should not be construed as a point in time indicating a sharp break in the patterns visible in Chaco Canyon. This date was first advanced by Hawley (1934: 22) as marking the introduction of the "narrow banded with core" type masonry at Chetro Ketl. The introduction of cored, faced masonry coincided with several major building periods in a number of the towns. It should be remembered, however, that most of the masonry styles have been dated on the basis of timbers from Chetro Ketl. While Chetro Ketl has more dated specimens than any other site in Chaco, canyon-wide adoption of a new masonry style at a specific date cannot be assumed on the basis of one site. Actually one specimen is dated at 1030 from Chetro Ketl (Bannister 1966: 149), and it appears that the first major building period of presently visible Chetro Ketl was between 1036 and 1040. Taking all available information into account, it is probably better to postulate that large-scale building projects using cored masonry in Chaco towns evolved sometime between 1000 and 1040.

Considering the date 1030 as more tentative than fixed, therefore, the following hundred years can be viewed as a continuation and culmination of the village and town pattern. The major characteristics of each during the final period are given below.

VILLAGE AND TOWN CHARACTERISTICS

It is difficult to estimate the number of eleventh-century villages present in the canyon, but there are probably no fewer than 200 and no more than 400. Many others can be found outside the canyon, especially to the south. Canyon villages occur in clusters and singly. The number of rooms per village is seldom more than twenty-five, and these are arranged in an amorphous plan. Kivas are often enclosed within the house-block, but there are no courtyards or plazas. Evidence for more than two-story construction is missing. Masonry is not cored, and walls are seldom well finished.

Kivas vary, but the predominant form is the San Juan or Mesa Verde type. Great kivas are not present within the sites, although the great kiva Rinconada, near several villages (Bc 50, 51, 59, and others), may have served some village sites.

Material items recovered from these villages are generally similar to those recovered from the towns, with the exception of luxury items. Cylindrical painted vases, mosaic, inlay work, large quantities of turquoise, copper bells, and parrots and macaws have not been recovered from village sites.

Burials, usually flexed and accompanied by grave goods, have been found in refuse areas and beneath floors at the villages.

Thirteen large towns are known to have been important during the eleventh century. Eight lie within a 9-mile section of the canyon or on the rim. Of those outside the canyon, one is near the head of the Chaco Wash about 15 miles east of Pueblo Bonito, three are some distance to the south and southwest of Pueblo Bonito, and the last is north of the canyon on the Escavada Wash. The densest cluster includes Old Alto, Pueblo Bonito, Pueblo del Arroyo, and Chetro Ketl, all of which lie within a mile of one another. The isolated great kivas Rinconada and Kin Nahasbas are architecturally similar to great kivas within towns and are considered as part of town development. Two other great kivas, one east of Wijiji and another near Kin Bineola, also are in this class of isolated great kivas.

Excavations in Pueblo Bonito, Chetro Ketl, and Pueblo del Arroyo have shown that major building projects were undertaken in the Chaco towns sometime after 1000. These projects were based on preconceived plans in which large units of the pueblo were constructed at one time. Judd (1964: 143-53) excavated an extensive foundation complex at Pueblo Bonito which was laid out and then abandoned in favor of another ground plan. As noted earlier, these construction programs included leveling of already existing structures.

Ground plans in most cases seem to have been based on an original linear compact mass of rooms to which blocks of rooms were added, forming L- and E-shaped pueblos. The arced front wall of many of the Chaco towns (Chetro Ketl, Hungo Pavi, Old Alto, and Pueblo del Arroyo) was one of the latest additions (see Fig. 1). The arced portion of Una Vida, Peñasco Blanco, and Pueblo Bonito, on the other hand, contains some of the oldest dated structures. Apparently, an original crescentic plan was maintained in these towns, but if it were present in the others, it was obliterated or made to conform to the new plan by alteration.

An open plaza surrounded by room-blocks was present in all the towns. These plazas became enclosed with the late addition of the arced row of rooms. Buildings ranged from two to at least four stories in height. Construction after approximately 1030 was in cored masonry with decorative wall veneers. The sandstone used in these buildings was not the most readily available, but a dark bedded variety found above the canyon walls.

Probably the majority of these towns developed in place over a long period of time. It is known that Pueblo Bonito, Una Vida, Peñasco Blanco, Kin Bineola, and possibly Chetro Ketl had a history of *in situ* development from at least A.D. 940. Pueblo Pintado, Old Alto, Hungo Pavi, Kin Klizhin, and Kin Ya-a may also have had a lengthy period of evolution. On the other hand, Pueblo del Arroyo and Wijiji were most likely late developments and may be preplanned offshoots of larger towns. Judd (1959: 172) conjectured that, "It is not beyond reason that Pueblo del Arroyo was built by a group migrant from the larger village (Pueblo Bonito), less than 300 yards distant."

67

Kivas are almost invariably in the Chaco style. At least one great kiva is also present in many of these towns and is usually located in the plaza. Developmental stages of the great kiva are known from the excavated sites of Pueblo Bonito and Chetro Ketl (Vivian and Reiter 1960), and in time excavation may demonstrate the existence and long development of great kivas in all of the towns. Isolated great kivas have been noted, and while they were most likely the creation of town residents, they may have served a town-village integrative function. Three tower kivas are also present. These poorly known structures are probably late, and only the Chetro Ketl example has been excavated. No tower kivas are known from village sites.

The material culture of town sites is marked by a particular richness. While ceramic types are similar to those found in villages, some ceramic forms, such as the tall cylindrical vases from Pueblo Bonito, are present only in the towns, and more ceramic effigy forms have been recovered from town sites. Luxury items in towns include large quantities of turquoise in mosaic, inlay, pendant, and bead form; carved and painted wood (primarily bird forms) from Chetro Ketl; painted cloisonné on sandstone; copper bells; and parrots and macaws.

Excavations in Pueblo Bonito, Chetro Ketl, and Pueblo del Arroyo produced only 121 burials. The proportion of burials recovered compared to the number of rooms excavated showed a discrepancy in the evidence for the population size. This discrepancy was not present in the village sites, and several extensive searches for town cemeteries have been made. None has been successful. Practically without exception, town burials were found in abandoned rooms or beneath floors. Most were in extended position and were usually accompanied by offerings of pottery, basketry, or jewelry. The majority had been disturbed (MacNitt 1957: 334).

The last construction in village and town sites was in the early years of the twelfth century. By 1130 the canyon was being abandoned and it is likely that by 1150 few persons were residing in the Chaco. With the exception of a few minor occupations in the canyon during the next two hundred years, pueblo occupation had ended.

The period from 1000 to 1100 was one of the greatest periods of growth affecting both towns and villages. Like the stimulus to growth, the causes of abandonment were felt equally by all the occupants of the canyon. The last construction (tree-ring dates) at Bc 59, a village, was 1110. Final construction at Chetro Ketl was 1116; at Kin Bineola, 1124; and at Pueblo Pintado, 1126.

CONSTRUCTION OF WATER CONTROL SYSTEMS

One additional major difference between the village and town patterns has been recognized in recent years. It is now apparent that there is an association of extensive water control systems with town sites, but there is no good evidence that systems for water control are associated with villages. The failure to recognize this important difference at an earlier date must be attributed to the fact that the majority of Chaco water control systems, though reported as early as 1901 (Holsinger 1901), have been ignored or not recognized in more recent times.

This situation was amended between 1963 and 1966 by R. Gordon Vivian, who mapped and photographed known water control structures in the Chaco area. A summary of his work appeared in 1966 in *Kin Kletso, A Pueblo III Community in Chaco Canyon, New Mexico.* Additional work was accomplished by me during the summer of 1967, under a project supported by a National Science Foundation Institutional Grant and the Arizona State Museum. This work was primarily a more intensive investigation of a single system. In view of the lack of published data, a brief review of known hydraulic structures in Chaco (Fig. 2) and a short description of one system (Fig. 3) are given below.

Farming Terraces

Evidence for farming terraces in Chaco is limited to one extensive system between the towns of Pueblo Bonito, Chetro Ketl, and Pueblo Alto. A portion of the terracing is shown in Fig. 3, where it is equated with the Pueblo Alto system. The terracing may have belonged to one community, or separate areas may have been claimed by individual communities. The terraces are long rock walls, many over 100 feet in length, and with a maximum height of 12 feet. They are constructed to capture runoff from the mesa top in gardens between the cliff edge and the terrace walls.

Grid Borders

Grid borders are used to hold soil against erosion and for controlling runoff after rains. Only one area of grid borders has definitely been identified in the canyon and is shown in detail in Fig. 3 near Chetro Ketl. Many other grid areas probably existed in Chaco but have been covered by

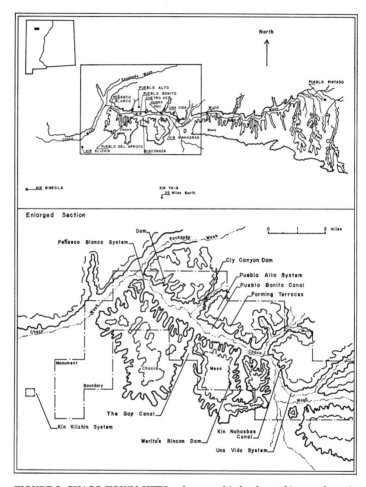

FIGURE 2. CHACO TOWN SITES and excavated isolated great kivas are shown in the upper small scale map. A section of the Chaco Canyon enlarged below shows the location of the densest cluster of water control features and systems in Chaco Canyon.

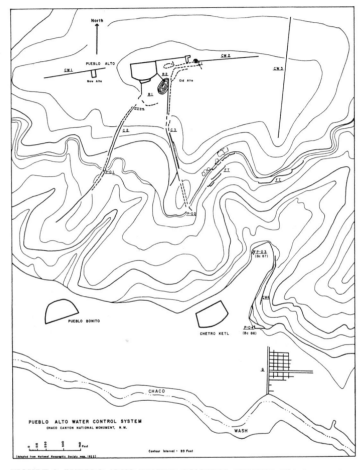

FIGURE 3. PUEBLO ALTO WATER CONTROL SYSTEM. This town system was developed sometime after A.D. 1000 and was probably used throughout the eleventh century. Features of the system are designated: CW, collecting wall; C, canal; R, reservoir; P-O, pour-off structure; FT, farming terrace; G, grid gardens.

heavy alluviation in the canyon bottom. The Chetro Ketl grid borders are earth ridges separating plots approximately 50 feet on a side. It is assumed that these plots were used for agriculture.

Dams

A masonry dam across one of the major tributary side canyons in Chaco Canyon was excavated in the summer of 1967. This dam collected runoff from the canyon and directed the water by means of a gate presumably into a canal. The dam was over 120 feet in length, and 20 feet in width, and stood at least 7 feet high. The gate measured 3½ feet in width and was near the center of the dam. The nearest towns were Pueblo Alto and Pueblo del Arroyo, both approximately a mile distant.

A similar but smaller dam was reported from a side canyon near Peñasco Blanco. Two other dams across a reentrant have been noted on the Chacra Mesa opposite Hungo Pavi. The center portion of each has been destroyed, so that it cannot be determined if the dams served to impound water permanently or to channel it through gates to farming areas.

Canals

The most impressive, and to date most widespread, evidence for water control in Chaco is the presence of canals. Ten canals have been located near nine of the town sites. Two canals are known at Pueblo Alto. Single canals definitely associated with a town occur at Pueblo Pintado, Una Vida, Pueblo Bonito, Peñasco Blanco, Kin Klizhin, Kin Bineola, and Kin Ya-a. The long "Gap" canal may be associated with Pueblo del Arroyo or both this town and Pueblo Bonito. Portions of these canals are known to range in length from 200 feet (the Kin Nahasbas section of the Una Vida canal) to more than 3 miles (Pueblo Pintado canal), and in width from 9 feet (Una Vida) to more than 50 feet (Pueblo Pintado) crest to crest. Depth ranges from 2 to slightly less than 5 feet. The variability in width and depth of canals probably reflects the differences between main canals and feeder ditches. Canals are either excavated and slab lined or are formed by slab and masonry walls where they could not be excavated. Diversion gates have been found in the Peñasco Blanco canal. The two Pueblo Alto canals are described below and shown in Fig. 3.

Reservoirs

Reservoirs are associated with canals and appear to have been designed to collect water from the canals for domestic use. As such, they frequently occur near the town. The best known example is at Pueblo Alto. Other reservoirs are reported from Pueblo Pintado, Peñasco Blanco, Kin Klizhin, and Kin Ya-a.

The Pueblo Alto Water Control System (Fig. 3)

This system like other Chaco water control systems was designed for the capture of surface runoff after rains. It was devised and constructed by the occupants of Old Alto; the small site of New Alto probably was built after the system was established.

Pueblo Alto occupies the mesa top above the canyon and like Peñasco Blanco, which is also on the mesa top, may have had farms in the canyon bottom. Water was collected to the east and west of Old Alto by long masonry collecting walls (CW 1, 2, 3, Fig. 3). These walls average 2 feet in width and height and are footed on bedrock which underlies the present ground cover at an average depth of 6 inches. It is conceivable that the mesa top, which in the vicinity of Pueblo Alto slopes slightly to the north, was at one time predominantly bedrock. The exact relationship of the collecting walls to each other has not been determined, but Collecting Wall 2 stopped northward flowing runoff and directed it west toward Old Alto. Near the town, it was channeled into Canal 1 (C1), which at one time was apparently connected with Canal 2 (C 2). Canal 2 was bounded by masonry walls (solid lines in Fig. 3) or cut through rock, sand, and gravel (dashed lines). The water from Canal 2 seems to have been directed into a small canyon west of the last wall remnant and then to the canyon bottom near Pueblo del Arroyo. Before water flowed into Canal 2, however, a reservoir, R 1, situated to the south of Old Alto, was filled by Canal 1. Surplus was then directed into Canal 2.

At some point in time, the canal-reservoir system was modified to direct water to the Chetro Ketl area rather than to the vicinity of Pueblo del Arroyo and Pueblo Bonito. It has not been positively established that Canal 3 did not exist contemporaneously with Canal 2. It is clear, though, that sometime after Canal 2 was established a wall was built from the corner of Old Alto to, and slightly over, the refuse mound southeast of

73

the town. This wall transformed an area bordering the town on the east into a new reservoir, R 2, and surplus water was channeled south through Canal 3. Like Canal 2, water in Canal 3 was carried to a point where it could be directed into a natural drainage and then to the canyon bottom.

All water after capture was diverted south and over two primary cliff edges requiring some means of controlling the water when it spilled over the escarpment. This was accomplished by "pour-off" structures, ramp-like masonry forms (P-O 1, 2, 3, 4) built against the cliff edge to delimit the water flow. Two of these structures (Bc 86, Bc 87) were classified as habitation sites by a University of New Mexico site survey. The structure at Bc 87 (P-O 3) diverted water from Canal 3, and Pour-off structure 4 channeled water collected from the mesa top along Collecting Wall 4.

Water from Canal 3 and from Collecting Wall 4 may have been intended in part for use in a garden grid area (G) southeast of Chetro Ketl. The alluviation in this area is not heavy, whereas the area directly south of Chetro Ketl shows much soil deposition. It is probable that grid areas extended west of the known plot to the vicinity of Pueblo Bonito.

In addition to canyon farming, some limited agriculture was carried out in terrace areas (FT) below the cliff edge southeast of Pueblo Alto. These gardens were watered from cliff-top runoff. To prevent gouging of the gardens, runoff was slowed at the point of pour-off by circles and rectangles of large stones laid in the drainage channels. This apparently slowed the water sufficiently so that it ran over the edge more gently instead of funneling over in a destructive manner .

A more detailed description of the Pueblo Alto system will not add significantly to an understanding of it. This description is intended to convey an impression of the size, complexity, and variety of parts involved in a single system. Two further points should be made regarding the Pueblo Alto system, however. First, as a result of the mesa-top location of many of its features, it is better preserved than most Chaco systems. Canyon-bottom canals, dams, and other features are usually detected only where arroyos have cut across and exposed them. Second, some form of interpueblo cooperation may be evidenced in this particular case where mesa-top water collecting is presumably linked with canyon-bottom farming. The shift in water diversion from the Pueblo del Arroyo-Pueblo Bonito area to Chetro Ketl may have social or political implications.

SOCIAL IMPLICATIONS OF WATER CONTROL SYSTEMS

In concluding this review, several points may be made. All known structures were designed to capture or control runoff that would have occurred only after rains. There was necessarily then a concern with rainfall, a concern not shared by farmers who irrigated from permanent streams or rivers. Water control provided better utilization of rainfall, but it did not insure crop production without rainfall. The development of a system for collecting rainfall runoff may reflect a need for additional water for increased croplands or a necessary reaction to changes in the rainfall pattern or both.

In general, most Chaco systems involved some means of capture of runoff and its transportation to fields by canals. Not infrequently some water was diverted from canals into town reservoirs for domestic use. There is no evidence for what might be termed small-scale water control. I refer to small check dams in intermittent drainages, short boulder linear borders, and short ditches reported from other areas of the Southwest (Schwartz 1960, Lindsay 1961, Hayes 1964).

With the possible exception of the Pueblo Alto systems, all systems seem to be community enterprises, and water control projects connecting several towns were not developed. Town-village cooperation on some systems may have occurred. The "Gap" canal, which brings water through a break in the Chacra Mesa, may be associated with Pueblo del Arroyo or Pueblo Bonito. Several village sites in the Gap, however, through cooperation in canal construction and maintenance, could have shared water with the towns. All evidence points to the fact, though, that major canals and reservoirs are closely associated with towns and were their creation.

Finally, construction of the water control systems in Chaco Canyon probably began sometime after A.D. 1000. Dating of these systems is tenuous and has been based on masonry styles and a limited number of sherds recovered from water-control structures. Recent climatological studies also tend to support a post-A.D. 1000 date for the development of water control systems in Chaco.

In 1962, on the basis of pollen analysis from 18 sites in eastern Arizona and western New Mexico, James Schoenwetter (1962: 182-209) proposed a series of climatic periods for the area and discussed the cultural implications that could be derived from climatic shifts. The two periods of interest are Period II, dated before A.D. 350 to circa A.D. 1000, and Period I, circa A.D. 1000 to the present.

Period II was a time when "summer rainstorms were not so numerous, water tables were higher, dissection of flood plains was not widespread and, possibly, winter rainstorms were more numerous than they are now" (Schoenwetter 1962: 198). With conditions of increased winter ground moisture for germinating crops and fewer destructive summer rains, Schoenwetter believed that early pithouse agriculturists were dry farming.

At approximately A.D. 1000, there was a climatic shift during which "a pattern of numerous summer rainstorms contributed the majority of available water to plants in the eastern-Arizona-western-New Mexico area and initiated conditions of sediment disturbance and arroyo-cutting" (Schoenwetter 1962: 198). Dry farming eventually became precarious under conditions of decreased winter moisture reserves and destructive summer rains, and Schoenwetter believed that conditions of predominantly summer rainfall about 1000 increased the potential for irrigation farming. He concluded by noting that if this interpretation of environmental changes were correct, "it should be possible to demonstrate that changes occurred over the entire area of the steppe climatic zone in the Southwest, ... One source of confirmation for the interpretation of the environmental shifts presented is the cultural record" (Schoenwetter 1962: 202).

Palynological data from the Navajo Reservoir District some 50 miles northeast of Chaco Canyon altered this scheme very little. Schoenwetter (Schoenwetter and Eddy 1964: 118) determined that:

> Between A.D. 700 and 800, our information on total annual rainfall is confused by the change from a winter dominated to a summer dominated precipitation pattern. However, we can recognize a brief rise in effective moisture values. From A.D. 800 to 975, the data indicate a trend of decreasing total annual rainfall. This trend appears to have reached minimal values about A.D. 1025. From that date to an estimated date of A.D. 1000, total annual precipitation appears to have increased.

A model of population dynamics constructed by Schoenwetter (Schoenwetter and Eddy 1964: 128) for "a specialized narrow canyon flood plain situation" suggests that, "Once the initial stage of winter dominant storms appears on the scene, man moves in to take advantage of the situation. The introduction of summer dominant storms allows subsequent population growth and a peak. Decline and abandonment of the area appears to follow continuance of the summer dominated storm pattern." He also notes (Schoenwetter and Eddy 1964: 128) that, "The totally limiting factors of summer dominant storms and completely dissected flood plain (in the Navajo Reservoir District) have been present twice (A.D. 1050-1550; A.D. 1775-1800), causing abandonment of the district."

Aboriginal reaction to the effects of a continued summer-dominated storm pattern in the Navajo Reservoir District was population movement before headward channel cutting, since cutting not only reduced cropland but lowered the ground-water level. There is no evidence in the Navajo Reservoir District for canals, reservoirs, or other water-control structures (Schoenwetter and Eddy 1964: 121).

At approximately A.D. 1000, systems for water control do appear in other areas of the Anasazi Southwest. Canals or ditches are reported from the Creeping Dune site, Utah (Sharrock, Dibble, and Anderson 1961); the Beaver Creek site, Utah (Lindsay 1961); Mesa Verde (Rohn 1963; Herold 1961; Stewart and Donnelly 1943; Stewart 1940); and Flagstaff (Breternitz 1957a, 1957b). Sites with ditches are noted by Bandelier for Fort Wingate, New Mexico (1892: 343), and Tule, Arizona (1892: 388). Bandelier's sites cannot be dated definitely but probably existed between 1000 and 1200.

Farming terraces are reported from the Beaver Creek site; Paiute Canyon, Utah (Adams and Adams 1959); Mesa Verde (Hayes 1964 and references cited above); Shihump Canyon, Arizona (Schwartz 1960); Walhalla Glades, Arizona (Hall 1942), and Flagstaff (Colton 1932b).

Linear and grid borders are present at Beaver Creek; Castle Creek, Utah (Adams and Adams 1959); Mesa Verde; Walhalla Glades; and Wupatki, Arizona (Steen 1949).

Reservoirs are reported from the Creeping Dune site; Mesa Verde; Fort Wingate; Mariana Mesa, New Mexico (Danson 1957); and Marsh Pass, Arizona (Kidder and Guernsey 1919).

If Schoenwetter's data from the south (1962) and north (1964) of the Chaco area serve as a possible indicator of climatic conditions in the intervening area, it might be expected that by A.D. 1000 the Chaco population was experiencing the effects of a summer-dominant storm pattern. The topographic features of Chaco Canyon were such that flood waters were best controlled by large substantial structures capable of holding and diverting the great quantities of water that occurred after summer rainstorms. Construction of these works could be carried out most effectively by groups accustomed to working as a unit. Once the importance of water control was established, the construction and continued maintenance of canals, dams, and other works would have assumed special significance for the continuation of a social system that permitted more efficient and reliable utilization of a changing environment. Community investment in water control not only provided better crop assurance but reinforced an organizational base designed for community undertakings. Probably the social structuring of town groups in the Chaco did not change but, under the stimulus of water conservation, took better advantage of integrative mechanisms inherent in the system.

DEVELOPMENT OF DUAL DIVISION HYPOTHESIS

Briefly reviewed, the empirical data from the Chaco indicate that from approximately A.D. 850 to 1150 two contemporaneous community types were present in Chaco Canyon. Differences in these community types are most evident in site plan and settlement pattern, architectural styles, burial practices, presence or absence of luxury goods, and association with water-control systems. These two community types have been designated as village and town sites. Chaco villages appear to be based on an organizational system that remained essentially unchanged, though in equilibrium with the natural environment, for at least two and a half centuries. During this period there was little change in site plan and settlement pattern, architectural styles, agricultural techniques, burial practice or level of technology. Chaco towns seem to have their roots in an organizational system that became more complex through time, allowing for increased nucleation rather than fragmentation in the face of changed environmental conditions. From A.D. 850 to 1150 towns were characterized by changes in site plan, architectural styles, agricultural techniques, and possibly level of technology and craft specialization.

Explanations for these differences either have not been offered or have been presented in very general terms. As stated earlier, it is my hypothesis that these dissimilarities reflect the operation of two different systems of social organization. The final portion of this paper is devoted to a consideration of this in terms of propositions and test implications. This procedure follows the methods suggested by Hill in this volume.

TEST IMPLICATIONS FOR LOCALIZED LINEAGES

Although localized lineages have not been spatially delimited in the Southwest in recent times (Dozier 1965: 40), it has been suggested (Steward 1955: 170-71; Chang 1958: 322; Eggan 1950: 299-300) that localized lineages were present in prehistoric times, that at one time clans and lineages may have been equivalent and localized, and that late prehistoric and historic Pueblo villages represent the delocalization and dispersal of lineages and the development of multilineage clans in multiclan towns. It is proposed that "village" sites in Chaco Canyon were the residence units of localized lineages, that these lineages were uxorilocal and exogamous, and that they were "the corporate group which [held] ritual knowledge and economic good in trust for future generations" (Eggan 1950: 299 in reference to clan characteristics).

If this proposition is correct, then one would expect to find the following evidence.

1. Villages should be of varying sizes reflecting the varying population numbers of lineages.

2. Villages should vary in length of period of occupation reflecting the fluctuating nature of lineage continuity.

3. Villages should be composed of several contemporaneous household units.

4. The number of contemporaneous household units should vary, and some units within the village may appear to be abandoned or reoccupied through time.

5. Household units should be composed of two or three rooms connected by doorways.

6. Household units should be separated from other household units by walls without connecting doorways.

7. Architectural styles of household units should tend to be heterogeneous.

8. Villages should contain at least one grinding room. If more than one exists, they may show temporal differences in use.

9. Villages should contain at least one storage room for maize. This room may connect with the grinding room, or maize storage facilities may be present in the grinding room.

10. Household units should contain storage facilities for nonmaize foodstuffs.

11. Wild plant and animal remains, indicative of a major dependence on hunting and gathering, should be present in village sites.

12. Tools associated with hunting and gathering should be equally distributed in all household units of a village.

13. Villages should contain at least one ceremonial room or kiva. If more than one exists, they should show temporal differences in use.

14. Architectural styles of kivas, if more than one exists, should tend to be heterogenous.

15. Architectural modifications of a kiva over time should tend to show heterogeneous architectural styles.

16. High status burials exhibiting marked differences in number and types of burial goods should not be found in village cemeteries.

The following test implications for uxorilocal residence are derived from Hill (see pp. 38-39). It is assumed that it will be demonstrated that spatial clusterings of style elements do not represent functionally different areas of the pueblo.

17. Nonrandom distributions of items or style elements within classes of items which delineate households of the village as being different from one another should be present but may be difficult to distinguish.

18. These elements should be associated with female activities primarily and not with male activities.

19. These items or elements within each household unit in the village should exhibit temporal continuity.

20. Nonrandom distributions of items or style elements within classes of items which delineate localized lineages (villages) as being different from one another should be present and should be relatively easy to distinguish.

Sources consulted for developing the above test implications include Eggan 1950; Dozier 1965, 1966a; Hill 1966; Chang 1958; Titiev 1944; and Longacre 1966.

TEST IMPLICATIONS FOR DUAL DIVISION SYSTEM

Dozier (1960: 158) has noted that there are many varied techniques for achieving community centralization without vesting authority in the lineage. Village associations or dual divisions charged with the responsibility of secular and religious functions are two forms that have been developed by Puebloan peoples. While the western Pueblos have utilized the kinship system as a primary integrating factor, "The eastern Pueblos, in contrast, have organized much of their social and ceremonial life in terms of non-exogamous but generally patrilineal dual divisions. . ." (Eggan 1950: 302). Eggan (ibid.) further remarks that "Dual organizations in a broad sense are devices to organize and regulate rivalry and opposition in order to serve the purposes of the group as a whole." Dozier (1960) has suggested that the differences in social organization between eastern and western Pueblos may be explained by differences in agricultural practices. Irrigation agriculture of the eastern Pueblos required centralized control of communal labor, whereas rainfall agriculture practiced by the western Pueblos did not necessitate communal labor but was more the concern of households and lineages.

It is proposed that "town" sites in Chaco Canyon were dual-division residence units characterized by nonexogamous moieties with a bilocal residence pattern. Social cohesion was achieved by moiety sharing in governmental and ceremonial responsibilities of the town and by community associations which cross cut moiety membership.

If this proposition is correct, one would expect to find the following evidence.

1. Towns should have two architecturally distinct units. (This attribute which appears to be present at Pueblo Bonito was given as part of the empirical data. It has not been noted at other town sites, however, and should therefore be considered a valid test implication.)

2. Each half should possess style peculiarities not shared by the other.

3. Within each half of the town, localized residence areas should not be capable of differentiation on the basis of distribution of items or style elements within classes of items. Distribution of female and male stylistic items should be random.

4. Each half should contain a number of contemporaneous extended household units separated from other similar units by walls without connecting doorways.

5. The number of contemporaneous extended household units in each half should vary and should not necessarily be equal.

6. Each extended household unit should vary in size and include several nuclear family residence units.

7. Each nuclear family residence unit should contain storage and grinding rooms.

8. Each half should contain several connecting rooms larger than other rooms in the moiety residence unit, which housed the moiety head or chief and which served as moiety association rooms and storage rooms for moiety foodstuffs used in communal feasting. These rooms should contain features and materials not found in other rooms.

9. There should be one great kiva in each town, used on a rotating basis by each moiety. (Although great kivas were noted in the empirical data, there are conflicting opinions on whether one or two great kivas should be present with dual division organizations, especially in the Chaco. The test implication is considered valid.)

10. Evidence for temporal differences in great kiva construction and use should be present in town sites with more than one great kiva.

11. A number of association kivas or ceremonial rooms should be present in town sites. They should vary in location within the town, size, features, and materials.

12. Architectural styles of association kivas and rooms should tend to be heterogeneous, and modifications(especially of kivas) should tend to be heterogeneous.

13. Style elements within classes of items found in association rooms and kivas may be random and not representative of particular residence units, small or large.

14. Architectural modifications of great kivas should tend to be more homogeneous than similar modifications in association kivas.

15. Two distinct cemetery areas should be present in town sites.

16. In addition to the spatial differentiation, differences in burial position, kinds of accompanying grave goods, and type of interment should differentiate one cemetery from the other.

17. Several high-status burials, exhibiting marked differences in number and type of burial goods, should be found in each of the town cemeteries.

18. Field areas, if detectable, should be divided into two large divisions, each sharing canal water. Garden plots within each division should vary in number and size.

19. Evidence for greater dependence on cultivated food crops should be present in town sites (as compared with village sites).

20. Racetracks for ceremonial racing should be present at each town site.

Sources consulted for aid in developing the above test implications include Eggan 1950; Dozier 1965, 1966a; Hill 1966; Longacre 1966; Parsons 1925, 1929; Ellis 1964; and White 1962.

In almost all situations, alternate propositions for explaining patterns of empirical data should be considered and tested. In this instance, only one proposition has been offered for each of what appear to be two distinct cultural patterns in the archaeological record from post-a.d. 850 Chaco Canyon. If the proposition that these patterns reflect the operation of two different systems of social organization is correct, the probability that a particular explanation is better than another can only be strengthened by testing other propositions. If, after testing, few of the propositions appear relatively valid, it may be necessary to revise the original hypothesis.

CONCLUSION

The above discussion of prehistoric social organization in Chaco Canyon has been offered not as an explanation for differences in the Chaco communities, but as an experiment in determining how archaeological data may be utilized to formulate testable hypotheses regarding prehistoric social organization. I have not attempted to develop other testable propositions, nor have I attempted to gather the data relevant to the test implications presented so that they might in fact be tested. I would hope that this initial inquiry into social structure in Chaco Canyon will stimulate the development of other testable hypotheses and the accumulation of data for testing. Unanswered questions raised by these propositions and their tests should be of significant value in providing some of the research goals for future archaeological investigations in Chaco Canyon.

NOTE

1. This paper benefited considerably from its review by the symposium members, especially the comments by William Longacre and James Hill. Paul Grebinger, a graduate student in the Anthropology Department, University of Arizona, has also offered much valuable criticism. I am indebted to the U.S. National Park Service for its cooperation in loaning me R. Gordon Vivian's field notes, maps, and photographs of water-control systems and for granting me permission to work in Chaco Canyon in 1967. Finally, the results of the 1967 Chaco field work are equally the product of my wife, Pat, and Greg Staley, a student at Northern Arizona University, Flagstaff, who assisted me in the field.

Anasazi Communities in the Red Rock Plateau, Southeastern Utah

WILLIAM D. LIPE

Department of Anthropology,
State University of New York
at Binghamton

INTRODUCTION

In this paper, I attempt to reconstruct some aspects of the social organization of the Anasazi groups that occupied the Red Rock Plateau at various times in the prehistoric past. The archaeologist is, of course, handicapped in the investigation of social organization, because he cannot observe the full range of social behavior as it is being carried out. He is left only with the material traces of that fraction of social behavior that impinges on the material world so as to leave traces. If, however, these traces can be identified, that is, if they can be seen as clues, the archaeologist may be able to infer that particular activities were carried out. From no single clue or kind of clue can more than a tiny fragment of a prehistoric social system be constructed, but if the archaeologist can assemble enough of these fragments, he can begin to rough out some parts of the system. What I have tried to do in this paper, then, is to set forth some of the Red Rock Plateau data that I see as clues to past social organization and to give some of the reasoning leading me to relate a particular observation to a particular inference. In some cases, I have tried to suggest what kinds of future observations we might make to acquire additional clues or to test the inferences we have already made. The paper is basically a long compilation of specific small inferences about specific items of data. There are, however, several themes or foci running through it, including (1) a regional approach to the problem, (2) an ecological emphasis on the ways in which the prehistoric social systems of this area interacted with and adapted to various physical and biological systems, and (3) an emphasis on reconstruction of localized residential groups, specifically the group of immediate domestic coresidence or household and the larger residential group or community.

The regional focus seems useful first because prehistoric Anasazi groups usually depended on utilizing the resources of a rather wide area. If the analysis of activity loci is a fruitful source of inference about prehistoric behavior, then we must be prepared to seek and to relate such locations in a large area. In much of the western part of the Anasazi area prior to the middle or late 1200s, the community and all but the most minimal social units were probably seldom localized in a single site.[1] Furthermore, regional studies usually allow one to sample more than one occurrence of a particular class of phenomena and thus should increase the reliability of the sample. Last but not least, the archaeological salvage project during which nearly all the data I have used were collected was by design and necessity a regional study. I consider this a blessing and have preserved this orientation.

The ecological emphasis stems from my belief that sociocultural systems serve to adapt their populations to their total physical, biological, and social environments. Therefore, a productive way to investigate sociocultural systems should be to attempt to understand their adaptive functions. In this paper, adaptation to physical, and to some extent, to biological environments has been stressed, because the Red Rock Plateau was climatically, physiographically, and biologically marginal for the Anasazi people. The requirements of successful adaptation here must have been both especially stringent and somewhat different from those of their usual highland habitat. Some of the distinctive characteristics of Red Rock Plateau community organization may be related to problems of coping with particular aspects of the natural environment, as discussed in the following pages.

An emphasis on residential units and communities was chosen because

85

the data lend themselves to this kind of analysis, and because I think this kind of information is crucial to our understanding the evolution of Pueblo social organization. The shift from a highly dispersed settlement pattern with short occupancy of small sites to a pattern of residence in large, permanent, highly nucleated, village communities was, it seems to me, a watershed in Pueblo history. It is inconceivable to me that some of the distinctive aspects of modern Pueblo social organization, such as the very tight systems of social control, could have developed prior to the appearance of large, permanent, densely populated communities. The concept of community that underlies my approach is largely derived from Arensberg (1961). The community is seen as a minimal, territorially based population aggregate, including individuals of the two sexes and at least three generations, capable of maintaining itself through time, including opportunities for enactment of or articulation with the main social roles present in the larger society, and including mechanisms for transmission from one generation to the next of the principal content of its culture.

Before moving into the body of the paper, I should also say something about how the data were collected. What we know archaeologically about the Red Rock Plateau is almost entirely the result of the work done by the University of Utah branch of the Upper Colorado River Basin Archeological Salvage Project (more conveniently referred to as the Glen Canyon Project), directed by Jesse D. Jennings and sponsored by the U.S. National Park Service. I was fortunate enough to have been an employee of this project from 1958 through 1960 and again in the summer of 1961, and to have been allowed to study collections and records in the project laboratory in Salt Lake City in the academic year 1962-63.

It seems to me that the philosophy behind the field work of the Glen Canyon Project was something like this: A salvage project cannot focus on any single specific problem, ignoring data not relevant to that problem. Because the sites under study will be irrevocably lost, the salvage archaeologist must collect the specimens and make the observations that will serve the greatest variety of important archaeological problems of which he is aware. Further, he must do his best to predict what kinds of problems, and therefore what kinds of data, will be important in the years to come. He is, in effect, working for the whole profession of archaeology rather than just for himself.

None of us who worked on the Glen Canyon Project was especially committed to trying to reconstruct prehistoric social organization; I know that I was considerably more naive about what data to look for than I am now. But I think all of us felt that cultural and societal reconstruction was one of our ultimate goals, and we did our best to make observations that might help us or someone else to eventually attain this goal. After reexamining the data, I find it surprising that so much that was relevant was collected; it is also clear that more and better observations would have been made had the theoretical orientations we brought to the field been different or our formulation of the problems more precise.

In using the Glen Canyon data as the basis for this paper, I am relying on the field work, notes, and publications of many people in addition to myself. In general, I have not given full citations when I have relied on material published by the project staff; the result would be too cumbersome. Tables specifying the published record for nearly all the sites discussed here, however, can be found in my doctoral dissertation (Lipe 1967; Tables 4 and 6). Jennings (1966) also provides a comprehensive bibliography of the rather extensive literature stemming from the Glen Canyon Project.

Archaeological survey and excavations were conducted in the Red Rock Plateau in the summers of 1958 through 1962 as part of the Glen Canyon Project. The Red Rock Plateau was but one part of the area encompassed by this project, which was designed to salvage archaeological materials in the area to be flooded by the Glen Canyon Dam at Page, Arizona. Jennings (1966) has summarized the objectives, methods, and accomplishments of the project.

Glen Canyon Project field teams located 512 sites in the Red Rock Plateau, of which thirty-six were only test-pitted and fifty-nine were excavated somewhat more thoroughly. Five phases of prehistoric occupation of the region have been recognized (Lipe 1967: 6), as follows:

	Phase	Estimated Date, A.D.	Stage/Period in Pecos Classification
1.	White Dog	200-300	Basket Maker II
2.	Klethla	1100-1150	Pueblo III
3.	Horsefly Hollow	1210-1260	Pueblo III
4.-5.	Jeddito and Sikyatki	1300-1600	Pueblo IV

Only the first three phases are discussed in any detail in this paper.

The site sample, on which the inferences discussed here are based, consists of all the identifiable components of the White Dog, Jeddito, and

Sikyatki phases, and the larger components of the Klethla and Horsefly Hollow phases. For these two phases, only components yielding 100 or more typologically identifiable potsherds were included. Although it represents only a small fraction of the Pueblo III sites located in the area, the selected list of sites includes nearly all the habitation and most of the frequently used campsites and special-function sites known for the Klethla and Horsefly Hollow phases. These sites also produced the great majority of the artifacts of these phases recovered in the region. Other admittedly important sampling problems are treated in detail by Lipe (1967, especially 115-20, 160-65, 268-79). It is sufficient to say here that the differences in site characteristics among the various phases seem to be due primarily to factors other than sampling error or differential site preservation.

THE REGION

The Red Rock Plateau (Figs. 4 and 5), an area of about 750 square miles, is a physiographic subdivision of the Canyon Lands section of the Colorado Plateau and is noted for a degree of dissection extreme even in the Canyon Lands. It is bounded by the Glen Canyon of the Colorado River, the canyon of the San Juan River, the Red House Cliffs, and Red Canyon (boundaries slightly modified from those of Gregory 1938).

Most of the areas immediately adjacent to the Red Rock Plateau apparently were less hospitable to Anasazi populations; to this extent the region was isolated, although its inhabitants were affected at times by events occurring elsewhere. To the south, the Red Rock Plateau was bordered by the San Juan Canyon. With a few exceptions (for example, the Beaver Creek community reported by Lindsay in 1961), this canyon and the lower parts of its southern tributaries lack evidence of substantial occupation, probably because of a general paucity of cultivable soil and of manageable water supplies for augmenting rainfall in agriculture. (Within 10 miles of the San Juan, however, exist large highland regions that were heavily populated at various times.) The Red Rock Plateau's northwestern boundary, the Glen Canyon proper, was also sparsely occupied, although for slightly different reasons, as discussed below. The lower parts of the tributaries entering the Colorado from the northwest also showed evidence of only light prehistoric occupation. The closest highlands in the northwestern direction lie at a considerable distance from the river. To the north, the Red Rock Plateau is bounded by the extensive drainages of

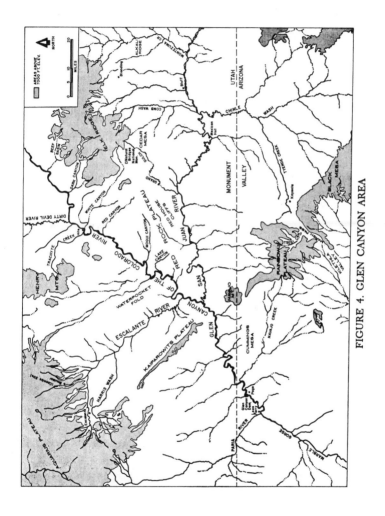

FIGURE 4. GLEN CANYON AREA

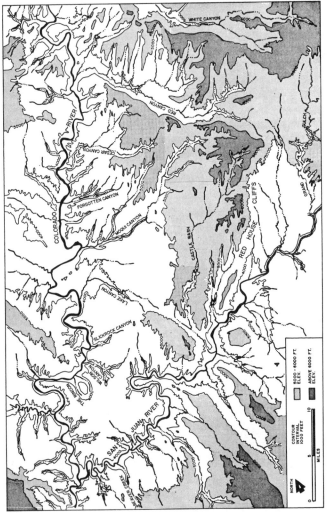

FIGURE 5. TOPOGRAPHY OF RED ROCK PLATEAU

Red and lower White Canyons; much of this is uninhabitable badlands of exposures of Chinle formation. To the east, there are also extensive exposures of Chinle, and there are few sites at the base of the Red House Cliffs. The bordering Grand Flats area is low and poorly watered. Only to the northeast does the Red Rock Plateau join an area that was probably well populated at the same times that the plateau was occupied. Here, Castle Creek and Steer Pasture Canyon head in a dissected but fairly extensive highland that is also drained by the heads of Steer Gulch, Grand Gulch, Red Canyon, and the southern tributaries of White Canyon.

The Red Rock Plateau itself is environmentally marginal in terms of the usual Anasazi requirements for settlement. Most of the region is considerably less than 5500 feet in elevation (Fig. 5), and thus is well below the normal zone of Anasazi occupation. All but a small fraction of the area is a true desert, receiving an average of from 5 to 10 inches of rainfall per year. Dry farming would have been out of the question everywhere in the region.

Special physiographic features serve, however, to concentrate water and cultivable soils in a number of the Red Rock Plateau canyons; Anasazi occupation was largely confined to these canyons. The most favorable canyons were those cut into the Glen Canyon sandstones—the Wingate, Kayenta, and Navajo formations. The Navajo and Wingate are permeable and are excellent aquifers; springs and seeps usually occur at their contact with underlying, less permeable formations. These spring-rich contact zones are most often exposed where canyons cut through the Navajo or Wingate formations; hence such canyons have good supplies of surface and ground water.

In this sparsely vegetated region, the Glen Canyon sandstones also provide much eolian sand, some of which is trapped in the canyons as it blows across the plateau surface. Much of this sand is reworked by water when the canyons flood after showers. Where these floods have lacked power to flush out all the sand, thick deposits of alluvium have accumulated. While these deposits were stable or aggrading, floods were probably not confined to a single channel but spread out over the floodplains. Most Anasazi farming in the Red Rock Plateau probably depended on these easily worked, occasionally flooded alluvial soils of the canyon floors. Nearly all these alluvial bodies are now deeply trenched by erosion, and thus are unsuitable for cultivation. There is evidence, however, that arroyo-cutting of the present magnitude did not occur during the period from about A.D. 200 to 1600 with which this study is concerned (Lance 1963). In addition to providing source material for alluvium, the dunes and sheets of sand derived from the Glen Canyon sandstones help store ground water. Nearly all the rainfall received by these sandy deposits sinks below the surface; much of it eventually percolates into the permeable Navajo and Wingate sandstones and may then contribute to spring flow. Some of the larger dunes in the canyons also have a water table sufficient to support springs at their bases.

The Red Rock Plateau canyons that are entrenched into the Glen Canyon sandstones have much better water and soil supplies than other canyons or than the barren plateau surface between drainages. Most of the archaeological sites found in the region therefore occur in or near such canyons. Of this group, the two (Fig. 5) most richly endowed with soil and water in prehistoric times were (1) Lake Canyon, particularly the broad, low-walled part around former Lake Pahgarit, and (2) the broad, shallow upper part of Castle Wash (including Steer Pasture Canyon). Moqui Canyon is also fairly well supplied with water and alluvium but is deeper and has a narrower floodplain than either Lake or Upper Castle Wash. The Glen Canyon proper has numerous relatively broad floodplain remnants preserved as low terraces, but its flood regimen is somewhat different from that of the tributaries. Farming lands would have been flooded only in the spring, in response to melting snows in the Rockies and the high plateaus; these floods tend to be prolonged and violent. The floods in the tributary canyons, on the other hand, follow any substantial local shower, including those occurring during the growing season. These floods are brief and are violent only in narrow, steep parts of the canyons, or where they are confined within arroyos.

Other Red Rock Plateau canyons possessing adequate water and soil are Wilson, Slickrock, Forgotten, and Alcove Canyons, as well as parts of the San Juan Canyon. The area suitable for farming in each is small. The total amount of cultivable land of whatever sort in the Red Rock Plateau is quite limited—probably no more than a thousand acres altogether.

In addition to scattered oases of good soil and water, the Red Rock Plateau offered Anasazi farmers a very long growing season, averaging about 200 days. A growing season this long would virtually eliminate frost danger and would enable food crops to be planted and harvested more than a month earlier than in the highlands. It would also favor the heat-loving cotton plant, which was poorly adapted to the cool highlands. Cotton bolls, seeds, and fibers have been found in a number of dry Horsefly Hollow phase sites, and weaving implements and loom anchors are even more common.

Minor factors that probably helped make the Red Rock Plateau habitable are:

1. There is an abundance of natural rock shelters—favored locations for habitations during the White Dog and Horsefly Hollow phases and for storage structures during both these phases and in the Klethla phase.

2. Numerous high Pleistocene gravel terraces near the Colorado and San Juan Rivers contain lumps of chert, jasper, and other siliceous rocks. These gravels furnished raw materials for chipped stone tools, not only for the local people but probably also for inhabitants of adjacent regions as far away as the Tsegi Canyon area (Turner and Cooley 1960).

3. The canyons incised into the Glen Canyon sandstones, because of their reliable water supply and varied physiography, have a rich flora, including many plants normally confined to the highlands, as well as those of the desert zone and some peculiar to the canyons. Thus, the Anasazi, though living outside the altitudinal zone they normally occupied, were not deprived of most of the wild plants that they normally used as raw materials, medicines, and supplementary foods. The main deficiency in the canyon flora for the Anasazi was probably the scarcity of piñon and juniper trees.

4. Wild animals were common enough in the Red Rock Plateau to permit regular hunting and to ensure that the region's inhabitants occasionally ate meat. Animal bone (most commonly bighorn sheep) and hunting gear (usually projectile points) occur at most Red Rock Plateau sites and generally seem much more common there in relation to other types of refuse than at most of the larger highland sites.

ANASAZI COMMUNITIES IN THE RED ROCK PLATEAU

The White Dog Phase (circa A.D. 200-300)

The Basket Maker II stage in the Four Corners area represents the earliest demonstrable occupation of this region by peoples possessing domesticated plants. In the western part of the Four Corners area, this stage is manifested by the White Dog phase, best known from sites near

93

Kayenta, Arizona; from Grand Gulch in southeastern Utah; and from Cave Du Pont in south central Utah. White Dog phase sites typically occur, or at least, typically have been found, in canyon environments, where spring- and flood-water farming on alluvial soils is possible and where natural shelters are abundant. Thus, the Red Rock Plateau canyons resemble the typical environments of sites of this phase, although they are somewhat lower in elevation.

The White Dog phase people seem to have been the first inhabitants of the Red Rock Plateau, and therefore must have migrated into the region. The most likely source area for this migration is the Grand Gulch region (Fig. 4), only a few miles to the east. Basket Maker sites are relatively frequent in the Grand Gulch, and some are apparently of sufficient size and depth to imply a long occupancy. Comparably large centers of White Dog occupation have not been demonstrated for other regions within a 10- or 20-mile radius of the Red Rock Plateau. Furthermore, as noted earlier, the highlands around upper Grand Gulch connect directly with the northeastern part of the Red Rock Plateau, whereas the other boundaries of the region are isolated to some extent from surrounding highland areas by barren lowlands.

If my dating estimate is correct, the White Dog occupation was brief and probably occurred in the third century A.D. After this, the region was largely or entirely unoccupied until the late 1000s or early 1100s. The dating of the White Dog occupation is anchored by a single radiocarbon determination of A.D. 250±80 (M. Stuiver, personal communication) and given general support by the finding of White Dog materials stratified below Pueblo materials at several sites. The inference that the occupation was rather brief is based on the sparseness of cultural remains at most of the sites. The inference that all or most of the sites were occupied during the same brief period is supported only by artifactual similarities among them.

The White Dog movement into the Red Rock Plateau may have been initiated by a prolonged period of somewhat above-average rainfall during the last part of the second and first part of the third centuries A.D. (Schulman 1956: Table 49; Lipe 1967: 129-30).[2] Such a favorable climatic period would have promoted population growth among the White Dog people, leading some families or bands to seek new territory, and would also have made the Red Rock Plateau canyons more attractive by raising water tables and strengthening spring flow. Withdrawal of White Dog people from the region and its subsequent long abandonment are hard to explain but may be the result of improved cultigens (Galinat and Gunnerson 1963), agricultural techniques (especially dry-farming techniques), and housing that made large areas of the open highlands more habitable and, conversely, canyon environments relatively less attractive. A decline in the amount and reliability of rainfall in the late third and the fourth centuries may also be involved in the abandonment of the Red Rock Plateau at this time.

White Dog sites in the Red Rock Plateau are not abundant, and most occur in two small clusters—in Moqui Canyon and Upper Castle Wash (Fig. 6). These areas have natural shelters, good deposits of occasionally flooded sandy alluvium, and numerous springs. Other canyons with these characteristics, however, apparently were not much used by the White Dog people, although later Puebloans found them attractive. Lake Canyon, for example, was the area most heavily occupied by Puebloans but seems not to have been used by the Basket Makers at all. The restricted distribution of the White Dog sites may be due perhaps to the fact that Moqui Canyon and Castle Wash are the only habitable canyons permitting easy access to the highlands north and east of the Red Rock Plateau; the other habitable parts of the Red Rock Plateau are cut off from these highlands by stretches of barren slickrock desert. The upper part of Castle Wash, where the White Dog sites occur, is located in the lower part of the juniper-piñon zone.

There seem to me to be two different (though not mutually exclusive) explanations for the location of White Dog sites on the margins of the highlands. The first is historical and sociological: the earliest inhabitants of the region settled in the parts most accessible from the east because they came from the east; because only a few families ever lived in the Red Rock Plateau, they had no need to expand into new areas, and the locations of the original settlements enabled them to maintain close contact with families of the same or related bands centered in the Grand Gulch area.

A second, and to me more probable, explanation is that the Red Rock Plateau was settled by a single, small, rather isolated band and that the pattern of site distribution reflects only the demands of the White Dog subsistence pattern. Although farming was probably the single most important means of livelihood during this phase, hunting and gathering clearly seem to have been more important than they were to the late

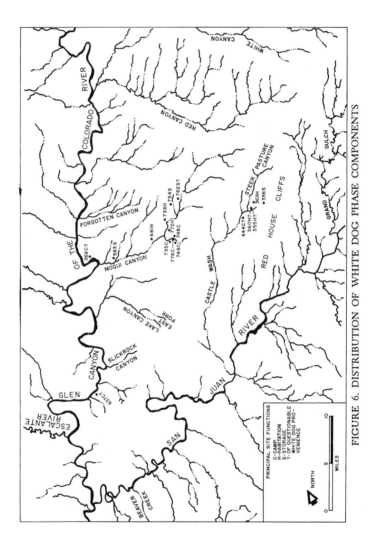

FIGURE 6. DISTRIBUTION OF WHITE DOG PHASE COMPONENTS

Puebloans. Thus, the canyons where the sites are located were probably best for the White Dog people's small-scale farming, but the inhabitants also needed access to the open highlands for the wild foods (especially piñon nuts, grass seeds, deer, and rabbit) more common there. An analysis of the functions of the White Dog sites in the Red Rock Plateau (see discussion below and in Lipe 1967: 138-48) indicated that some of these sites were the result of hunting and gathering activities; this supports the inference of a mixed farming-collecting economy. In addition, piñon nuts, which must have come from the highlands, were found at a White Dog storage site in Moqui Canyon (Sa754). The White Dog sites in Castle Wash occur in a canyon setting, but Castle Wash at this point near its head is actually in the juniper-piñon zone. The one and perhaps three shallow pithouse dwellings noted in Castle Wash may even have been the result of winter occupation dependent on the piñon nut harvest. Surface indications of similar houses in the uplands near the head of Grand Gulch have been observed by the writer. The rock-shelters of the deeply entrenched Grand Gulch itself have, of course, yielded abundant remains of the White Dog phase.

Under this interpretation, the White Dog subsistence and settlement patterns in the Red Rock Plateau show several striking resemblances to patterns ethnographically recorded for the nomadic Southern Paiute bands that historically frequented parts of the Glen Canyon region (Kelly 1964). These Paiute bands received domesticated plants during the nineteenth century but continued to rely heavily on collecting wild foods. They farmed only small plots near springs, usually in sheltered and low-lying canyons. Seldom living near their fields all year, they preferred to move to the highlands in the fall and winter to harvest seeds and to hunt. Houses usually were built only in the highlands.

Some progress in weighting the two hypotheses stated above might be made if further surveys could be carried out in the highlands between Castle Wash and Grand Gulch. If this area proved to have been substantially uninhabited in White Dog times, an interpretation of the Red Rock Plateau sites of this phase as representing a single, somewhat isolated, band would be strengthened, and the first hypothesis would be disfavored. If, on the other hand, White Dog occupation is continuous between Upper Castle Wash and Grand Gulch, the first hypothesis, which sees the Red Rock Plateau occupation as essentially an extension of territory by a Grand Gulch-based band, would be favored. The ecological interpretation of site distribution would not be disproved, but it would require additional support from demonstration that it is a recurrent adaptive pattern in the general area.

Two main geographic site clusters and three main functional or activity classes of White Dog sites have been distinguished in the Red Rock Plateau (Lipe 1967). An examination of all the data on the White Dog occupation of the region has yielded a few rather tenuous hints on the composition of the social units occupying the site clusters and carrying out the activities associated with the site types. These "hints" are briefly inventoried below.

Moqui Canyon Cluster

The Moqui Canyon site cluster is centered on a group of three habitation and burial sites, located in natural shelters within an area of about 2½ miles in diameter. Four small food-collecting campsites are located in a small tributary to Moqui Canyon about 12 miles from the habitation sites. Two storage sites are also peripheral to the habitations; one is located several miles down the canyon from the habitation sites, the other several miles upstream from them.

1. *Habitation and Burial Places.* Three sites, all natural shelters, contained White Dog habitational residue and burials: Bernheimer Alcove (Sa736), Rehab Center (Sa681), and Sa772. All are located near the upper end of the canyon's body of floodplain alluvium and amid the major concentration of springs occurring above the mouth of North Gulch. Painted pictographs adorned the walls of all three shelters, and at all three were rather heavy midden deposits. Evidence of fire was abundant at Sa736 and Sa681. Sa772 was excavated by the 1929 Bernheimer expedition; the composition of the midden deposit was not recorded. Although a cache of whole corn ears was recovered at Sa736, storage structures as such were not found at any of the three sites.

Of the approximately twenty burials found at the three sites, twelve were at Sa736, which probably was the most heavily occupied (although Sa681 yielded much more food bone and more elaborate hearth structures). A full range of ages was shown by the Sa736 burials, but most interesting for our purposes was an undisturbed group of five infants under three years old (ages about 2½ years, 1 year, 6 months, and two newborn) discovered at the bottom of a crevice. The infants were crowded together in a small space, suggesting that they were buried at about the same time, which in turn indicates that at least three nuclear families, and probably more, were using the shelter at the same time. This inference must be qualified, however. The burials were tied onto cradle boards, and the location was dry enough so they had not entirely decomposed after 1500 to 2000 years. Conceivably the grave could have been opened repeatedly over a number of years and new interments made without noticeable derangement of the earlier burials taking place (a relevant ethnographic example of repeated infant burials in the same grave by the same Hopi family is given in Simmons 1942: 261, 270, 284, 290). On the other hand, the sand around the burials was fairly clean even though overlaid by a trash deposit; this suggests that the grave was not opened repeatedly.

That habitation residue is concentrated in a fairly small space in all three sites indicates that the population using each site was small. It seems reasonable to postulate that two to four nuclear families used each site. The coresidence of three generations is suggested by the juxtaposition in a single grave at Sa681 of an adult female, a newborn infant, and a middle-aged to elderly male.

Whether or not the three habitational sites were used by three coexisting social units is not clear, in the absence of precise absolute dating for each. I would guess that they were occupied contemporaneously, because all seem to have been used for more than a brief interval and because they appear functionally equivalent, rather than complementary, to one another.

2. *Food-Collecting Camps.* The four shallow, essentially "surface" sites in Camp Canyon all yielded a number of thin sandstone grinding slabs (mostly broken), one-hand manos, and projectile points, as well as a considerable quantity of flaking debris. All these items are rare in the habitation sites. The camps, on the other hand, have little or no midden deposit and few traces of fire; this is true even in spots where wind erosion has not been active.

These sites do not appear to have been connected with farming. Camp Canyon, though well watered, is choked with huge falling sand dunes, has little alluvium, and was ignored by the later Puebloan farmers of the region. It seems likely to me that these camps reflect the gathering and grinding of wild seeds, perhaps of the Indian ricegrass or Indian millet (*Oryzopsis hymenoides*), which now is fairly common on the Camp

Canyon dunes and which must have been more abundant before the introduction of cattle. Seeds of this plant were a staple for most Paiute groups (Steward 1938), including all the Southern Paiute bands (Kelly 1964: 41-42, 153, 170, 179), and were collected by the Hopi in times of famine (Whiting 1939: 65). Caches of these seeds have been found in Basket Maker sites (Morris 1939: 15). The time of harvest seems to have been June, at least for the Hopi (Nequatewa 1943). This would probably have been a time of food shortage for the White Dog people, because it lies after planting, when the people would have to stay fairly close to their fields, but before the earliest crop harvests.

Among the Southern Paiute, Indian rice was often ground shortly after collection; this practice would explain the quantities of grinding slab fragments at the Camp Canyon sites. Several complete grinding slabs were found at each of the sites; at Sa748 these were turned face down as if their users anticipated a return in the future. The numbers of unbroken grinding slabs at these sites suggest that several persons, probably women, shared the grinding of the seeds that had been collected.

As previously noted, the Camp Canyon sites also contained a number of projectile points and considerable flaking debris (including chips, cores, and hammerstones). These seem clear evidence that the work parties using these sites included men as well as women. Perhaps after helping collect seeds, the men made or repaired hunting equipment while the women prepared the seeds for eating. Sweeney and Euler (1964) report that sites identified by their (male) Southern Paiute informants as "hunting camps" had thin sandstone grinding slabs as well as points and flaking debris on the surface.

The Camp Canyon sites were probably not often used for overnight stays, because none of the three main habitation sites was far away; this may explain the general scarcity of traces of fire at these sites. The fifth probable food-collecting camp in the Moqui Canyon cluster, Sa369, at the mouth of Moqui Canyon, shows abundant evidence of fire; there are stone-lined hearths and the fill is stained with ash and charcoal. This site may have been an overnight camp used by wider ranging collecting parties.

3. *Storage Sites.* Two sites, Echo Cave (Sa583) and Honeycomb Alcove (Sa754), fall into this class. The former is located well downstream from the cluster of habitation sites, the latter upstream from them. Both consist largely of pits and jar-shaped cists dug into natural clay-like hard-

pan on the floors of dry shelters. Echo Cave contained 16 storage features ranging from a few inches to 5½ feet in diameter. With the exception of one shallow pit containing a caked organic substance, all had been cleaned out by the Basket Makers, by rodents, or by later Puebloans, who had utilized the cave in a minor way. The small amount of trash present is mostly attributable to the Pueblo occupation.

Honeycomb Alcove, which apparently was not reused by Puebloans, contained 58 pits and cists ranging from a few inches to about 3½ feet in diameter. All had been fairly thoroughly cleaned out in prehistoric times. The few items left included piñon nuts, corn kernels, squash fragments, a flint core, a digging stick, a bundle of unworked bighorn sheep metatarsals, fragments of a large carrying basket, and pieces of juniper bark and yucca matting probably once used to wrap cached materials. There was no habitational residue and virtually no trace of fire.

The sites apparently were used to store paraphernalia used in hunting and gathering and in cultivation, as well as foods and other materials obtained through these activities. The peripheral locations of the storage caves with respect to the habitation sites is difficult to explain. It may have something to do with the demands of the food-collecting component of the subsistence pattern, or with the cultivation of outlying fields, or both. Or perhaps the locations were simply dictated by the presence of suitable hardpan floors. Such caves are not particularly common in the region.

The question of who was using these sites and the various storage features in them is a perplexing one. The considerable spatial separation of the sites from one another and their lack of spatial correlation with particular habitation sites suggest that the whole local community had access to them, that one was for "downstream" activities, the other for "upstream" activities. Despite the large number of pit and cist features, neither site had a very large total storage capacity. Most of the features are small, rather shallow pits; the jar-shaped cists, on the other hand, tend to be larger; most have diameters of between 20 and 48 inches. These cists seem better designed for storing food than the pits, but whether food actually was stored in the cists is conjectural, since clearly a variety of items was stored at the sites.

Despite the large number of storage features at these two sites, their capacity is not large; probably neither has greater capacity than one of the small two- or three-family pueblos of the Horsefly Hollow phase. The storage requirements of the Puebloans were probably greater, however. A study of the volumes of storage features in relation to other kinds of structures for all phases in the Red Rock Plateau is under way, but no patterns have emerged as yet.

Castle Wash Cluster

In contrast to the Moqui Canyon cluster, the Upper Castle Wash White Dog phase sites occur in a much smaller area, are fewer in number, and include at least one constructed house.

1. *Habitation Sites.* The only clearcut example is the Lone Tree Dune site (Sa363), a single shallow circular pithouse about 20 feet in diameter with a nearby deep jar-shaped cist about 5 feet in diameter. Only one small firepit was found in the house, located slightly off center. Filled with charcoal rather than ash, it may not have been a true indoor fireplace. A large outdoor slab-lined hearth was found, however, about seventy feet from the house. According to Naroll's (1962) cross-culturally derived formula relating house-floor area to household size, an occupancy by only three or four adults, or perhaps a married couple with several children, is indicated.

Two unexcavated nonceramic sites on adjacent sand ridges several hundred yards away show surface evidences similar to Sa363, although they are more eroded. If they represent similar structures, a local residential unit of several nuclear families, probably related by marriage or descent, is implied. Since no attempt was made in the field to test this postulated similarity of the three sites, it must remain speculative.

Two other unexcavated house structures probably similar to Sa363 in size and construction were noted recently by the author during a brief unsystematic survey of a highland area near the eastern rim of Grand Gulch. These two structures were about a half mile apart; cursory examination of the intervening area failed to reveal any other houses.[3] Caves with pictographs, probably Basket Maker in style, were noted less than a mile away in Grand Gulch proper.

2. *Storage and Camp Site.* Only one site of this sort, Sa356, was found. Located in a dry alcove, it contained three slab-lined cists, one unlined storage pit, and two slab-lined firepits. The thin layer of trash yielded corncobs, squash fragments, piñon nuts, and a few perishable artifacts, but little animal bone and almost no stone artifacts.

3. *Camp Site.* The several thin nonceramic strata at the Greenwater Spring site (Sa444) may relate to the White Dog phase. Little was found here except three slab-lined hearths and a few nondiagnostic chipped flint artifacts. As the name indicates, the site is close to a spring, probably the best one in this canyon.

Conclusions

The rather meager evidence assembled above indicates that the White Dog phase inhabitants of the Red Rock Plateau maintained, for at least part of the year, local coresidential groups of probably no more than two or three nuclear families. It seems reasonable to suppose that these families were linked by kinship, either of common descent or of marriage, or a combination of both.

If the three habitation sites in Moqui Canyon were occupied simultaneously, the existence of a local community larger than the unit of immediate coresidence seems evident. Storage sites, but not individual storage pits, may have been used by the whole Moqui Canyon community. There is no other evidence of any other means of community integration. It seems quite likely that the small residential units occupying the canyon were also integrated by kinship ties, but I can present no evidence to support this proposition.

The relationship between the site cluster in Moqui Canyon and the one in Upper Castle Wash is far from clear. One speculation is that the pithouse, or possibly pithouses, in Castle Wash were winter residences for some of the families that occupied Moqui Canyon in the summer. The move to the highlands for the winter would have been to take advantage of the piñon nut harvest. A similar adaptive pattern was followed by some of the Southern Paiute in the nineteenth century.

Studies of associated pollen, growth-ring stages in charcoal from hearths, artifact functions, and so forth, might produce evidence on whether or not these two groups of sites were occupied seasonally. These studies have not been carried out, and it is unlikely that the relevant data are included in the collections made from these sites. Even if it were to be shown, however, that the two site clusters were used at different seasons, it would still remain to be demonstrated that the same group of people was responsible.

If there were three house structures in the Upper Castle Wash cluster, this would indicate that the local residence unit here was similar to the one reconstructed for Moqui Canyon. A scant bit of evidence from the Grand Gulch area further east, however, suggests that in that area, similar houses were somewhat widely scattered rather than being clustered. This is in accordance with the ethnographically described Paiute winter-settlement pattern.

The apparent partial dependence of the White Dog people of this area on food collecting implies that a fair part of their time was spent in mobile hunting and/or gathering groups. Analysis of several sites in Camp Canyon, a tributary of Moqui, led to the tentative identification of seed-gathering parties composed of both men and women. The amount of artifactual material at the sites suggested that the parties were composed of more than a single family. Small food-collecting camps located at some distance from the habitation sites have also been tentatively identified.

SITE DISTRIBUTIONS AND SITE CHARACTERISTICS OF THE KLETHLA AND HORSEFLY HOLLOW PHASES

The basic data for the discussions in the next two sections are presented in maps, Figs. 7 and 8, and in tables, Figs. 9 and 10. The site sample used here consists of the fifty-six Klethla and Horsefly Hollow sites that yielded 100 or more sherds of a list of frequently occurring pottery types. This rather arbitrary measure was chosen because site dating was based on identification of complexes of pottery types; this could not be reliably done with extremely small samples. The sample so selected includes most of the sites of this size that are to be found in the region, as well as the great bulk of the artifactual material collected in the Red Rock Plateau. These sites are probably where the majority of the prehistoric inhabitants of this region during the Pueblo III period spent most of their time. The principal weakness of the sample for reconstructing prehistoric activity patterns is that it is biased toward habitation or residential sites and against the smaller camp sites, isolated small storage sites, isolated petroglyph panels, hand-and-toe-hold trails, and other kinds of sites that did not result in much accumulation of artifactual material. Another weakness of the sample is that, in some areas, a number of sites may have been lost through burial in alluvium or by erosion. For several reasons (Lipe 1967), I estimate that the loss of sites has not been substantial in most parts of

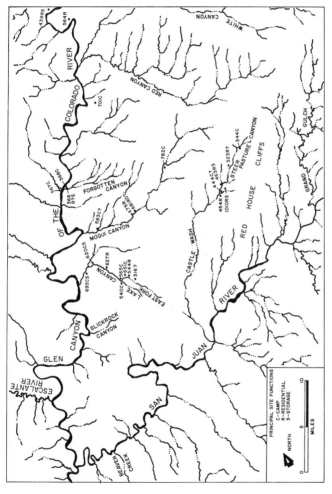

FIGURE 7. DISTRIBUTION OF KLETHLA PHASE COMPONENTS

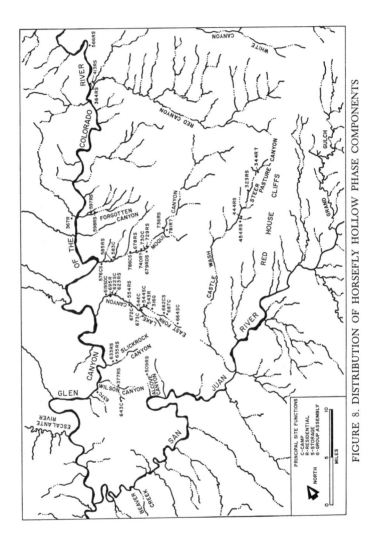

FIGURE 8. DISTRIBUTION OF HORSEFLY HOLLOW PHASE COMPONENTS

AREA	PHASE	SITE	ELEVATION	SHELTER	SUBSTANTIAL ROOMS With Hearth	SUBSTANTIAL ROOMS Without Hearth	INSUBSTANTIAL ROOMS With Hearth	INSUBSTANTIAL ROOMS Without Hearth	KIVAS	EXTERIOR HEARTHS	STORAGE STRUCT.	DEFENSIVE STRUCT.	SHERD COUNT	PRINCIPAL SITE FUNCTIONS
WILSON CANYON AREA	HORSEFLY HOLLOW	643 (E)[1]	Low Bench	Alcove			1			2			129	C[3]
		633 (E)	High Talus	Alcove	5		3	4	1	1	6		448	R[4],S
		509 (S)[2]	High Talus	Alcove	1?				1?		4?		180	R,S
		635 (E)	High Ledge	Alcove	2	1	1			1	1	2	426	R,S
		377 (E)	High Ledge	Overhang	1		1			1		2	159	R,S
		637 (E)	Canyon Floor	Open									197	C
LAKE CANYON AREA	KLETHLA	693 (E)	Canyon Floor	Alcove							6		134	C,S[5]
		565 (S)	Canyon Floor	Open									160	C
		651 (E)	Canyon Floor	Open									1076	C
		544-2 (E)	Canyon Floor	Open	2								248	R
		627 (E)	Canyon Floor	Open	1?			2					3070	R
		620 (E)	Canyon Floor	Open							1		584	C,S
		540 (E)	Canyon Floor	Open						1			161	C
		316 (E)	Low Bench	Open	2					1			1199 (M)[6]	G[7]
		672 (S)	Low Bench	Open				1?					259	C
	HORSEFLY HOLLOW	664 (S)	Low Bench	Alcove				1?			2		167	S,C
		695 (E)	Canyon Floor	Open	2			1			2+		319	R
		544-1 (E)	Canyon Floor	Alcove						4	14+		2034	S,C
		623 (E)	Canyon Floor	Open	1		1	1	1?		1		325	R,S
		619 (E)	Low Ledge	Alcove		1				1	2	1	190	S,D,C

[1](E), Excavated; [2](S), Survey Only; [6](M), Badly Mixed Collection; [3](C), Campsite; [4](R), Residential Site; [5](S), Storage Site; [7](G), Group Assembly Site

FIGURE 9. CHARACTERISTICS OF KLETHLA AND HORSEFLY HOLLOW PHASE SITES

(a) Lake Canyon and Wilson Canyon areas

AREA	PHASE	SITE	PHYSIOGRAPHIC SETTING ELEVATION	SHELTER	SUBSTANTIAL ROOMS With Hearth	SUBSTANTIAL ROOMS Without Hearth	INSUBSTANTIAL ROOMS With Hearth	INSUBSTANTIAL ROOMS Without Hearth	KIVAS	EXTERIOR HEARTHS	STORAGE STRUCT.	DEFENSIVE STRUCT.	SHERD COUNT	PRINCIPAL SITE FUNCTIONS
LAKE CANYON AREA	HORSEFLY HOLLOW	673 (E)	Low Bench	Open									166	C
		622 (E)	Low Ledge	Alcove							2		174	S,C
		662 (E)	Talus	Alcove			1	2			1		539	C,S
		543 (E)	Canyon Floor	Overhang	1		1				1		494	R
		554 (E)	High Ledge	Overhang	1	1		1			1	1	207	R,S
		687 (S)	Low Bench	Open				1?					161	C
MOQUI CANYON AREA	KLETHLA	782 (E)	Canyon Floor	Open									154	C
		681 (E)	High Talus	Alcove	1	2		1			1	1	332	R,D
		675 (E)	Canyon Floor	Open	1					1	2		284 (M)	R
		583 (E)	Low Bench	Alcove				1			1		256 (M)	C
		576 (E)	Low Bench	Alcove				1			4	1	265	C,S
		786 (S)	High Ledge	Alcove				1?				1	458	C,S
	HORSEFLY HOLLOW	585 (E)	Low Talus	Alcove	2	1		1-3	1	1		3+	1269	R,S
		730 (S)	High Ledge	Overhang				3?					116	C
		729 (E)	High Ledge	Overhang	1		1	1				3	305	R,S
		736 (E)	Low Talus	Alcove	1		1	4	1			4	211	R,S
		678 (E)	High Ledge	Overhang	2			1	1	1		2	352	R,S
		781 (E)	Canyon Floor	Open	1						1		209	R?
		679 (E)	High Ledge	Open, Overhangs	1		1				1	4	869	R,D,S
		740 (S)	High Ledge	Open				7?					228	R?

Fig. 9, continued. (b) Moqui canyon and Lake Canyon areas

AREA	PHASE	SITE	PHYSIOGRAPHIC SETTING		ARCHITECTURAL FEATURES								SHERD COUNT	PRINCIPAL SITE FUNCTIONS
			ELEVATION	SHELTER	SUBSTANTIAL ROOMS		INSUBSTANTIAL ROOMS		KIVAS	EXTERIOR HEARTHS	STORAGE STRUCT.	DEFENSIVE STRUCT.		
					With Hearth	Without Hearth	With Hearth	Without Hearth						
FORGOTTEN CANYON AREA	KLETHLA	367-1 (E)	Canyon Floor	Overhang						10			416	C
		366 (E)	Low Talus	Alcove					1?	1	1		979	R?,S
		368 (E)	Canyon Floor	Open						2			388	C
	HORSEFLY HOLLOW	367-2 (E)	Canyon Floor	Overhang	2					2			823 (M)	R
		597 (E)	High Talus	Alcove	1		1	1	1	1	3		110	R,S
		598 (E)	High Talus	Alcove	3		1	1	1		4		569	R,S
UPPER CASTLE WASH	KLETHLA	1010 (E)	Canyon Floor, Ledge	Open, Shelter	2	1		1		3	1		389	R,S
		454-1 (E)	Canyon Floor	Open	2?	1?							552	R
		463 (E)	High Talus	Overhang	1					2	1		363	R,S
		344-2 (E)	High Dune	Open									176	C
	HORSEFLY HOLLOW	323-1-2 (E)	Canyon Floor	Boulder	1?			1?		5			913 (M)	R?
		444-1 (E)	Canyon Floor	Open									274 (M)	C?
		344-1 (E)	High Dune	Open				2?	1				101 (M)	R?
		454-2-4 (E)	Canyon Floor	Open	2	2			1		1		1094 (M)	R,S
		444-2 (E)	Low Talus	Overhang	1	1?					2?		257	R,S
		323-3 (E)	Canyon Floor	Boulder	1			2	1		4		528	R,S
UPPER GLEN CANYON	KLETHLA	564 (E)	Canyon Floor	Boulder	3								753	R
		701 (E)	Canyon Floor	Open			1	1?		2			2359	C
	HORSEFLY HOLLOW	439 (S)	Low Bench	Open	3?						5+		100	R,S
		413 (E)	Low Talus	Overhang	2					1+	1		100 (M)	R,S
		566 (E)	Ledges	Overhang	2			1			2		135	R,S
		364 (E)	Low Bench	Open	4-6	3?				1	3?		1239	R,S

Fig. 9, concluded. (c) Upper Glen Canyon, Upper Castle Wash, and Forgotten Canyon areas

SUMMARY

AREA	PHASE	SITE ELEVATION		SITE SHELTER		ARCHITECTURAL FEATURES						SITE FUNCTIONS			
		CANYON FLOOR	OTHER	OPEN	SHELT. ERED	SUBST. ROOMS	INSUBST. ROOMS	KIVAS	EXTER. HEARTHS	STORAGE STRUC.	DEFEN. STRUC.	CAMP	CAMP & STORAGE	RESI- DENTIAL	GROUP ASSEM.
WILSON CANYON AREA	K.¹														
	H.H.²	1	5	1	5	11	9	4	4	14		2		4	
LAKE CANYON AREA	K.	7		6	1	3	2		1	7		3	2	2	
	H.H.	4	10	7	7	9	12	1	9	23	2	4	5	4	1
MOQUI CANYON AREA	K.	2	1	2	1	4	1	1	3		1?	1		2	
	H.H.	1	10	2	9	10	25	3	8	18	1	2	2	7	
FORGOTTEN CANYON AREA	K.	2	1	1	2			1	13	1		2		1	
	H.H.	1	2		3	6	4	2	3	7				3	
UPPER CASTLE WASH AREA	K.	4	2	4	2	8	2		10	2		2		4	
	H.H.	2	2	2	2	7	7	3		7				4	
UPPER GLEN CANYON AREA	K.	2	1	2	1	6	2		2	5		1		2	
	H.H.		3		3	13	1		3	4				3	
TOTALS	K.	17	5	15	7	21	7	2	29	15	1?	9	2	11	
	H.H.	9	32	12	29	56	58	13	27	73	3	8	7	25	1

¹(K.), Klethla Phase; ²(H.H.), Horsefly Hollow Phase

FIGURE 10. SUMMARY OF SITE CHARACTERISTICS BY AREA

the region, and has not biased the sample significantly, but alternative viewpoints have been expressed (for example, Jennings 1966).

An explanation is needed for the architectural feature labels used in Fig. 9. Substantial rooms have (or can be inferred to have had) (1) solidly built walls of masonry or sometimes of jacal, (2) roofs, and (3) adequate interior space for comfortable habitation. Most of the "substantial" rooms that were excavated had hearths, but some did not. Insubstantial rooms usually have rough dry-masonry walls and were probably never roofed; only a few of these structures that were excavated had hearths. Many were probably just low windbreaks.

Kivas were in some cases difficult to identify (see Smith [1952: 154-65] for a discussion of "when is a kiva?"), but in general, this rubric was applied to large well-built pithouses having a deflector, ventilator, and central firepit, and sometimes, pilasters or a southern recess. "Exterior hearths" include fireplaces noted at camp sites, as well as those appearing in courtyards and outdoor work areas at residential sites. This category is probably underrepresented at sites known only from survey and at large canyon floor sites which seldom were as completely excavated as rock-shelter, ledge, or talus-top sites. "Storage structures" include cists and small substantially built aboveground masonry buildings whose interior dimensions or doors were too small to permit comfortable habitation. Buried pottery vessels, most of which were probably used for storage, were not tabulated.

"Defensive structures" refers to a specific type of building element, found at only four sites. This element is a substantial masonry wall enclosing the front of an alcove or part of an open site and breached only by a narrow door and by small "peephole" openings at irregular intervals. Residential sites located in defensible positions were not classed as defensive structures, although many may well have been built in hard-to-reach places for defensive reasons.

The "principal site functions" are rather speculative and provisional. The main division of functions is into residences versus camps. Residential functions were assumed if the site contained one or more substantial rooms with hearths. Camps lack such rooms. Storage and defensive functions are also noted when structures of these sorts occur.

This assignment of functions may not be very realistic; particularly troublesome is the distinction between "residential" and "camp" sites. Many of the camp sites yielded more artifacts than residential sites with numerous structures. If artifact quantities are any indicator of the length of time a site was occupied and/or the number of people using it, then it seems apparent that in some areas of the Red Rock Plateau, many of the people spent most of their time away from formal complexes of substantial structures.

In general, architectural features are probably underrepresented in the record at canyon floor sites and other open sites because of the greater chance for structures to be obscured or obliterated by the elements or to escape the excavators' spades. Klethla architectural features, especially, are probably underrepresented in the tabulations, because (1) these sites tend to be in the open and on the canyon floors, (2) Klethla sites are older and so have been longer exposed to damage, and (3) the Klethla people more frequently built small slab-and-jacal constructions which decompose rapidly.

The Klethla Phase (circa A.D. 1100-1150)

Five hundred to 800 years after its abandonment by the White Dog people, the Red Rock Plateau was reoccupied, in the late 1000s or early 1100s. The new inhabitants belonged to the Klethla phase of the Kayenta branch. Although other explanations cannot be ruled out at this point (see Lipe 1967: 246-51), the hypothesis best supported by the available fragmentary evidence is that the Red Rock Plateau was reoccupied at this time because populations in the highlands to the east and south had increased to the point of "spilling over" into the environmentally marginal Red Rock Plateau. This hypothesis can probably be confirmed or refuted to the extent that the site distributions it implies could be checked by properly designed surface surveys in the highlands.

In addition to the scanty evidence that now exists of site distributions in the highlands, there is also some evidence that a long period of consistently above-average rainfall occurred between about 1050 and 1150 (Fig. 11) and that a warming trend took place concurrently (Baerreis and Bryson 1965; Lipe 1967). Both these developments would probably have led to population growth in the highlands.

The Klethla occupation of the Red Rock Plateau was only part of a general movement of Kayenta peoples into the Glen Canyon area as a whole. Substantial numbers of early Klethla phase sites were also established on the Kaiparowits Plateau and Cummings Mesa and on the south-

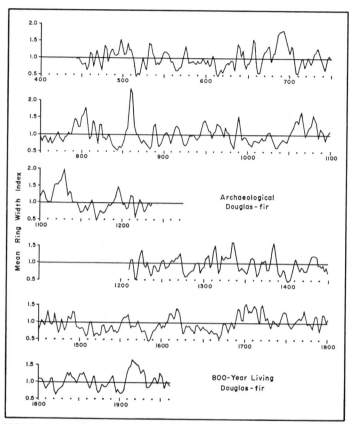

FIGURE 11. TREE-RING INDICES FROM MESÁ VERDE (after Fritts et al. 1965)

eastern fringes of the Aquarius Plateau near Boulder, Utah. This period was also the time of maximum northward and westward (if the Virgin branch is considered a Kayenta subbranch) geographical extent of the Kayenta Anasazi.

About 1150, Kayenta population in southern Utah apparently declined sharply. The Red Rock Plateau seems to have been either entirely or nearly abandoned at this time, as was most of the northern and western part of the Glen Canyon area. This abandonment of much of the Glen

Canyon area about 1150 correlates with a general southward retreat of the northern boundary of the entire Kayenta branch, with the disappearance of the Virgin subbranch (Aikens 1966a: 56), with the eclipse of the Fremont culture of central Utah, and probably with continuing population decrease on the Mesa Verde (Hayes 1964). The Coombs site, located in a highland setting near permanent streams, seems to have continued to be occupied during this period, and perhaps until A.D. 1200. Some Fremont communities in north central and northern Utah may also have survived, continuing until perhaps as late as the 1400s (Aikens 1966b). In general, however, the population of southern Utah seems to have declined sharply about 1150.

These events correlate well with the onset, at about 1150, of a severe drought, as recorded in the Mesa Verde tree-ring record (Fig. 11), which indicates that this drought was extremely intense and lasted about 40 years. Schulman's (1956) tree-ring chronology does not record such a severe drought but does indicate a marked decline in moisture relative to the preceding period. Other dendrochronological evidence indicates substantial regional variation in rainfall in the northern Southwest in the late 1100s (Jeffrey Dean, personal communication).

During the Klethla occupation of the Red Rock Plateau, sites were much more numerous and were less restricted in distribution than in the earlier White Dog phase (Fig. 7). The principal Klethla site clusters are in Lake Canyon and in the Upper Castle Wash area; a smaller cluster is at the mouth of Forgotten Canyon, and there are scattered Klethla sites in the Upper Glen Canyon and Moqui Canyon. The number of Klethla sites recorded from Moqui Canyon may be misleadingly small—the sample from this canyon has probably been disproportionately diminished by arroyo-cutting and alluviation. Nevertheless, it is doubtful that Moqui Canyon was as intensely occupied as Lake Canyon or Upper Castle Wash.

Klethla sites tend to concentrate in the few areas where the canyons are accessible and open and where relatively large patches of flood- and/or spring-watered soils occur. It appears that the Klethlans, unlike the earlier White Dog people, occupied all the parts of the Red Rock Plateau most favorable for farming. Other potentially habitable areas, chiefly in the deeper and narrower canyons such as Wilson, Slickrock, and Upper Forgotten, were largely ignored. These canyons were probably less desirable because their soils occur in small scattered patches and because fields were more subject to violent flooding.

None of the sites of the Klethla phase has more than a few structures, including sites yielding large numbers of artifacts. The largest Klethla site in pottery yield—Dead Tree Flats in Lake Canyon—had only one substantial room, a large masonry-lined pithouse that may have been a kiva. This room may have been constructed during a light Horsefly Hollow occupation of the site, for it closely resembles a definite pithouse or kiva of this phase found at the nearby Lyman Flats (Sa623) site. Fairly extensive trenching at the Dead Tree Flats site revealed only insubstantial structures; however, the site was not fully excavated. The second largest collection of Klethla sherds comes from the Creeping Dune site (Sa701) in the Upper Glen Canyon. Here, a rather elaborate reservoir and system of ditches had been built to irrigate plots of land with springwater (Sharrock et al. 1961). Pottery was scattered over several acres, but only two small room-like structures were found. Extensive trenches failed to reveal any pithouses.

Lake Canyon, the most heavily occupied part of the Red Rock Plateau during Klethla times, judging by numbers of sites and artifacts, had only a few structures assignable to Klethla origins. The only definite Klethla house in Lake Canyon is a small (10 foot diameter) slab-lined, shallow pithouse on a dune in front of the Horsefly Hollow site (Sa544); it apparently had a jacal or pole superstructure. Associated was a small deep unlined pithouse that seems not to have been finished.

More extensive building during Klethla times seems to have gone on in Upper Castle Wash and the Upper Glen Canyon. At the Steer Palace site (Sa454) in Upper Castle Wash, there is an unlined pithouse with five mealing bins on the floor, arranged in a semicircle around a central firepit. One and possibly two slab-based jacal surface rooms seem to have been levelled and rebuilt by later Horsefly Hollow occupants of the site. The disturbance produced by this later occupation makes it difficult to determine whether other Klethla structures were present or not. At the nearby Scorup Pasture site (Sa1010), a single small shallow slab-outlined pithouse like the one noted from Sa544 was found. Nearby, under a ledge, were the remains of one to three vertical-slab and jacal structures; masonry structures built atop them had largely obliterated their traces. The rebuilding was probably done during the later Horsefly Hollow phase.

The largest and best preserved Klethla structures in the region are in the Upper Glen Canyon, at Daves site (Sa564) and Ga439. Daves site consists of three surface masonry rooms built around a large slump boulder. Ga439, which was previously excavated by unknown parties and reported only from surface observations (Steward 1941: 335-36; Lister 1959: 120), consists of three or four contiguous surface masonry rooms located near the mouth of Trachyte Creek.

Kivas are rare at the Klethla sites. Other than the questionable one at Sa627, only two structures are likely to have served as kivas. The most clearly identifiable one, at Sa675 in Moqui Canyon, is deep and masonry-lined and has a southern recess, ventilator, deflector, and central firepit. The Husteds Well site (Sa366), at the mouth of Forgotten Canyon, also has these features, but is smaller and not fully masonry-lined. The only other structure at Husteds Well was a collapsed jacal storage room. Klethla remains at Sa675 were largely buried in alluvium and the site was not fully excavated. One other room, probably of Klethla age, was found.

The probably misnamed Fortress site (Sa316) in Lake Canyon, which may have served what I have called a group assembly function in the Horsefly Hollow phase, may have also been so used in Klethla times. The walled plaza and large masonry rooms at the site almost certainly date to the later phase, but Klethla pottery does appear, although it is not predominant. Furthermore, the peculiar scarcity of gray ware sherds characterizing collections from the Fortress is present among the Klethla as well as the Horsefly Hollow types, suggesting that this location may have had a similar special function in both phases.

One of the "defensive wall" structures may possibly belong to the Klethla phase. At site Sa681 in Moqui Canyon, one of the few Klethla components located in a high cave, a large well-built masonry wall with peepholes closes off part of the cave floor. Since some Horsefly Hollow pottery does occur in the site Sa681 deposits, and a probably Klethla jacal room at the back of the cave had been burned and levelled, it may be that the "defensive" wall was built during the later phase.

Storage structures are rare at Klethla sites, at least in comparison to their frequency in Horsefly Hollow sites. Of course, some of the small coursed-masonry granaries that occur throughout the canyons in sheltered spots may be of Klethla origins. Such granaries are built into many Horsefly Hollow sites, but their association with Klethla sites is not so clear. The only case of probable association is at Ga439 in Upper Glen Canyon at the mouth of Trachyte Creek, where Lister (1959: 120) reports several masonry granaries under ledges near the main structures.

Large campsites are more abundant in Klethla times than in the Horsefly Hollow phase. The Buried Olla site (Ga367) is a large campsite that may have been a stopping place on a popular trail during Klethla times. It is located in Glen Canyon at a point where there is a good fording place and where two tributary canyons lead in opposite directions away from the Colorado, providing a convenient pathway for east-west travel across the canyonlands area. One of the largest panels of petroglyphs in Glen Canyon is also associated with the Buried Olla site, as if each traveller had left some mark of his passage. The levels of the Buried Olla site at which Klethla pottery was dominant contained ten hearths and several buried storage jars but no house structures. Later, during the Horsefly Hollow phase, two masonry pithouses were built, but the site probably continued in use as a trail stop as well.

Because of the scarcity of definite structures and because potentially relevant data on artifact variation and distribution were not collected, the nature of the social units and activities of the Klethla people are difficult to infer. In the few sites where houses have been found, the evidence points to a very small unit of coresidence. The several small, isolated pithouses noted from Lake Canyon and Upper Castle Wash could have been occupied only by small nuclear families. The largest Klethla sites, in architectural elaboration, have shelter space for only two or three families. The grinding room at Sa454, with its five metates, could have been staffed by the women of two or three families. The other Klethla structures discovered at the site do not seem to provide enough living space for more than this number.

In sum, the scanty evidence available on living arrangements suggests that despite a larger total population, despite greater dependence on what must have been a more productive agriculture, the unit of coresidence during the Klethla occupation of the Red Rock Plateau was no larger, and perhaps not as large, as it had been during the White Dog phase, hundreds of years earlier. The Klethla immigrants into the region probably came as single nuclear families, or in small groups of two or three families. Probably the individuals coming into the region were young pepole unable to secure suitable farming land in their home areas. So, at least at first, residential units including three generations would have been rare, and the total number of people in a given residential unit would have been small.

There is some evidence of the occasional formation of larger groups of people and of mechanisms for integrating several minimal residential units. The Creeping Dune site (Sa701) in the Upper Glen Canyon (Sharrock et al. 1961) affords perhaps the best evidence of this. Here, a masonry reservoir some 27 by 12 feet in plan, with walls up to 6 feet high and 5 thick, was built to collect water from a now defunct spring. Ditches extended from this reservoir and perhaps from other springs in this area for a distance of at least 400 feet downslope, along sandy spurs extending out from the cliffs. Artifacts are thinly scattered over an area of 6 or 7 acres, and it seems probable that an area one-third to one-half this large was irrigated. The construction and maintenance of the irrigation system at this site and the farming of the irrigated plots must certainly have drawn labor from a group consisting of more than a single extended family.

The two or possibly three Klethla phase kivas recorded for the Red Rock Plateau seem not to be associated with particular groups of residential structures. It seems likely that the kivas, too, served to integrate groupings larger than the coresidential unit, or household. If the kiva at Dead Tree Flats was in use during Klethla times, it is associated with what appears to be a very large Klethla campsite; the total amount of pottery present here is probably greater than at any of the Klethla sites having definite house structures. Perhaps gatherings here were related to use of the kiva. The importance of kivas in the early Klethla phase probably should not be overemphasized, however. Kivas are rare in the western Kayenta area before the end of the Klethla phase and do not appear at all in some of the northwesternmost early Klethla phase settlements, such as those of the Kaiparowits Plateau and Coombs village near Boulder, Utah (Aikens 1966a: 47).

The Fortress site (Sa316) in Lake Canyon has already been referred to as a possible place of group assembly, perhaps for dances or other ritual activities. This site is on the edge of a prominent bench overlooking the broadest and probably the most productive part of Lake Canyon. The large plaza and room structures at this site probably belong to the Horsefly Hollow phase, but Klethla pottery is also fairly abundant at the site, although not predominant. The distinctive characteristic of the pottery here—both for Klethla and for the later type—is that decorated wares are much more common than are gray wares; the reverse is normally true.

Another site in the same part of Lake Canyon that shows similar pottery frequencies is Sa540, the Pahgarit Dune site. This is simply an open, essentially surficial "camp" site, on the edge of what was, in the late nineteenth and early twentieth centuries, a shallow lake dammed by an alluvial fan or falling dune. There is some question as to whether a lake existed here in prehistoric times (Lance 1963), but the area was probably at least swampy. In any case, Sa540 yielded materials attributable to the Klethla and Horsefly Hollow phases, to Pueblo IV period Hopi, perhaps to nineteenth-century Utes, and certainly to nineteenth- and twentieth-century Mormon cowboys. The bulk of the pottery found is attributable to the Klethla occupation, however. A historically known north-south trail leading to the Navajo Mountain area crosses Lake Canyon at about this point; if it were in use in prehistoric times as well, this might account for the great variety of materials at Sa540, though not necessarily for the skewed pottery frequencies.

Although it seems certain that communities spatially more extensive than the individual sites existed, there seems no way of precisely delimiting these at the present stage of analysis. A distributional study of pottery style variation at the attribute level, such as Longacre (1964a, 1964b) has carried out, might be fruitfully applied to this problem.

In summary, a review of the evidence from the early Klethla phase occupation of the Red Rock Plateau indicates that the only identifiable residential unit was small, consisting of no more than one to three nuclear families, that the people may have been living as often in temporary shelters or open camps as in houses, and that a certain amount of integration of the small coresidential units into larger communities may have derived from cooperation in irrigated farming and from participation in group rituals. At this point the data do not seem to permit postulation of community boundaries within the region.

The above analysis has implicitly assumed that the Klethla migrants into the Red Rock Plateau stayed there the year around and became independent to some extent of their parent communities outside the region. Obviously this analysis is misleading if these people were in fact only seasonal occupants of the region, migrating annually to and from villages in the adjacent highlands so that their highlands communities could have the benefits of both the highland and lowland environments in cultivation and food collecting. Hypotheses of this sort have been used by Long (1966) and Adams and Adams (1959: 36) to account for various groups of small sites in the Glen Canyon area.

A fuller statement of the seasonal occupation hypothesis would hold that the canyons of the Red Rock Plateau (with the possible exception of Upper Castle Wash) were only seasonally occupied by the Klethla people, who maintained larger, permanent habitations in the surrounding uplands. In the spring, small parties (perhaps only of men) would have left their home villages, traveling several tens of miles across rough desert terrain (again excepting Upper Castle Wash) to the low-lying, hot, but well-watered canyons of the Red Rock Plateau. These parties would have camped near the fields while the plants were maturing, as required by the intensive nature of Pueblo cultivation. Small houses might occasionally have been built for shelter. After harvest, part of the yield would have been carried back to the home village, the rest being left in storage to provide food and seed for the next spring.

A hint that seasonal occupation was being followed in the Red Rock Plateau comes from Daves site (Sa564) and the Creeping Dune site (Sa701) in Upper Glen Canyon. At both, pottery is abundant, but food-grinding tools are rare. None were found at Daves site, and only seven manos and no metates were recovered at Creeping Dune. Either women were not available to grind corn, or it was taken elsewhere for grinding; both interpretations imply seasonal use of the sites.

That scarcity of grinding tools is not universal in the Red Rock Plateau Klethla sites. This was demonstrated at Sa454 in Upper Castle Wash, where, as previously noted, a pithouse containing five mealing bins was found; many manos and several metates occur in the total collection from the site. This site is at the lower margin of the highland zone where the postulated home base villages would have occurred. As was also noted, however, the Upper Castle Wash sites do not seem significantly larger or more permanent than do the postulated summer farm houses located elsewhere in the region.

The biggest disadvantage of the seasonal occupation hypothesis, in my opinion, is the logistical prowess it requires of the Pueblo farmer. So that he and his dependents could enjoy during the winter the fruits of his summer labors, he would have had to make several trips back to his home village, heavily laden, over long stretches of dry, rugged country. Also, food and seed for the next spring would have had to be stored unattended in the canyons for use the following spring. As previously noted, there is little evidence of the requisite storage structures in association with the Red Rock Plateau Klethla sites.

An alternative interpretation is that the ephemeral Klethla settlements of the Red Rock Plateau were more or less typical of the western Kayenta Anasazi (including the so-called "Virgin Branch") at this time in their prehistory. This involves discarding our assumption that the typical settlement of this period should be a solidly built village that was continuously occupied for a number of years. Recently, Jennings (1963, 1966) has questioned this assumption for the Anasazi in general and for the Kayenta in particular. He suggests that the assumption derives from the South-western archaeologists' concentration on only the larger sites of all periods and from the attention given to the very large sites occupied just prior to the abandonment of the northern Southwest (a time when population definitely does seem to be aggregating in increasingly large settlements). I might add that the Southwesternist's familiarity with the large, seden-tary modern Pueblo villages has probably helped lead him to expect that villages of this sort were also typical well into the past. Jennings (1963: 12-13) has stated his point of view as follows:

> One forgets that [the] huge centers are rare and scattered, found only in very favorable locations. . . . Most settlements are small family settlements; they consist of one or two dwellings and a cluster of storage rooms, which can be most descriptively called little ranches or *rancherias*. The settlement pattern can be described as a scattered single family homestead type. . . . If the Pueblo can be seen as sub-sistence gardeners representing a culture whose limits were closely geared to some minimal rainfall line, if we can see the Pueblo as ex-panding and contracting territorially in almost annual response to climatic/rainfall conditions . . . then perhaps we can understand [their lifeway's] survival and better understand its details. . . . The real Anasazi were clever, ingenious small ranchers whose ability to exploit the environment was equal to, and possibly derived from, the desert culture ancestor whose skills were retained in large degree.

In this perspective, then, the small size and transient quality of the Klethla Red Rock Plateau sites is not surprising. The lack of abundant and well-made house remains may be no more than a reflection of the region's relatively warm winters. The numerous contemporaneous early Klethla sites on the Kaiparowits Plateau southeast of the Red Rock Plateau are small, and none yielded more than about 1000 sherds during thorough excavation (most produced much less pottery), yet each site has, on the average, two or three masonry rooms. At 7000 feet, the Kaipar-owits is considerably colder, both summer and winter, than the low-lying Red Rock Plateau. Houses would be much more useful at the higher elevation.

Jennings' hypothesis, then, is that the large sites of this time period, such as the Coombs site, are atypical and require special explanation. The Coombs site does have some unusual features that may help explain its size. In the first place, it is very well-favored ecologically, being in a high valley with abundant good soil and permanent streams small enough for easy diversion. It was also on the extreme northwest frontier of the Kayenta branch and is one of the few sites with evidence for substantial and continuing contact between Anasazi and people of the Fremont culture. Village size and permanency may have been especially advantageous here for defense or in establishing trading relations with the Fremont people.

A test of the seasonal farming hypothesis with respect to the Red Rock Plateau sites will require further fieldwork in the highland regions. If Klethla sites approaching the Coombs site in size are relatively numerous in the highlands near the Red Rock Plateau, then it seems to me the seasonal farming hypothesis would be favored. If, on the other hand, most highland sites are like those of the Red Rock Plateau, or like the two- or three-room-plus-courtyard Kaiparowits variety, then the interpretation derived from Jennings' ideas would be favored.

Jennings' hypothesis about the nature of Kayenta Anasazi settlement patterns during the Pueblo II and III periods is an important one that could be tested by systematic surveys designed to gather quantitative information on settlement patterns. Because of the highly variable nature of Kayenta settlements, care would have to be taken to sample a number of locales within the Kayenta area.

The Horsefly Hollow Phase (circa A.D. 1210-1260)

After a 50- or 60-year period of complete or near abandonment, the Red Rock Plateau was repopulated and saw its heaviest occupation in the early and middle 1200s. The southeastern part of the Glen Canyon basin also seems to have gained population at this time, as indicated by data from Cummings Mesa, where sites became larger and much more numerous in the early 1200s (Amber, Lindsay, and Stein 1964). The western part of the Glen Canyon area, including the Kaiparowits and the Southern Aquarius Plateau, remained unoccupied.

Several factors probably favored repopulation of the Red Rock Plateau in the early 1200s: (1) The extreme drought of the late 1100s was broken. (2) The environmental zone available to Anasazi farmers may have been contracting at the highest elevations, because of the onset of the cool neo-Pacific climatic episode (Baerreis and Bryson 1965). This put more population pressure on the habitable parts of the medium-level highlands and on entrenched canyons, including those of the Red Rock Plateau. (3) More land was being destroyed by a cycle of arroyo-cutting that was trenching alluvial floodplains. Canyons that remained unchanneled, such as those of the Red Rock Plateau, were therefore relatively more attractive than before. (4) Population may have been increasing in the Navajo Mountain area in the early 1200s, as it became a refuge for groups abandoning other parts of the shrinking Kayenta territory. The southern Red Rock Plateau may have received some population surplus from the Navajo Mountain area.

Pottery type distributions indicate that the populations entering the Red Rock Plateau in the early 1200s came from several directions. The southern and westernmost sites have high frequencies of the Kayenta pottery common in the highlands around Navajo Mountain to the south, while the northern and western sites have high frequencies of Mesa Verde-like pottery resembling that found in the highlands to the northeast around Elk Ridge. Many sites in the central Red Rock Plateau have substantial frequencies of the ceramics of both traditions. The Horsefly Hollow phase, which includes all this variation, was named after a site in Lake Canyon where both Mesa Verde and Kayenta pottery were abundant.

As noted earlier, the Klethla people had settled primarily in areas where the canyons are relatively broad, shallow, and accessible, and where the alluvial soils are present in fairly large, continuous plots. The Horsefly Hollow people heavily occupied the same areas but also settled the narrower, deeper, less accessible canyons—Moqui, Wilson, Slickrock, Upper Forgotten, and Alcove (Fig. 8). Here, the cultivable areas are smaller, more dispersed, and more likely to be damaged by violent floods. This pattern of settlement supports my earlier contentions that (1) the Horsefly Hollow phase was a time of maximum population for the region, and (2) because fewer potential farming locations were now available in surrounding areas, the Horsefly Hollow people were forced to make fullest possible use of the land resources of the region.

The Horsefly Hollow sites, compared to the earlier Klethla sites, tend (1) to be located more often in elevated, sheltered positions than on the canyon floor, (2) to have more structures, with greater use of masonry, (3) to have kivas more often, (4) generally to have considerably more provision for storage, and (5) at least in some areas, to show more clear-cut functional differences among sites.

Several site clusters of the Horsefly Hollow phase can be distinguished by geographic distribution, interaccessibility among the sites, and similarities in pottery and architecture. Each of these clusters perhaps may represent a small community.

The site cluster/communities postulated on this basis are (1) Wilson-Slickrock-Alcove Canyons, (2) Moqui Canyon, (3) Forgotten Canyon, (4) Upper Glen Canyon, (5) Upper Castle Wash, and (6) Lake Canyon. The clusters on the margins of the Red Rock Plateau perhaps may be part of communities outside the region, either through such mechanisms as seasonal occupation or because the cluster extends outside the boundaries of the region studied and therefore was not fully mapped. The latter possibility seems applicable only to the Castle Wash cluster. The treatment of these six site clusters as separate communities in no way implies that they were isolated from one another; on the contrary, contacts must have been fairly frequent.

Below, attempts are made to reconstruct some of the social characteristics of these communities. Site Clusters 1-3 can be discussed together, since their site characteristics are rather similar, although they are geographically separated.

Analysis of Site Clusters

Site Clusters 1 (Wilson-Slickrock-Alcove Canyons), 2 (Moqui Canyon), and 3 (Forgotten Canyon). The most common site in these three clusters is a small residential pueblo, with structures standing alone or in small groups, rather than being built in a compact block. The structures are usually strung out along a narrow ledge or talus top. In two cases, however (Sa679 and Sa740 in Moqui Canyon), such sites were built in the open on the edge of a rock bench or spur. Of the twenty Horsefly Hollow sites from these three clusters (Fig. 9), twelve are of this type.

Characteristically, these sites have: (1) one to five substantial living rooms with a firepit and sometimes also with a mealing bin; (2) a small courtyard or open-air work area, often with a fireplace, and sometimes with a mealing bin or set of loom anchors; (3) usually a kiva, sometimes with loom anchors in addition to the regular central firepit, deflector, and ventilator; (4) several insubstantially built rooms, probably never roofed, occasionally containing a hearth or other floor features, and (5) several well-built masonry storage structures in a variety of sizes and shapes. The number of potsherds recovered from these sites is never very great, with the exception of Doll Ruin (Sa585), perhaps in part because refuse was usually thrown over the edge of the living area and well scattered. Other kinds of artifacts, such as food-grinding tools, hammerstones, and chipped stone tools, are occasionally quite abundant, but not always. The small numbers of habitation rooms at these sites suggest that they were generally occupied by only a few nuclear families, probably comprising an extended family or minimal lineage. The smallest sites may have sheltered only a single nuclear family.

Within the group of canyons considered here, the number of these small residential sites to be found in a particular canyon varies rather closely with the size of the area available for farming. The smallest canyons contain only one or two, whereas the largest canyon of the group—Moqui —has five. Two other sites of this sort, known only from surveys, would probably have become incorporated in the Moqui Canyon sample had they been excavated or had the surveyors made larger collections. In general, the Moqui Canyon sites listed here are smaller than the small-canyon pueblos. Only four or perhaps five of the seven sites mentioned have a kiva. Although all are located above the canyon floor, Sa678 and Sa679 are the only ones in high, easily defensible positions. In contrast, all the residential pueblo sites from the smaller canyons are in high locations.

Other residential sites from the site clusters discussed here include Tamarix Dune (Sa781), a canyon-floor pithouse in Moqui Canyon, and the Buried Olla site (Ga367), located in Glen Canyon opposite the mouth of Forgotten Canyon. This site, used as a trail-side camp in Klethla times, was "improved" during the Horsefly Hollow phase by the construction of two small canyon-floor-level masonry houses. The site probably continued to be a trail-stop camp as well, however. An indication of this is that a large outdoor masonry firepit was built in Horsefly Hollow times; it contained much animal bone (mostly bighorn sheep), as if it had been regularly used by hunting parties bringing in fresh game.

As noted in the previous Klethla phase discussion, site Sa681 in Moqui Canyon contained a defensive structure, a large wall with loophole perforations that closed off part of the cave. This may have been constructed during the Horsefly Hollow phase, but the evidence is not conclusive.

The pottery at the site clusters discussed here varies somewhat. The Wilson-Slickrock-Alcove canyons cluster produced pottery very predominantly of Kayenta branch types. Both Moqui Canyon and Forgotten Canyon, on the other hand, showed various mixtures of Kayenta and

Mesa Verde types. In this, they resemble Lake Canyon and Upper Castle Wash.

The separation of the Moqui Canyon and Forgotten Canyon clusters is questionable perhaps, because the two areas are close together, the Forgotten Canyon cluster is very small, and the pottery from both areas is a mixture of both Mesa Verde and Kayenta types. The separation was made on a geographic basis; a traveler going directly from the main part of the Moqui Canyon site cluster to the principal Forgotten Canyon site, Sa598, would have to cross dry, deeply entrenched North Gulch. Access from Moqui Canyon and into Forgotten Canyon at their closest approaches to one another would also be difficult. A route via the mouths of the two canyons would be easier, but much longer. In other words, in travel time, Forgotten Canyon is probably as far away from Moqui as is Lake Canyon.

Site Cluster 4: Upper Glen Canyon. Three sites from the sample of fifty-seven are here. The largest by far is the Loper Ruin (Sa364), which sits on the edge of a low bluff overlooking the Colorado River and the flats at the mouth of Red Canyon. This site, partly two-story, is L-shaped in plan, with five ground-floor rooms and a kiva in the angle of the L. Under the overhanging edge of the bluff are several substantial masonry rooms that were probably used for storage. Artifacts, especially pottery, are plentiful. This small "unit pueblo" differs in a number of respects from the small pueblos previously discussed. It has better masonry, its rooms are built together rather than being essentially independent structures, and the courtyard work areas and insubstantial unroofed "rooms" common at the other sites are lacking. The structural differences may relate partly to the nearby outcropping of tabular Moenkopi sandstone, which makes excellent masonry and is not generally available elsewhere in the region. In terms of the number of people the site could shelter, Loper Ruin is probably equivalent to the largest cliff dwellings, such as Widow's Ledge (Sa633) in Slickrock Canyon or Defiance House (Sa598) in Forgotten Canyon. The principal differences, however, are in site plan and construction, rather than size or function.

The other sites in this cluster, Ledge Ruin (Sa566) and Forked Stick Alcove (Sa316) are more similar to those of Clusters 1-3. Ledge Ruin consists of three small, poorly constructed rooms and a granary, widely scattered along a sheltered ledge. Forked Stick Alcove has a crudely built pithouse, a small surface room, and a small granary. Despite their architectural differences, all three sites in this cluster had very similar pottery profiles, with almost all pottery being Mesa Verde in style.

Site Cluster 5: Upper Castle Wash. The four Horsefly Hollow sites from this area that were included in the sample were all occupied during the Klethla phase as well, so it was difficult in some cases to determine which structures related to which occupation. The size of these sites and the variety of structures present at each—rooms, kivas, storage structures— are about the same as in the cliff dwellings of Clusters 1-3. The site plan is also typically loose, with scattered structures or groups of structures. The chief differences between these sites and those of Clusters 1-3 are that the Castle Wash sites are either in the open or are not completely sheltered and are either on or not far above the canyon floor, differences perhaps primarily related to the physiographic setting. Upper Castle Wash is rather shallow in comparison with the deep canyons of the first group, which offered numerous sheltered and canyon wall site locations.

Site Cluster 6: Lake Canyon. The site groupings described above are dominated by sites having residential rooms. In Lake Canyon, on the other hand, the thirteen Horsefly Hollow sites contained in the sample include only four small sites with residential structures. Three of the remaining nine were considered to be primarily camps. Another five showed evidence of both camping and storage functions. The last of the thirteen is the previously discussed "Fortress" (Sa316), interpreted as a place of group assembly. In addition to these sites, seven other probable Horsefly Hollow phase sites were excavated but produced too little pottery to be included in the sample on which this discussion is primarily based. Tentative classification of these "unproductive" sites indicates they do not contradict the pattern shown by the thirteen larger sites mentioned above.

Because of the distinctiveness of the Lake Canyon site cluster, I will discuss each of the functional site types occurring there. Emphasis will be on the sites from the basic sample, but some information from the seven low-pottery-yield sites will also be used.

1. *Residential Sites.* These are relatively rare and are uniformly small; none has more than two substantial rooms with hearths, and artifacts are not very abundant. The only ledge or talus-top dwellings are Rogers House (Sa554) and Wasp House (Sa373). (The latter, one of the seven sites from outside the regular sample, is less than a mile from the canyon mouth and is the most solidly constructed residential site in the canyon.) The other residential sites are on the canyon floor or canyon rim.

These Lake Canyon residential sites have a loose layout, with some or all the structures being built as separate units. Kivas are found only at Wasp House (Sa373) and (probably) at Lyman Flat (Sa623). Storage structures are found at some but are not nearly as common as at the residental sites of Clusters 1-3. Since there seems to be a tendency for residential sites to be built on the canyon floor, the sample may be somewhat biased against them, for reasons previously given.

2. *Camp Sites.* Sites of this sort large enough to yield substantial artifact collections are uncommon in Lake Canyon during the Horsefly Hollow phase. Most of the camp sites that were excavated contained a few loosely built structures, probably windbreaks. Exterior hearths were not common.

3. *Camp and Storage Sites.* This group includes the Horsefly Hollow site (Sa544), the highest pottery-yield site in the canyon and by this standard one of the largest in the region. Although it is evident from the several hearths and numerous potsherds and stone tools found here that the site was a favored camping and/or working place, its primary function was storage. Eight large masonry-lined storage cists, ranging from about 3 to 5 feet in diameter and up to 5 feet deep, were sunk into the sandy floor of a small alcove overlooking the broad alluvial flats of lower East Fork. Several smaller cists and thirteen large storage vessels were also found. Since only about two-thirds of the sheltered area was excavated, other cists and vessels probably remain. I speculate that the large storage cists held food for individual households or other small residential groups, while the storage jars and small cists may have been the seed corn repositories for individual farmers. The corn undoubtedly was grown on the extensive alluvial flats in front of the cave.

The remaining camp and storage sites, most of them in the lower part of Lake Canyon, also show primary emphasis on storage. In these sites, however, the storage structures, instead of being at the canyon floor level as in the Horsefly Hollow site, are usually in high, dry shelters. Typically, the storage structures are small tightly built rooms of masonry or sometimes of jacal.

One of these storage sites—Gourd House (Sa619)—has several small rooms built in a shallow alcove, but also includes a massive masonry wall, unbroken except for a narrow door and numerous peepholes, that closes off the front of the shelter. Although it is not high above the canyon floor, the alcove can be entered only by pecked hand-and-toe holds. Inside the area enclosed by the 5-foot high wall is a large firepit and a set of loom anchors. The site thus appears to have been a place of refuge as well as of storage. I have observed a strikingly similar site in Fable Valley, in the highlands of the Elk Ridge area to the northeast. It is Pueblo III in date and has Mesa Verde pottery very similar to that from the Loper Ruin (Sa364).

4. *Defensive Site.* Gourd House probably had defensive functions, but this interpretation could be questioned. There seems little room for alternative explanations of the function of Sa655, one of the "low-yield" excavated sites noted earlier. This site is built across the narrowest part of a steep-sided rock peninsula that extends into old Lake Pahgarit from the canyon's right bank. The single structure at the site is a masonry room about 10 feet wide and 60 feet long, constructed of tabular limestone brought from ¾ mile away. A line of holes pecked in the rock leads from one end of this building down the more gently sloping side of the rock peninsula, suggesting that a fence was built here to complete the blocking of entry to the peninsula. The few artifacts found at the site consisted of several sherds of characteristic Horsefly Hollow pottery types, plus two sherds of Jeddito corrugated. The latter indicates that Jeddito phase Hopis visited the site. The remains of three small campfires found inside the building atop a layer of what appeared to be melted roofing clay, mortar, and/or plaster may derive from this visit.

5. *Group Assembly Site.* The probably misnamed "Fortress" site (Sa316) consists of a large walled rectangular plaza, 75 by 50 feet in dimension, oriented roughly east-west, with two large masonry rooms at its west end. Over most of its length, the plaza wall seems never to have been high enough to have served a defensive function. In the center of the plaza is a circular fireplace 4 to 5 feet in diameter. Each of the two long walls of the plaza is breached by a doorway just opposite the fireplace. The symmetry of the two rooms exiting onto the plaza and because there are two symmetrically opposed outside doorways to the plaza, each giving equal access to the central hearth, suggest that a dual social segmentation was recognized at whatever assemblies were held here. Chang (1958: 307) has noted, on the basis of a cross-cultural survey, that segmented communities, usually composed of several lineages, often have a large common plaza or other place of community assembly. The two rooms at the west end of the site are similarly built, and both open only onto the plaza, through separate doorways. The sills of both doors are built up above the room floor and plaza level, so that one must step up

and over them to enter or leave the room. In both rooms, the fireplace is built against the front wall immediately adjacent to the doorway, a mode of fireplace location not quite like anything observed elsewhere in the Red Rock Plateau, though it may be related to the Kayenta entry-box complex (Lindsay et al. 1966), which does appear in the region. A person stepping up to the plaza from one of these rooms would pass through the smoke of the fire, much as would someone climbing up through a kiva hatchway. The relative rarity of kivas in Lake Canyon suggests that the structures at Sa316 may have been performing some of the ceremonial functions conducted elsewhere in kivas. Further indications that Sa316 may have had some ceremonial use are (1) the finding of a *tchamahia* stuck in between wall stones in one of the rooms, and (2) the presence of a rough dry-laid masonry structure in the plaza in front of the rooms. This feature, little more than a pile of large stones, is similar to structures that Hayes (1964: 113-14), on the basis of ethnographic analogies, has called "shrines." If the structure at Sa316 is a shrine, it must have been built sometime after the site's abandonment.

As already noted, a further indication of the unusual nature of Sa316 is the abnormally low frequency of gray ware sherds in the collections. The great bulk of the sherds are from painted types. If large gray ware jars were used primarily for cooking, holding water, and for dry storage, and the decorated vessels primarily as eating utensils, then perhaps we may surmise that already-cooked foods were brought to the site from elsewhere and that the storage functions of large jars were not needed because the site was only occasionally occupied.

COMPARISON AND DISCUSSION OF SITE CLUSTERS

In contrast to the other site clusters, Lake Canyon is distinguished by greater segregation of special-function structures. Elsewhere in the Red Rock Plateau, the dominant sites are small pueblos generally including not only residential but also storage and ceremonial-assembly (kiva) structures. Lake Canyon, on the other hand, has one large, and probably several small, specialized storage sites, a large specialized group assembly site, and at least one special defensive site. The relatively few sites with residential structures tend to lack associated kivas and storage buildings.

These differences indicate a higher level of community organization in the Lake Canyon area than elsewhere in the Red Rock Plateau during the Horsefly Hollow phase. The storage structures of a small cliff dwelling such as Defiance House (Sa598) in Forgotten Canyon were probably used only by the one or two households that lived there. The numerous storage structures of the Horsefly Hollow site, however, must have belonged to several different households, none residing at the site. The Sa316 plaza likewise must have been used by many different residential groups, none of them living at the site. The development of large, functionally specialized sites probably depended on the greater size and compactness of the Lake Canyon population, which in turn depended on the greater amount and more compact distribution of alluvial farmlands in Lake Canyon. Especially important in concentrating population must have been the extensive alluvial deposits in lower East Fork and around Lake Pahgarit; it is significant that the three most functionally specialized sites (Sa544, 316, 655) all occur in this area.

This is not to say that the people of the other canyons lacked social mechanisms for integrating families and households into larger groups, but merely that only in Lake Canyon was it possible for a number of families to farm in a relatively small area so that they could easily come together for various kinds of group activity. In the other areas, farmlands were limited to smaller patches, which were usually strung out at intervals along narrow canyons, so that only a small number of people could conveniently live close to each patch of cultivable soil.

The surprising thing about the Lake Canyon development is that the people did not choose to establish larger residential units—true pueblos. This seems to contradict a trend, during the 1200s in the western Four Corners area, for previously dispersed populations to become increasingly concentrated into larger residential units. On Cummings Mesa, for example, at a time correlative with the Horsefly Hollow phase, sites of ten to fifteen rooms are not uncommon. This trend could, of course, take effect only in areas where resources could support a fairly large localized population, but Lake Canyon seems to have been such an area. Certain functions, notably storage, group assembly-group ceremonial, and defense, seem to have been spatially aggregated, but residence apparently was not. Furthermore, dwelling structures of any sort are rare altogether. The central problems, then, of interpreting the Lake Canyon settlement pattern are to determine (1) why residence did not undergo localization as other functions seem to have, and (2) where the people actually lived.

These problems are not easy to resolve, and I have no satisfactory answers. With regard to the problem of where people lived, the typical dwellings may have been pithouse rooms scattered widely over the canyon floors. This kind of pattern is suggested by the three excavated canyon-floor residential sites—Sa543, 623, and 695. If this is the case, then the salvage crews may simply have missed most dwelling places, either because they were covered with blowsand, had been removed by arroyo-cutting, or simply seemed too insignificant to warrant further investigation beyond making a small surface collection and reporting another "campsite." Alternatively, the Horsefly Hollow people may have spent most of their time at small campsites.

Both these interpretations assume, however, that Lake Canyon was somehow exempted, not only from the trend toward large multiroom residential sites but also from general trends toward increasing use of masonry in building, increasing use of site locations above the canyon floor, and increasing numbers of aboveground structures—trends evident not only elsewhere in the Red Rock Plateau but also in surrounding highlands such as Cummings Mesa. If we view the evidence from the Red Rock Plateau in isolation, there is some indication that these trends most readily asserted themselves in isolated areas where populations were smallest—so the largest residential pueblos, with the greatest use of masonry and aboveground construction, and with locations well above the canyon floor, occur in the most isolated and smallest site clusters—at the mouth of Red Canyon, in Upper Forgotten Canyon, and in Slickrock, Wilson, and Alcove Canyons. This further implies that all four trends may relate to defense, perhaps specifically to the need to have storage structures in safe places, guarded by on-the-spot residents.

In this interpretation, then, we see the Red Rock Plateau Puebloans clinging most tenaciously to their old pattern of living close to their fields in dispersed single households and reluctantly abandoning this pattern only when the need for security required it. Another facet of this interpretation would see these Puebloans as hesitant to build substantial masonry residential structures purely for shelter from the elements. To the highland-oriented Pueblo people, the climate of the low-lying Red Rock Plateau must have seemed extraordinarily hot in the summer and mild in the winter. Consequently, even where residential structures were built, they often were flimsy, apparently thrown together with a minimum of effort. That this was by choice rather than lack of skill is shown by the juxtaposition, in some of these sites, of shoddy houses and stout, excellently finished storage structures. Really well-made residences occur in a few places, but these tend to be in isolated spots, where defense was perhaps a factor.

The above arguments, however, are seemingly contradicted by evidence from adjacent regions. On Cummings Mesa (Ambler, Lindsay, and Stein 1964), for example, a population concentration probably larger and hence more secure than the one in Lake Canyon was at this time building large multiroom pueblos with storage, ceremonial, and residential rooms.

Another hypothesis about the anomalous Lake Canyon residence pattern, not necessarily contradictory to those previously offered, is that most occupation of Lake Canyon was seasonal, with small groups coming in to farm from neighboring canyons or even from outside the Red Rock Plateau. It seems unlikely to me, however, that what must have been the best farming area in the region should have been seasonally occupied, while less favorable areas were occupied the year around.

In conclusion, the most basic division within the Red Rock Plateau during the Horsefly Hollow phase seems to be between the Lake Canyon site cluster on the one hand and the rest of the area on the other. The less pronounced differences among the site clusters outside of Lake Canyon seem to boil down to differences between the clusters occupying narrow deep canyons and those in relatively broad, shallow ones.

THE PROBLEM OF KAYENTA-MESA VERDE POTTERY RELATIONSHIPS

As previously noted, pottery from two major Anasazi traditions was in use in the Red Rock Plateau during the Horsefly Hollow phase. Sites of the Upper Glen Canyon cluster have almost all Mesa Verde pottery; those of the Wilson-Slickrock-Alcove cluster have almost entirely Kayenta. The remaining clusters show substantial amounts of both traditions, although Upper Castle Wash definitely leans to the Mesa Verde side. The Red Rock Plateau during this period seems to be on the boundary between an extensive distribution of Mesa Verde style pottery to the northeast and east and of Kayenta style pottery to the south and southeast. It is reasonable to infer that the people who occupied the Red Rock Plateau during the Horsefly Hollow phase either came from both the adjacent pottery-style areas, or engaged in extensive importation of one or the other styles of pottery, or both.

It might be postulated that in the situation described above, culturally plural communities would have existed in the central part of the Red Rock Plateau during the Horsefly Hollow phase, with perhaps part of a site or site cluster being occupied by people using one kind of pottery, another part by people using a different kind. Such seems not to be the case, however; the same people seem to have been using both kinds of pottery. Inspection of the horizontal distributions of the sherds did not reveal spatial segregation of Mesa Verde and Kayenta types within a single site or among neighboring sites. There are a few possible exceptions. The Crumbling Kiva site (Sa597) had very little Mesa Verde pottery, while it is common at Defiance House (Sa598) less than a mile upstream. Also, Rogers House (Sa554) is the only Horsefly Hollow site in Lake Canyon that completely lacked Mesa Verde black-on-white, although other Mesa Verde types occur in small numbers. These cases suggest some site-to-site segregation of the two kinds of pottery within a single area, but the evidence is not very convincing. Both Sa597 and Sa598 yielded only small sherd samples (110 and 207, respectively), so their departure from the norm could be the result of sampling error.

The evidence of recurrent distributional homogeneity cited above comes largely from refuse or room deposits, which may reflect fairly long spans of time and which are subject to mechanical admixture. Better evidence of the close association of Kayenta and Mesa Verde types comes from deposits reflecting single events or very short time spans and from which chance admixture is excluded.

At the Ivy Shelter site (Sa738), a small Horsefly Hollow phase cemetery in Moqui Canyon (Sharrock, Day, and Dibble 1963: 144-25), one burial contained three bowls, all of Kayenta types, while a second burial had two Mesa Verde black-on-white bowls. This seeming Kayenta-Mesa Verde segregation was contradicted, however, in the third pottery-yield burial; it had a Mesa Verde black-on-white mug resting inside a Moenkopi corrugated (a Kayenta type) jar. Furthermore, these three burials lay close together in the same small cemetery, the only true cemetery found in the Red Rock Plateau. This suggests it was being used by the same group of people. At the Horsefly Hollow site (Sa544) in Lake Canyon (Sharrock, Dibble, and Anderson, 1961: 39-66), a large Tusayan black-on-white (a Kayenta type) sherd covered the head of a burial, while a Mesa Verde black-on-white jar appeared in the fill just above it, apparently part of the grave goods. The Horsefly Hollow site also had many buried storage jars of both Kayenta and Mesa Verde types that must have been in use contemporaneously. The spatial distribution of the jars appeared random with respect to the Mesa Verde-Kayenta dichotomy.

The coherence of the two pottery design style traditions seems well maintained. That is, distinctive Mesa Verde attributes almost never appear on vessels decorated basically in the Kayenta style, and vice versa. I think the possibility of massive style acculturation can be ruled out. This indicates that the mixture of pottery in the site clusters in the central part of the Red Rock Plateau is due either to (1) extensive trading of pottery into the area, (2) the residence of some number of potters (women) schooled in each tradition in the several site clusters where the mixture occurs, or (3) a combination of the first and second situations. Some progress might be made in sorting out these alternative explanations if technical studies could be carried out that determined where the pottery was actually made (or at least where the clay came from); the trading hypothesis might be tested in this way.

If widespread trade were not occurring, and the mixture of pottery is due to the residential association of women trained in different traditions, then some further understanding might be gained by trying to identify stylistic features that can be associated with male activities, and then by comparing the distributions of such features to the pottery distributions. As a start in this direction, I would propose as a working hypothesis that most of the structures in Lake, Moqui, and Forgotten Canyons and in Castle Wash were built by men from the Kayenta area. Evidence supporting this interpretation is the occurrence in the central part of the Red Rock Plateau of the entry-box complex, extensive use of jacal in combination with masonry, and great variation in the form of kivas, all traits common in the Kayenta area at this time. Then, if we can exclude trade, we must infer that a virilocal marriage rule was generally being followed and that Kayenta men were marrying women from both Kayenta communities to the south and Mesa Verde communities to the north or northeast. If such a study emphasizing architectural features were carried out, one of the first things that would have to be done would be a survey of architecture in the Mesa Verde sites of the Beef Basin-Elk Ridge highlands northeast of the Red Rock Plateau, because this area has received little study.

We cannot simply assume that the architectural practices of the Mesa Verde proper hold true for this westernmost extension of the culture.

THE ABANDONMENT OF THE RED ROCK PLATEAU

Most Horsefly Hollow sites in the Red Rock Plateau seem to have been abandoned by about 1260, although a few may have been occupied somewhat longer. The evidence suggests that the withdrawal from the region was gradual and unhurried. At two sites, Sa598 in Forgotten Canyon and Sa364 in Upper Glen Canyon, there was evidence that the groups occupying these sites departed one family at a time—at the end of occupation some of the dwelling rooms had already been vacated and partially filled with trash.

If my dating estimate of 1260 for abandonment is about ten years too early, then the onset of the so-called "great drought" may have been a factor in the exodus of population from the region. On the Mesa Verde, this dry period started about 1270 and lasted nearly until the end of the century (Fig. 11). Its occurrence is also well attested in tree-ring records from elsewhere in the northern Southwest. Although this drought may not have been as severe as the one recorded in the Mesa Verde records for the late 1100s, the Red Rock Plateau would probably have been difficult to inhabit during the period because of depleted ground and surface water.

Also instrumental in the abandonment of the area may have been an increase in the violence of floods, which would have disrupted floodplain farming. The Red Rock Plateau seems to have escaped a thorough cycle of arroyo-cutting, but evidence from Moqui Canyon indicates that stream regimens may have been somewhat disturbed (Lance 1963). This disturbance is not dated precisely enough, however, to allow us to say whether or not it correlates well with the abandonment date. Furthermore, the Lake Canyon alluvium does not record a change in stream regimen (Lance 1963); yet this canyon was abandoned about the same time as Moqui.

Probably implicated in the withdrawal of population from the Red Rock Plateau were whatever pressures that lay behind the area-wide trend toward residence in large multifamily and multilineage pueblos. In the 1200s, the Anasazi populations remaining in the northern Southwest were drawing increasingly together in and around large pueblos. The reasons for this change in settlement pattern are not well understood, although they have been debated for many years. Cooling climates, drought, and arroyo-cutting were probably acting separately or together to make a number of previously habitable areas uninhabitable. Larger communities may have been necessary to provide for the fullest exploitation of remaining soil and water resources. Defensible site locations become common in this period, too, and it has often been suggested that warfare of some kind may have been responsible for a shift to larger communities. That many communities continued to live in essentially indefensible locations, plus the scarcity of direct evidence of violence anywhere in the area, argues against the defensive hypothesis, however.

Whatever the reasons for the formation of larger communities at this time, the process was widespread. The Red Rock Plateau is unusual in that a dispersed settlement pattern was followed until the time of abandonment in the middle 1200s. It seems unlikely that the meager and scattered soil and water resources of the Red Rock Plateau would have supported any really large nucleated communities; the people who left the region in the middle or late 1200s probably joined or founded large pueblos somewhere to the south. The nearest likely area for such resettlement would have been the Navajo Mountain area, where Kayenta Anasazi lived nearly until the end of the 1200s. Lindsay et al. (1966) show that about 1270 several large pueblos were built or greatly enlarged in the area north and east of Navajo Mountain. Red Rock Plateau emigrants probably contributed to the peopling of such sites, although this is presently a hypothesis for further testing rather than a demonstrated fact.

As noted above, drought or other environmental factors may have been primary agents in dislodging the Horsefly Hollow people from the Red Rock Plateau. On the other hand, defensive needs or other nonenvironmental pressures to join larger residential aggregates, if strong enough, could probably have depopulated the region even without significant environmental deterioration.

THE JEDDITO AND SIKYATKI PHASES (CIRCA A.D. 1300-1600)

After the Horsefly Hollow occupation, the Red Rock Plateau was never again settled by the Anasazi. During the Pueblo IV period, however, the region was briefly visited a number of times by small parties of Hopi, some perhaps descendants of the earlier inhabitants. Twenty of the 512 Red Rock Plateau sites yielded distinctive Jeddito and Awatobi yellow ware sherds, evidence of these visits. The sites cannot be precisely dated, but the majority appear to be from the 1300s.

The Jeddito-Sikyatki components are small, have on the average very few sherds, and lack structures other than an occasional firepit. The sites tend to be in the open on the canyon floor or in other unelevated positions and usually occur in the broader, more open parts of canyons or outside the canyons altogether. Deeply entrenched canyons were apparently avoided. The distribution of sites suggests that some may be associated with an old trail running from the Navajo Mountain area north across the Red Rock Plateau.

The Pueblo IV Hopi utilization of the Red Rock Plateau obviously did not involve farming, but the precise reasons for the visits are not entirely clear. Petroglyphs at a Hopi site in Moqui Canyon show hunting scenes (Day 1963: 246-47, 290); Turner's (1963) Hopi informants also suggested that the Pueblo IV travelers may have been visiting shrines, perhaps some of those established during earlier occupation of the area by their ancestors. Also, Hopi trading expeditions to the Southern Paiute are ethnographically documented (Kelly 1964) and cannot be ruled out as an explanation. It may well be that the Red Rock Plateau was not itself the destination of the Hopi parties; they may simply have detoured into the region because of its relatively abundant sources of surface water.

CONCLUSIONS

My principal conclusions are (1) that something resembling, in size and probably in composition, the modern western Pueblo extended-family-based household was both the regular and the maximal unit of co-residence in the Red Rock Plateau from Basket Maker through Pueblo III times; (2) that mechanisms of community integration grew stronger and more extensive through time, but that the Red Rock Plateau Anasazi maintained until the end of permanent occupation an older pattern of settlement in geographically dispersed households, probably located close to their fields; and (3) that the Red Rock Plateau environment, with its limited and dispersed soil and water resources, was probably an important factor in helping maintain a dispersed residence pattern into a period of

Anasazi Communities in the Red Rock Plateau

increasing residential aggregation elsewhere in the western Four Corners area.

NOTES

1. I think this generalization holds for Kayenta and "Virgin Branch" communities in southeastern Utah and northeastern Arizona and perhaps for the very westernmost Mesa Verde communities in Utah as well. Jeffrey Dean (personal communication, and in his paper in this volume) disputes this with respect to Tsegi Canyon. He finds that in the Tsegi, fairly large nucleated communities occur in Basketmaker III and Pueblo I times. These do, however, break down by about A.D. 1000, and a dispersed residence pattern with small sites is common until large nucleated communities appear again in the late 1100s and the 1200s.

2. It is risky to rely on Schulman's tree-ring data alone, because they are compiled from different species which may have reacted differently to precipitation, and because the earlier part of Schulman's chronology depends on specimens collected 100 miles or more from the Red Rock Plateau (Jeffrey Dean, personal communication). On the other hand, Schulman's chronology provides the best data available so far for this time period.

3. Systematic survey and excavations in this area in the summer of 1969 have confirmed these initial impressions.

Aspects of Tsegi Phase
Social Organization:
A Trial Reconstruction[1]

JEFFREY S. DEAN

Laboratory of Tree-Ring Research,
University of Arizona

Significant advances have recently been made in the theory and techniques of reconstructing certain aspects of extinct sociocultural systems from archaeological data. A developing body of relevant anthropological theory, accumulating knowledge of local archaeological assemblages and traditions, and more sophisticated techniques of data extraction have made it possible to formulate and test hypotheses relating to prehistoric social organization. While attempts to reconstruct sociocultural systems on the basis of archaeological evidence are fraught with hazards created by the nature of the data, the archaeologist would be remiss if he ignored these problems simply because of their inherent difficulties. As others have pointed out (Longacre 1966: 101; Hill 1966: 27), it is not necessary to accept the results of these attempts as final answers. It is sufficient that sociological inferences based on sound data and techniques of analysis sharpen our focus on these problems, indicate alternative or supplemental hypotheses, and improve our techniques for extracting pertinent data.

Aspects of Tsegi Phase Social Organization

This paper presents the results of one such attempt based on data from several late Pueblo III sites in Tsegi Canyon, northeastern Arizona. Primary interest centers on the largest of these sites, Betatakin and Kiet Siel, but data from other sites contribute to the analysis. I want to stress that many of the inferences summarized here are propositions (Hill, this volume) that must be subjected to rigorous testing before they can be considered as demonstrated. Most of these propositions are amenable to testing against data independent of those by which the propositions were generated, although the opportunity to do so has not yet arisen.

Before proceeding with the analysis, it is necessary to specifically define several terms that appear throughout this paper.

The *Kayenta Branch* (Gladwin and Gladwin 1934) has long been recognized as a distinct, geographically bounded manifestation of the Anasazi cultural tradition in the plateau Southwest. Although the Kayenta Branch is recognized primarily by a diagnostic ceramic tradition, other fairly consistent divergences between it and other Anasazi branches exist. For this presentation, I have chosen to deal with only a small portion of the vast Kayenta area (Lindsay and Ambler 1963: 86) to minimize the possible effects of the considerable regional diversity that characterizes this branch. Unless otherwise qualified, the statements made in this paper apply only to the *Tsegi area*, that is, the area drained by Laguna Creek and its tributaries west of Kayenta, Arizona.

The *Tsegi Phase* is the terminal unit in Colton's (1939: 51-59) phase sequence for the Kayenta Branch. The spatial extent of this phase is limited to the Tsegi area as defined above. These geographical restrictions exclude similar and contemporaneous Kayenta Branch manifestations near Navajo Mountain and in the Hopi area but have the advantage of ensuring a high degree of uniformity among the sites included. The Tsegi Phase can be precisely dated to between A.D. 1250 and 1300 on the basis of 386 tree-ring dates from thirteen sites representative of the phase in whole or in part (Dean 1969).

The term *habitation unit* was defined by Bullard (1962: 101) to refer to the grouping of pithouses and surface rooms that is characteristic of the Anasazi tradition from Pueblo I through Pueblo III times. I use the modified definition of the term provided by Rohn (1965: 67): "The specific association of a small number of contiguous rooms with a pit house or a kiva."

THEORY AND METHOD

Considerable attention has recently been given to the theoretical and methodological aspects of deriving sociological inferences from archaeological data (Sears 1961; Binford 1962, 1964, 1965) and to analyses of the nonrandom distributions through time and within single sites of artifacts, features, and stylistic elements as indicators of patterned behavior (Deetz 1965; Longacre 1964a, 1964b, 1966; Hill 1966, 1967). Hill (1966: 10) states the basic assumption that underlies any effort to comprehend aspects of prehistoric sociocultural systems through archaeological data:

> The basic theoretical model employed is simply that human behavior is patterned or structured. . . . people do certain things in certain places within their communities, and they leave behind them many of the structured remains of these activities. . . . The spatial distributions of cultural materials are patterned or structured (nonrandom), and will be so within an archaeological site.

Since Betatakin and Kiet Siel are "cliff dwellings," the data available for analysis differ considerably from those normally recovered from open sites. A circumstance that conditions the data is that all the sites involved were more or less completely excavated before refined techniques of data control were commonly employed, and the collections are useless for distributional analyses. However, the dryness of the rock shelters has preserved many features not normally available for study; thus, the architectural features are essentially intact.

Sampling procedures were determined primarily by the objectives of the research program and secondarily by the limitations of the available data. The research was conceived as a methodological experiment to explore the contributions that precisely controlled dendrochronological data could make to all types of archaeological analysis as opposed to their use solely as chronological indicators. The primary data-gathering objectives were the collection of large numbers of tree-ring specimens, along with minutely detailed provenience, associational, and architectural information as a basis for a controlled analysis of the interrelationships among these categories of data. Fortunately, the excellent preservation of the sites permitted nearly 100 percent sampling of the timbers and architectural data at Betatakin and Kiet Siel, eliminating sampling error as a factor in the analyses of these sites.

Aspects of Tsegi Phase Social Organization

There are two major aspects of the analyses of the Betatakin and Kiet Siel data: architectural and temporal. Patterning of architectural features at the two sites provides the foundation for the inference of certain types of social units and their interrelationships. The intrasite distribution of tree-ring dates and their relationships to the architectural units provide complementary sets of data that relate to some historical and functional aspects of the architectural units. We have then for each site an architectural (or horizontal) matrix of relationships crosscut and articulated by an absolute temporal (or vertical) matrix of relationships to form a two-dimensional relational structure that may be used as a basis for some sociocultural inferences. Analyses of the tree-ring collections as populations of artifacts (beams, posts, firewood, and so forth) provide the basis for a number of nonchronological inferences, some of which are relevant to understanding the activity organization of the villages.

A final contribution of the analyses of the spatial and temporal distributions of subvillage architectural units is the recognition of specific events. In addition to constructing accurate histories of the sites themselves, it is often possible to recognize and date events in the histories of individual rooms or groups of rooms. These events, of course, are the results of the activities of the inhabitants of the villages. The activities revealed by the events, especially those activities that occur repeatedly, are important indicators of the nature and frequency of certain types of patterned behavior.

While analyses of the types described above are capable of revealing patterns in the spatial and temporal distributions of cultural items, features, and events, they tell us little about the "behavioral meanings" associated with the identifiable patterns (Hill 1966: 10; Rohn 1965: 65). To get at these meanings, we must resort to inferences based on analogy with comparative ethnographic data (Thompson 1958: 1-8; Sears 1961: 226; Binford 1967a; Hill 1966: 10). Since analogy involves consideration of similarities in relationship as well as in form, its use presupposes the view of "a culture" as a system of structurally and functionally integrated subsystems whose interrelationships provide the means for inferring behavioral aspects of the culture from the patterning of cultural items, features, stylistic elements, activity loci, and "ecofacts" that can be perceived by the archaeologist (Binford 1964: 425-26).

The most useful analogies in dealing with archaeologically observed results of patterned behavior are those made with functioning sociocultural systems or subsystems rather than the units of which such systems are composed. While analogies involving formal attributes of specific items of material culture, for example, are extremely instructive in certain contexts, they are of limited value here, for we are interested in the relationships of the parts and not primarily in the parts themselves. Therefore, analogy should provide models of systems comparable to those perceived in the archaeological data. A number of suitable models may be generated in a number of ways depending on how they are used and the orientation, either synchronic-functional or diachronic-evolutionary, of the research. Such models provide the bases for generating propositions to be tested by the archaeological data.

Since there is demonstrable continuity between the Kayenta Anasazi and the modern Hopis, and since similar adaptations to similar environments are involved in both cases, the Hopis may be used as a model for the Tsegi Phase expression of Kayenta Branch culture. While specific analogies may be made between the Tsegi Phase and the Hopis, it must be remembered that the two are not directly comparable because of the temporal variable. In the 500-year interval between the Tsegi Phase and the ethnographically described Hopis, a number of sociocultural changes have undoubtedly taken place in response to changing environmental conditions, migrations, population fluctuations and amalgamations, and interaction with other groups. More suitable analogies might be made with models of early stages of Hopi social organization as inferred from their present organization. Eggan's (1950: 123-33) comprehensive treatment of the development of Hopi kinship organization provides a number of potentially significant analogs, as does Titiev's (1944: 46-48) more theoretical reconstruction of the ancestral Hopi kinship system. Though generally similar, the two models differ in one important respect: whereas Eggan (1950: 62) attributes the development of phratries to the amalgamation of previously unrelated clans, Titiev (1944: 57) attributes them to the segmentation of lineages and clans brought about by the geographical expansion of an increasing population. We will return to this important difference later.

To the direct ethnographic models provided by Eggan and Titiev may be added other models derived from more general considerations of worldwide ethnographic data. Among these are models based on Steward's (1955) and Service's (1962) analyses of ethnographic data in terms of their respective theories of cultural evolution and on Chang's (1958) cross-cultural comparison of settlement and community patterning among a number of societies considered to represent a neolithic way of life. Steward's (1955: 151-72) and Chang's (1958: 317-23) applications of their models to Anasazi culture-history are especially relevant to the Tsegi Phase problem.

Although analyses of the intrasite patterning and the inferred behavioral meanings of these patterns permit the description of certain aspects of the social structure of a prehistoric community, they are limited in their capacity to generate explanations of the inferred structures. To explain the structures that are perceived in the archaeological data, we must consider the dynamics of the cultural system; that is, the ways in which various subsystems are articulated with one another and the ways in which changes in one subsystem affect other subsystems (Steward 1955: 30-42; Binford 1962: 217-18, 1964: 425). From an archaeological standpoint, the most useful way to view a culture for consideration of its dynamic aspects is as a mechanism that adapts the people who participate in it to their physical and social environments (Binford 1962: 218). An adequate understanding of the workings of such an adaptive system demands adequate knowledge of the effects of a number of variables, including the physical environment; the techniques used to exploit the environment; the nature, intensity, and frequency of the interaction of the people involved with other groups of similar or different character; and the developmental history of the system that is being studied as a synchronic phenomenon. Without sufficient control of these and similar variables, the functional-structural reconstructions will stand isolated in time and space and will contribute little to our understanding of the processes of cultural change and stability.

THE ENVIRONMENTAL SETTING

The Tsegi Canyon-Marsh Pass area is a region of high plateaus and mesas gashed by deep narrow canyons and broad open valleys. The highlands range between 7000 and 8000 feet in elevation, while the elevation of the canyons varies between 5500 and 6500 feet. The largest of the southward flowing canyons is the Tsegi, a great dendritic canyon system incised into the Shonto Plateau and Skeleton Mesa. The canyon is drained by Laguna Creek, a perennial, spring-fed stream. At the mouth of the Tsegi, Laguna Creek makes a sharp eastward bend, flows through the narrow defile of Marsh Pass, and debouches into the broad arid Chinle Valley where it continues on past Kayenta to empty into Chinle Wash. Springs and seeps developed along the contact between the eolian Navajo sandstone, an excellent aquifer, and the underlying flat-bedded Kayenta formation in the walls of Tsegi Canyon provide Laguna Creek with a constant supply of water.

Except for Black Mesa, the highlands of the Tsegi area were not important loci of prehistoric settlement, primarily because they consist of vast expanses of baldrock stripped of any soil mantle and because they lack permanent supplies of water. The canyons and valleys, however, were occupied from Basketmaker II through Pueblo III times, undoubtedly because of the abundance of potential farmland and a relatively stable water supply.

The canyons and valleys are filled with deep deposits of Pleistocene and Recent alluvium that are now dissected to depths of 50 to 80 feet by a fully integrated system of arroyos. Since the end of the Pleistocene, there have been at least two periods each of alluviation and erosion (Hack 1942, 1945; Cooley 1962). A long but not uninterrupted period of aggradation that terminated about A.D. 1150 was followed by a period of degradation that was at first characterized by generalized stripping but which culminated sometime after 1250 in a developed system of arroyos similar to that which prevails today. A subsequent period of alluviation was terminated by the present episode of arroyo-cutting which began in the Tsegi in the 1880s. Hydrological conditions in the Laguna Creek system were a significant factor in the exploitative adaptation of man to the environment of the Tsegi area, and changes in these conditions had serious adaptive consequences for the residents of the area.

Under present climatological and hydrological conditions, the Tsegi is not capable of supporting a large population of primitive subsistence agriculturalists. Since the annual precipitation is neither adequate (average 11.4 inches) nor regular (range 6.8 to 18.8 inches) enough to support maize agriculture (Hack 1942: 23), techniques of water conservation and control are necessary to supplement the rainfall. Although at present there is plenty of water and an abundance of land in the Tsegi, the former lies 50 feet lower than the latter, and sufficient quantities of water cannot be applied to the fields without advanced techniques of water transport. However, before the cutting of the Tsegi-Naha arroyo about 1300, the alluvial surface extended unbroken across the canyon and the water table was high, perhaps high enough to support a permanent stream that meandered across the canyon floor (Hack 1945: 156; Cooley 1962: 48, Fig. 18.1). Under these conditions fields could have been planted in cleared areas throughout the canyon, with reliance for water being placed on the high water table or on irrigation from flowing streams rather than on precipitation.

CULTURAL-HISTORICAL BACKGROUND

The sociocultural system of the Tsegi Phase was a product of a series of developments that were influenced by the environment and by contacts with other groups of people living in nearby areas. Therefore, I present a brief resume of the development of Kayenta Branch culture in the Tsegi area, primarily focusing on those aspects of the evidence that give some insight into the adaptive circumstances and the nature of the sociocultural integration that was achieved at various points in time. In the absence of data from controlled surveys or excavations, this discussion is limited to the changing patterns of settlement through time and is organized within the framework of the concepts of settlement and community patterning developed by Sears (1961: 226). The discussion is admittedly subjective and tentative, since it is based on unsystematic personal observations, on the pertinent literature, and on information contributed by others who have worked in the area.

Little is known of settlement or community patterning in the Basketmaker II period, since no domiciliary structures have yet been discovered. We do know that these people used dry caves and rock shelters for storing surplus food, for burying their dead, and perhaps also for temporary habitation. I would guess that the Basketmaker II people practiced a mixed hunting-gathering-horticultural economy with emphasis on gathering toward the beginning and on farming toward the end of the period. This period is poorly dated in the Tsegi area, but it persisted until at least A.D. 700 to the west near Navajo Mountain.

The Basketmaker III period is marked by the introduction of a number of material items, including pottery. The manufacture and use of pottery probably indicates increased sedentism brought about by a greater reliance on farming for subsistence. Further evidence of increased sedentism is the appearance of recognizable dwellings, in this case pithouses. A tendency toward nucleation is shown by the development of fairly large villages made up of scattered pithouses, each with one or more associated slab-lined cists. The pithouse-storage cist units probably represent a cooperative social unit of economic production and consumption, undoubtedly a household of one type or another (Chang 1958: 302-03, 319). The presence at the Juniper Cove site (Cummings 1953: 62; Vivian and Reiter 1960: 101-02) of a great kiva that appears to have served a number of villages suggests a certain degree of intervillage integration. This pattern of multivillage great kiva association has a distinctly Mogollon cast, and in view of the number of Mogollon elements that appear in Basketmaker III sites throughout the Anasazi area, it might be inferred that the Anasazi groups were experimenting with a foreign technique of intervillage organization between A.D. 600 and 800. Known Basketmaker III settlements in the Tsegi area are generally situated along the peripheries of then aggrading stream channels, although other as yet undiscovered Basketmaker III sites may lie buried in the alluvium. The Basketmaker III period in this area dates between about A.D. 600 and 850.

The site community patterning of the Pueblo I period is similar to that of the preceding period with one important difference: there are no great kivas. If the apparent absence of great kivas is not a function of sampling, there must have been either a disintegration or a significant restructuring of intervillage organization. The Pueblo I villages are made up of individual habitation units, each of which consists of a pithouse and a surface room-block of contiguous storage chambers. If our sampling is not at fault, a significant change took place in the settlement pattern. Villages were no longer situated on the margins of the valleys; instead they were located directly on the aggrading floodplains. The Pueblo I movement out onto the floodplains may indicate a growing dependence on agriculture or some sort of change in aggradational conditions. The Pueblo I pattern persisted from A.D. 850 to about 1000.

The period between A.D. 1000 and 1150 is characterized by a development from relative heterogeneity to almost rubber stamp uniformity in site community patterning. At the beginning, there seems to have been a fission of the Pueblo I villages into small "homesteads," such as RB-1006 (Beals, Brainerd, and Smith 1945: 24-42), usually composed of a localized habitation unit consisting of a pithouse-kiva, a rectangular surface storage facility, an outdoor work area, and a formalized trash dump. Later in the period the site community pattern became highly standardized in the habitation unit form represented by RB-551 (Beals, Brainerd, and Smith 1945: 42-62), which consists of a rectangular masonry room-block containing living, storage, and work rooms; a kiva; and a trashmound arranged in the typical Anasazi "front oriented" fashion (Reed 1956: 11). There is evidence that in addition to the living rooms in the surface room-blocks, pithouses were associated with communities of this type. This suggests the presence of more than one nuclear family, with the family that occupied the masonry living room being of primary importance because of its direct association with the kiva. This widespread uniform site community pattern suggests a highly structured residence unit, such as an extended family based on a rule of residence (Service 1962: 120-23), or a rule of descent (Steward 1955: 151-54; Chang 1958: 322), or both. Although residence may have been the primary factor in determining the composition and form of these households (Titiev 1943; Service 1962: 117-18, 122), as soon as ownership of land or possession of a symbol of solidarity such as a fetish and/or a name became important, rules of inheritance and descent must have developed, at which point the unit became a corporate body (Titiev 1944: 46-48, Figs. 1, 2), in other words, a lineage or a clan.

The habitation unit settlements of this period conform perfectly to Chang's planned village type of community (Chang 1958: 306, 318). That Chang found in his cross-cultural survey of neolithic community types a perfect positive association between the planned village pattern and a monolineage community suggests the proposition that the habitation units of the Tsegi area represent lineally based residence units. Since the Hopis are so strongly matrilineally oriented, it seems likely that these communities were based on a matrilocal rule of residence and possibly also on matrilineal reckoning of descent. Presumably, test implications can be developed to strengthen or reject at least some of these propositions. As an example, one might expect the intersite distributions of stylistic elements and male- and female-associated artifacts to cluster in ways that support or refute some of these hypotheses.

The increasing standardization of these residence units throughout the period probably reflects the growing strength of the (matri)lineal organization as an integrative device. The reduction of variation throughout the period probably also indicates that an economically productive adaptation to a relatively stable environment had been achieved. If ever the ancestral Hopi household, lineage, and clan were coterminous and localized (Titiev 1944: 46; Eggan 1950: 299-300; Dozier 1965: 40), it was during this period. The processes of lineage and clan segmentation described by Titiev (1944: 46-48, Figs. 1, 2) were probably in operation at this time as the pressures of growing populations caused new families to separate from their "parent" units and occupy neighboring areas that were not already claimed by some other group. The number of the habitation unit sites and the fact that each seems to be an independent self-contained unit support the proposition that they originated by the segmentation of "daughter families" into unoccupied areas adjacent to that of the "parent family."

Although the above hypotheses about the localized habitation unit villages are still unverified, it should be possible to generate test implications relevant to testing these propositions. For example, if this model were correct, one might expect the intersite clusterings of artifacts, features, and stylistic elements from a spatially distinct group of habitation unit sites to indicate a series of intersite relationships "radiating" on a scale of increasing "associational distance" from one particular site. Furthermore, if the model were correct, one would expect that the pattern of "associational distances" among sites would be duplicated by the pattern of "temporal distances" as indicated by some sort of independent chronological control, and here only tree-ring dating would provide results refined enough for this type of analysis. Presumably, other test implications could be developed as well, but these should suffice as examples of the types of data that might serve to test the propositions.

At this point, as the Kayenta people are enjoying a period of prosperity and apparent tranquility, it might be well to look at what was happening in other Anasazi areas at about A.D. 1100 to 1150, for the Kayenta development did not take place in a vacuum. To the east, beyond the Chuska Mountains, the Chaco development of huge towns and complex ceremonial organization was at its peak. In the Mesa Verde region to the northeast and in the upper Little Colorado (Longacre 1964c: 209) and Puerco River valleys to the south people had begun to gather in large villages. It appears then that up to about 1150 the Kayenta people, in the Tsegi area at least, were going their own way with little regard for what their Anasazi neighbors were up to.

Unfortunately, we know next to nothing about the period between 1150 and 1250 in the Tsegi area, except that the localized habitation unit community type seems to have disappeared with surprising suddenness after 1150. In the Navajo Mountain region localized habitation units persisted into this period (Ambler, Lindsay, and Stein 1964: 21-29) alongside a new community type consisting of a number of rooms or pithouses arranged around the sides of a large enclosed plaza that contained one or more kivas (Ambler, Lindsay, and Stein 1964: 53-83). In the Tsegi area large pueblo villages appear for the first time in this period, but since none have been completely excavated, we know nothing of their internal patterning or their interrelationships. About all that can be said of this period is that it was one of rapid and significant change, which culminated by 1250 in the developed village organization of the Tsegi Phase.

It is important to note here that the middle and late 1100s were a time of important changes and population movements throughout the plateau Southwest: the distinctive, highly organized Chaco culture "collapsed," and the Chaco area was all but abandoned; the Virgin Branch development came to a close and that area too was deserted by Anasazi peoples (Aikens 1966a: 56); the Cohonina area west of Flagstaff was abandoned (Schwartz 1966: 479); the Kayenta withdrawal from north of the San Juan began; the higher regions of Black Mesa were apparently abandoned; and the first evidence of Southern Paiute penetration into former Anasazi territory in northwestern Arizona and southwestern Utah is noted (Euler 1964). It is apparent that some widespread factor or factors were influencing the inhabitants of most of the Colorado Plateau. It cannot be entirely coincidental that these events occurred simultaneously with the end of alluviation and the initiation of sheet erosion in large areas of the San Juan drainage (Hack 1945; Cooley 1962). In addition, pollen analyses indicate shifts in the amount of moisture available for plant growth in this time period (between A.D. 1000 and 1200) in the Navajo Reservoir District (Schoenwetter and Eddy 1964), in the Chuska Valley (Schoenwetter 1967), and in the upper Little Colorado area (Schoenwetter 1962; Hevly 1964). Such environmental changes, whether or not they were related or precisely contemporaneous, could have upset the delicate balance between man and the land and triggered population movements and adaptive changes in the cultures of the inhabitants of the plateau Southwest. In this regard, we must not overlook the possibility that the activities of man caused some local environmental changes that upset the adaptive balance. At any rate, the Pueblo peoples were not to achieve a stability comparable to that of the late eleventh and early twelfth centuries until they reached their present homes, and that is a stability at least partially imposed by the encroachment of European civilization.

THE TSEGI PHASE

Although Tsegi Canyon was continuously occupied from Basketmaker II through Pueblo III times, it was only sparsely populated just prior to 1250 (Colton 1939: 50; Beals, Brainerd, and Smith 1945: 19, Table 1), and the Tsegi Phase represents a substantial immigration. This immigration began about 1250 with the founding of Kiet Siel and with the seasonal agricultural use of parts of the canyon by farmers who apparently lived in villages outside the canyon. More people moved into the Tsegi in 1267 and founded Betatakin. The biggest population influx, however, occurred between 1272 and 1276 when Betatakin and Kiet Siel received major population increments and a number of other villages such as Scaffold House, Lolomaki, Batwoman House, and Twin Caves Pueblo were founded. The population curve reached its peak in the early 1280s, when there were at least 700 people resident in the canyon. Shortly after 1285 the population trend was reversed, and people began to leave the canyon. By 1300 at the latest, the Tsegi was deserted, bringing to a close 1000 years of occupation by the Kayenta Anasazi. In a period of less than 50 years, 700 people moved into the canyon, constructed about twenty villages, some of which were occupied for fewer than 25 years, and moved out again.

The brief but intensive Tsegi Phase occupation of Tsegi Canyon was but an episode in the continuing efforts of the people of the area to adjust to a physical environment that, by about 1150, had become inimical to their way of life. The massive immigration into the canyon and the subsequent emigration may best be viewed as responses to the deteriorating agricultural potential of the alluvial valleys, produced by the headward cutting of the arroyos of the second phase of the Tsegi-Naha erosion interval. The Tsegi, much less suitable than the open valleys for agricultural exploitation, was probably occupied as a last resort as the agricultural potential of the valleys was destroyed by the developing arroyo system. The advance of the arroyos into the canyon would have rendered it unsuitable for intensive agriculture, and, since the exploitative techniques of the Tsegi Phase people were no longer capable of supporting their village organization, they probably went south to join their relatives in the Hopi Mesas area where the land-water relationship is much more stable than in the Tsegi (Dean 1966).

Aspects of Tsegi Phase Social Organization

Settlement Pattern

The environment of Tsegi Canyon and the exploitative techniques of the Tsegi Phase people combined to produce a distinct pattern of settlement (Dean 1969: 21-23). Almost invariably the sites are in rock shelters in the heads of side canyons near the junction of one or more tributaries with the main canyon. These confluence areas provide much more extensive areas of arable land than do the reaches of the canyon where no tributaries breach the confining walls of the narrow gorge. Furthermore, runoff for use in floodwater farming or irrigation is channeled toward the confluence areas by the tributaries as well as the main channel. The choice of rock-shelters rather than open sites for occupation was probably due primarily to two factors: (1) the regular association of flowing springs with caves in the Tsegi, since nearly all the "cliff dwellings" are in caves that had springs and few caves without springs show any evidence of Tsegi Phase occupation, and (2) the shelter from the elements afforded by the rock overhangs. The general absence from the cave pueblos of features that could have served defensive functions, the location of many of the sites in caves far removed from possible farming areas, and the general dissociation of the rooms from the springs combine to indicate that defense was not a primary factor in the choice of rock-shelters for habitation. Proximity to arable land and the presence of springs were probably the most important determinants of the Tsegi Phase settlement pattern.

Site Community Pattern

Five functionally different types of room may be recognized in Tsegi Phase sites. Rooms of various types are associated with one another to form two types of multiroom subvillage architectural unit. The following abbreviated discussion of the form, function, and interrelationships of the various types of room summarizes data that I have presented in detail elsewhere (Dean 1969: 23-26); the statements made here are generalizations that do not reflect the full range of variation that may be found in Tsegi Phase sites.

Living Rooms. Features that typify living rooms are one or more jacal walls, low-silled doorways, leveled and plastered floor, firepits, entry-box complexes (Jennings 1966: 59), mealing bins, masonry shelves, interior wall plaster, and interior smoke-blackening. This constellation of features indicates that these rooms were used for domestic activities, including the preparation and consumption of food, sleeping, and shelter from the elements. Few living rooms are large enough to have accommodated very many people, and, in the absence of auxiliary sleeping chambers, it is unlikely that they served a social unit larger than a nuclear family.

Courtyards. These unroofed, irregularly shaped areas usually exhibit several of the following features: leveled and plastered floors, firepits, mealing bins, storage(?) pits, and abrading grooves. Courtyards are usually surrounded by living and storage rooms, all of which open onto the court. The courtyard was a locus of domestic activities identical to some of those that took place in the living rooms, as well as an outdoor work area.

Granaries. Rooms of this type are characterized by features designed to keep insects, rodents, and the weather out: high-silled doorways, door jambs grooved to receive stone slab doors, with loops set at either side of the doorways to hold bolts shot across the doors to secure them in place, heavy clay coping around the doorways, finely finished and profusely chinked exterior masonry, and exterior wall plastering. Granaries obviously were designed for storage and protection of perishable foodstuffs.

Storerooms. These chambers are recognized by the absence of the features characteristic of dwellings and granaries. Most of these rooms are too small to have served as auxiliary sleeping chambers and were probably used for storage of nonperishable items such as tools, ceremonial paraphernalia, pottery, and the like.

Grinding Rooms. Rooms of this type are characterized by the presence of batteries of two to four stone-slab bins that held a series of graded metates and by the lack of features diagnostic of other types of room. These chambers were obviously used for grinding corn into meal, probably by groups of women as is the practice among the modern Pueblo Indians. The number of grinding rooms at any one site is always far less than the number of room clusters, although most grinding rooms are definitely associated with a room cluster. This distribution suggests the proposition that each of these chambers was the locus of grinding activities that involved individuals from more than one room cluster, perhaps the women of a single lineage or clan; however, this hypothesis cannot be tested with the data presently at hand.

Ceremonial Chambers. Although Kayenta Branch kivas are notoriously heterogeneous and difficult to identify (Smith 1952: 154-65), it is possible to recognize structures of this type at most of the Tsegi Phase sites. Kivas vary from circular to rectangular in shape, from fully subterranean to completely above ground, and exhibit a bewildering variety of features, although the firepit-deflector-ventilator complex oriented toward the south or southeast always seems to be present, and loom anchors and southern recesses are common. Tsegi Phase kivas exhibit much more variability of form and internal features than do their Mesa Verde and Chaco Canyon counterparts.

A second type of ceremonial structure, which I call a ceremonial annex, can be recognized. These are D-shaped surface rooms that occur in contiguous association with some kivas. The curved wall of the ceremonial annex is always of masonry construction, while the straight wall is of jacal and is always oriented in the same direction as the ventilator of its associated kiva. Interior features of ceremonial annexes vary, but they generally include items such as firepits, deflectors, ventilators, loom anchors, and slab-paved floors. The exact function of the ceremonial annex is not obvious; however, it does not seem to have been an obligatory part of a "kiva complex," for a number of kivas do not have annexes.

An occasional association between kivas and granaries may be noted. In such cases, the granaries are situated directly behind the kivas in the manner of the old habitation unit, although there usually are no associated living rooms. The people themselves seem to have symbolized this type of relationship by constructing the granaries with extra care and by adding special touches such as decorative rows of spalls, incised geometric design panels, or painted bands to the exterior walls of the granaries. Three of the four Tsegi Phase kivas that have associated granaries also possess ceremonial annexes. Since every room cluster has its own granaries, the granaries associated with kivas probably held food for a social unit that had an interest in the particular kiva involved. Such a social unit must have included people from a number of room clusters and could have been a multihousehold residence unit, a nonlocalized descent group such as a lineage or a clan, or a ceremonial sodality.

Room Clusters. A room cluster consists of at least one living room, one to six storage chambers (granaries and storerooms), occasionally a grinding room, and in all but a few cases a courtyard (Fig. 12). The rooms of a cluster open directly onto the courtyard or are connected with other rooms that do; consequently, a room belonging to a particular cluster can usually be entered only from its courtyard. The room cluster is the basic architectural unit of the Tsegi Phase village. The sites are not agglomerations of individual rooms, but are formed by the amalgamation of a number of

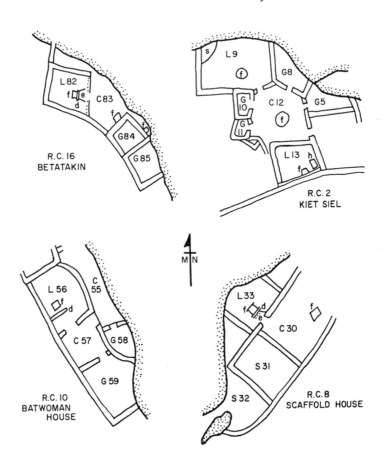

TSEGI PHASE ROOM CLUSTERS

L = Living Room   f = firepit
C = Courtyard   e = entrybox
G = Granary   d = deflector
S = Storeroom   s = shelf
R.C. = Room Cluster   h = roof hatch

NOT TO SCALE

FIGURE 12. TSEGI PHASE ROOM CLUSTERS

room clusters. Architectural units similar to the room cluster occur in Kayenta Branch sites near Navajo Mountain (Lindsay et al. 1968: 6-7) and at Mug House on Mesa Verde (Rohn 1965: 65-67).

Courtyard Complexes. These units consist of two or more room clusters grouped around a single courtyard. The room cluster is the fundamental unit in this association, because rooms were added to one or the other of the clusters and not to the courtyard complex itself.

Larger Subvillage Units. No subvillage units larger than the courtyard complex can be identified in any Tsegi Phase cave pueblos. The habitation unit, which forms a subvillage architectural unit in many late Mesa Verde sites (Fewkes 1909: 8; Rohn 1965: 67), does not occur as a recognizable entity in the Tsegi Phase. Distributional analyses of the artifact populations of Tsegi Phase sites, if they were possible, might indicate the existence of localized or nonlocalized units larger than the courtyard complex, but a test of this possibility must await the controlled excavation of a relatively undisturbed Tsegi Phase site.

The Village. The largest identifiable localized unit is the village. From an architectural standpoint, the village is a structural articulation of a number of essentially identical units, room clusters, and a few specialized units such as kivas and their associated rooms. The kivas are usually in front of and lower than the main blocks of secular rooms, but occasionally a kiva is found within a group of domestic rooms. The compact plans of the villages place them in Dozier's (1965: 42) category of centralized or tightly integrated villages. The sites also appear to belong to Chang's (1958: 304-07) unplanned village type, as the households (room clusters) are not grouped into spatially distinct larger units.

Dynamic Aspects of the Site Community Patterning

The absolute temporal relationships among architectural units and the specific historical events revealed by the dendrochronological analyses provide a number of insights into the dynamic nature of the identifiable architectural units. Brief histories of Betatakin and Kiet Siel are presented here to demonstrate the ways in which the various architectural units, as representative of social units, "behaved" under varying circumstances. It is not possible to include in this short paper the data and analyses upon which these village histories are based; a detailed presentation of this information is available (Dean 1969: 40-150).

Betatakin is a large arc-shaped pueblo of 135 rooms and courtyards and at least two kivas (Fig. 13) in an immense cave near the head of Betatakin Canyon, a southern tributary that joins the Tsegi about six miles upstream from Marsh Pass. Betatakin Cave was first occupied about 1250 by a small group of people who built a few structures that did not survive the subsequent occupation of the cave. This occupation may have been transient, with the cave serving as a seasonal camping spot for men who had penetrated into the Tsegi to plant fields at some distance from their home villages. The village of Betatakin as it is now known was founded in 1267, when three room clusters were built at intervals across the vast floor of the cave. A fourth cluster was added in 1268. This group of perhaps twenty people felled a number of trees, cut them to standardized primary and secondary beam lengths, and stockpiled them, presumably for use by future immigrants to the village. This task was performed in 1269 and again in 1272. The precut beams were not used until 1275, the beginning of a three-year period of immigration that resulted in the construction of more than ten room clusters and probably one or more kivas. After 1277 Betatakin grew at a slower pace, probably as a result of internal population growth and the creation of new families by marriage rather than by any

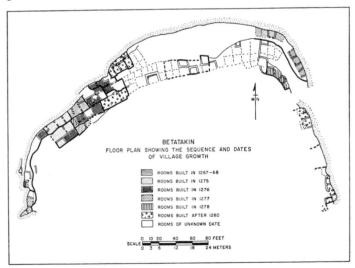

BETATAKIN
FLOOR PLAN SHOWING THE SEQUENCE AND DATES
OF VILLAGE GROWTH

ROOMS BUILT IN 1267–68
ROOMS BUILT IN 1275
ROOMS BUILT IN 1276
ROOMS BUILT IN 1277
ROOMS BUILT IN 1278
ROOMS BUILT AFTER 1280
ROOMS OF UNKNOWN DATE

SCALE
0 10 20   40   60   80 FEET
0   3   6   12   18   24 METERS

FIGURE 13. BETATAKIN FLOOR PLAN

significant immigration, until it reached its population peak of about 125 persons in the mid-1280s. The village was abandoned sometime between 1286 and 1300, but there is no evidence as to how this event took place.

Several lines of evidence indicate that Betatakin was settled by a group of people who already constituted a functioning community; that is, "Betatakin," *as a social unit*, existed somewhere else prior to the founding of the village now known by that name (Dean 1969: 82-84). The careful planning and execution that went into preparing the cave for habitation indicates that a community decision was made and that social sanctions powerful enough to produce compliance with the decision were operative. The preplanned move must have involved some sort of leadership structure to give it direction and cohesion, but the social basis of this leadership can only be speculated upon. There probably were no full-time political or religious leaders with coercive powers, and the decision probably involved some sort of consensus brought about by the operation of whatever decision-making mechanisms were available.

The dating of Betatakin strongly supports the architectural evidence that the room cluster is the basic unit of village composition. The first settlement of Betatakin took the form of three or four spatially isolated room clusters, and subsequently the village grew by the accretion of room clusters rather than larger units. Rooms added singly were tacked on to extant clusters, and courtyard complexes were formed by the amalgamation over a period of years of two or more room clusters that remained distinct from one another.

Kiet Siel is larger than Betatakin, consisting of at least 155 rooms and courtyards and six kivas in a rincon that overlooks Kiet Siel Canyon about five miles upstream from its confluence with Laguna Creek opposite the mouth of Betatakin Canyon. The Tsegi Phase occupation of the cave may be divided into five periods. The first of these began with the founding of the village in the late 1240s or early 1250s. The internal chronology of this period is poorly known because of the almost exclusive use of aspens, an undatable species, for construction beams. However, by the end of the period in 1271, Kiet Siel consisted of twelve room clusters scattered along the back wall of the cave (Fig. 14a). The few available tree-ring dates for this first period indicate that it was a time of fairly regular accretion and not one of mass immigrations, except for the initial occupation, which involved an unknown number of room clusters. During the second period, 1272 through 1275, Kiet Siel experienced a major immigration. Many new

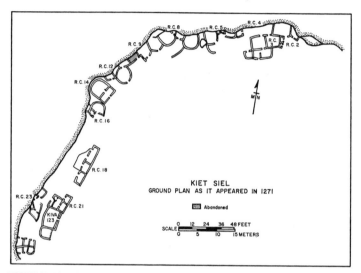

FIGURE 14. KIET SIEL GROUND PLANS
(a) A.D. 1271

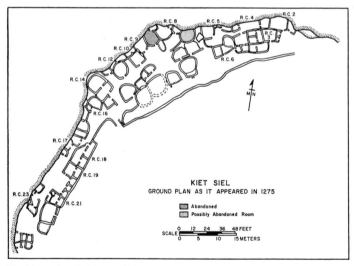

Fig. 14, continued. (b) A.D. 1275

160

room clusters were built, six extant clusters were augmented or modified, the great front retaining wall was constructed, and three kivas were sunk into the artificial fill behind the wall (Fig. 14b). The 1272-75 immigration significantly altered the ceramic industry of Kiet Siel (Anderson 1966) as well as the appearance of the village. The third period, 1276 through 1282, was characterized by reduced construction activity, although three or four more room clusters were added (Fig. 14c), to bring the population of the village to its maximum of about 150 persons. Three room clusters were abandoned, and the deserted rooms were either converted into granaries or used as sources of building material by the people who remained in the village. The fourth period, 1283 through 1286, was characterized more by reconstruction and remodeling than by new building (Fig. 14d). Four clusters were added, two of which involved the reoccupation of abandoned rooms. At the same time, other abandoned rooms were converted into granaries. This was a period of stress and instability as individual households moved out of the village and the residents that remained were increasingly concerned with the accumulation of stored food reserves. The fifth period was characterized by a lack of constructional activity and the gradual abandonment of the village, which was accomplished by 1300 at the latest.

The history of Kiet Siel contrasts sharply with that of Betatakin in a number of respects. The general lack of evidence for planning and preparation in the various immigrations into Kiet Siel suggests that it was composed of people from a number of different sources rather than one primary source as was indicated at Betatakin. This inference is supported by the heterogeneous assemblage of architectural forms and techniques on display at Kiet Siel, the number and formal variability of the kivas, and the fact that the village seems to have grown by the nondirected accretion of relatively independent household units. The Kiet Siel data reflect even more strongly than those from Betatakin the fundamental and basically independent nature of the social unit that occupied the room cluster.

Social Organization of the Tsegi Phase Villages

The highly standardized composition of the room cluster and its invariable occurrence in Tsegi Phase sites suggest that its associated social unit occupied a well-defined position in the social structure of the village. The nature of the rooms that form the cluster indicates that it was basi-

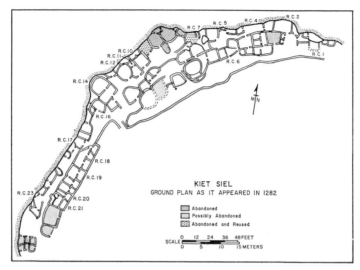

Fig. 14, continued. (c) A.D. 1282

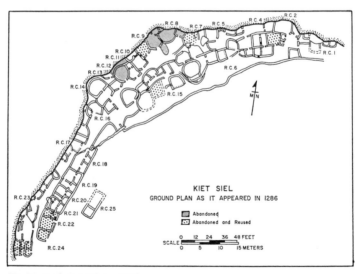

Fig. 14, concluded. (d) A.D. 1286

162

cally a unit of residence that provided shelter from the elements, delimited the more or less exclusive "territory" of the resident social unit, and served as the locus of a number of domestic activities including storage, preparation, and consumption of food and manufacture of tools, basketry, and perhaps pottery.

The room cluster was undoubtedly occupied by a household, the basic localized unit of modern Pueblo society. Dozier (1965: 38-40) notes the existence in the Southwest of two basic types of household: nuclear family and extended family. Those room clusters with only one living room must have been occupied by nuclear families, since the dwellings are too small to have accommodated very many people. Despite the existence of many single-family households, the Tsegi Phase household was probably not of the nuclear type. Room clusters with more than one living room, the addition of second and third dwellings to extant clusters, and the existence of courtyard complexes all indicate that multifamily households were common. Since single- and multiple-family room clusters occupy identical positions within the architectural structure of the village, I infer that they represent social units that occupied identical positions within the social structure of the village. The multifamily and single-family households were structurally identical and represent but one type of household, the extended family type. Analogy with the Hopis suggests the hypothesis that the Tsegi Phase extended family households were based on a matrilocal rule of residence (Eggan 1950: 29-30), but this proposition has not as yet been adequately tested.

The archaeological data show that the household was just as fundamental a unit in the Tsegi Phase as it is among the modern western Pueblos (Eggan 1950: 29-31; Titiev 1944:7-11). The stability of this social unit is shown by the fact that at Kiet Siel and other sites individual households came and went, taking their places within the village structure for short periods before moving on. Strikingly similar behavior that demonstrates the strength of the household occurred during the disintegration of Oraibi in 1906, where cleavage took place along household rather than clan lines (Titiev 1944: 89). Significant similarities may be noted between conditions that prevailed during the Tsegi Phase and those postulated by Eggan to have obtained in the Hopi area in the early fourteenth century when a general amalgamation of diverse population elements was under way. His hypothesis that newcomers to the Hopi Mesas "arrived as communities or fragments of communities such as household groups, and not as lineages and clans as such" (Eggan 1950: 130) accords well with the evidence for population movements in the Tsegi a half-century earlier. Dozier (1965:40) points out that among the western Pueblos the extended family always occurs within the context of a larger sociopolitical unit, the lineage; however, there is no Tsegi Phase architectural unit that could correspond to a lineage. The habitation unit, often equated with a localized lineage (Steward 1955: 163, 166; Aikens 1966a: 56), is absent from Tsegi Phase sites. Therefore, if lineages existed during the Tsegi Phase, they must have been nonlocalized, and their presence cannot be perceived in the archaeological data that are presently available.

Eggan believes that lineage and clan organization were not highly developed among Kayenta Branch peoples until they arrived in the Hopi area in the fourteenth century, where "by using matrilineal descent and matrilocal residence, they could maintain a certain amount of their group integrity and ceremonial possessions while integrating themselves with the other groups already there" (Eggan 1950: 130). He holds that the clan and phratry systems developed as mechanisms for the integration of new arrivals into the established social system. We have already noted the marked similarities between population conditions that prevailed during the Tsegi Phase and later on the Hopi Mesas; the people of Kiet Siel had just as much of a problem in absorbing newcomers as did the people of the Hopi Mesas area a half-century later. It does not seem unreasonable to infer that like pressures on peoples with similar cultures in similar environments produced similar responses. Since these processes of integration already seem to be in operation by the beginning of the Tsegi Phase, I would go so far as to propose that nonlocalized lineage and clan organization may have developed during that virtually unknown period between 1150 and 1250, after the breakdown of the independent habitation unit communities. The readaptation to rapidly changing physical and social environments and the major population shifts of this period must have produced significant changes in the existing social organization if the formerly independent localized lineage/clan units were to be integrated into the large unsegmented villages of the Tsegi Phase. This reorganization would undoubtedly have taken place insofar as possible in terms of the old structure, and, since it would have been impossible to maintain common residence under the conditions of population mobility that prevailed, it is likely that clan identity was maintained through the (matrilineal?) reckoning of descent and the possession of one or more symbols of group solidarity such as a name and a fetish. The lack of evidence for localized lineages in Tsegi Phase sites, then, may be due to a restructuring of the social organization toward a more Hopi-like configuration of non-localized lineages and clans that took place shortly before the sites were founded.

It should be noted here that it is not yet possible to reject alternative hypotheses relating to the development of nonlocalized clans among the Tsegi Phase people. In fact, it is not yet possible to reject the proposition that there actually were localized residence units larger than the household. Distributional analyses of artifacts and stylistic elements might possibly reveal clusters indicative of larger residence units that could not be observed in the internal architectural patterning. I would maintain, however, that most of the hypotheses advanced above are testable with data carefully collected from a relatively undisturbed Tsegi Phase site.

Beyond the room cluster and courtyard complex, the only Tsegi Phase architectural unit that can be isolated is the village itself. The identification of community structures and village-wide cooperative activities at Betatakin and Kiet Siel indicates that they were functioning communities that possessed mechanisms for mobilizing and directing the cooperation of the villagers in tasks thought to be in the common interest. The compact and fairly standardized layout of the sites implies that they were of the tightly integrated type as defined by Dozier (1965: 41-42). There are a number of ways in which this integration could have been accomplished, but, as among all the Pueblos, ceremonialism was probably an important factor.

The formal attributes and intrasite distribution of kivas and their associated structures provide some insight into the ceremonial component of Tsegi Phase village integration. The lack of spatial or architectural relationships between kivas and subvillage residence units indicates that the former must have been associated with some sort of nonlocalized social unit that included members of a number of households. The kiva-associated social units could have been the nonlocalized clans inferred to have been present in the villages, ceremonial sodalities whose memberships cut across those of the clans, or both. There is no direct evidence as to the manner in which the households and kiva-units were integrated into the functioning whole that was the village. However, analogy with Hopi village organization suggests two possibilities: (1) ceremonial sodalities, if present, would have served a strong integrative function because their membership would have cut across residential and kinship lines; and/or (2) the development of the concept that ceremonies were performed for the benefit of the entire community rather than for one of its component units would have strengthened village integration.

There are a few clues as to how village integration was not accomplished. There is no evidence for dual residence divisions such as those reported for Mug House on Mesa Verde (Rohn 1965: 69) or for dual ceremonial divisions such as those inferred from the intrasite distributions of great kivas in Chaco Canyon sites (Eggan 1950: 314; Wendorf 1956: 19-20). The lack of single-village-level religious systems may be inferred from the absence of great kivas and the probable absence of the kachina cult, which is indicated by the fact that none of the characteristic artifacts associated with it have ever turned up in the extensive collections from the cave pueblos.

While the above statements relative to Tsegi Phase religious organization are as far as we can go on the basis of the data from the sites themselves, a consideration of the evidence in culture-historical perspective permits some inferences about more specific aspects of the religious component of village organization. These inferences are highly speculative and are offered as propositions that may be tested at some future date providing the necessary test implications can be generated and data adequate to test them can be recovered from appropriate sites. On the basis of ethnographic data, it may be inferred that at some time in the past a clan-kiva-ceremony-fetish complex existed among the ancestors of the Hopis (Eggan 1950: 96). Although these elements are now somewhat dissociated from one another and do not form a "complex," it is significant that among the Hopis a kiva is "owned" by a clan, certain ceremonies belong to certain clans, and each clan has a symbolic fetish that is kept along with other ceremonial paraphernalia in a "clanhouse." If the clan-kiva-ceremony-fetish complex ever existed in pristine form in the Tsegi area, it was probably during the period between 1000 and 1150 when localized monolineage communities were typical. In this period, each local lineal unit probably had a fetish of its own and a ceremony that was performed in a kiva that served the functions of the Hopi kiva and clanhouse.

The population movements and amalgamations of the period after 1150 would have destroyed the local integrity of the complex, and the ceremonial organization would have had to be restructured to fit the new social conditions that prevailed. The dissociation of the performance of the ceremonies from the clan memberships may have developed in response to the fluctuating composition of the clans at any one village, which was due to the mobility of individual households. It is easy to visualize clan membership being so reduced at a particular village that members of other clans had to be used for the proper performance of rites deemed necessary for village welfare. Religious sodalities might have developed to offset the effects on clan composition of the changing household composition of the villages. The increasing participation of outsiders in clan ceremonies might have led to the development of the ceremonial annex as a center of strictly clan religious activity, in other words, a "clanhouse." The ceremonial annex might later have been replaced by a clanhouse that was removed from direct association with the kiva because of the growing importance of the ceremonial societies in the kiva performances.

Tsegi Phase religious organization probably represents a transition between localized lineage community organization and the present Hopi village organization, and this may account in part for the formal variability of the kivas and their inconsistent relationships with other architectural units. Ceremonial annexes may be nothing more than "clanhouses" built in direct association with the clan's kiva but kept separate to keep clan ritual property away from members of other clans who participated in ceremonies held in the kiva. The presence of kivas without ceremonial annexes may indicate that in some cases either the process of clan disjunction from the kivas had not yet begun or it had been completed. Clans associated with kivas without ceremonial annexes may have had special rooms set aside in the pueblo for exclusive clan use, but such rooms cannot now be identified. This hypothetical reconstruction, if generally accurate, suggests that Tsegi Phase religious organization was similar but not identical to that of the Hopis. The existence of nonlocalized clans and probably also ceremonial sodalities associated with kivas is indicated, and the overlap of these two types of unit probably exerted a strong integrative force within the community.

There is considerable evidence that the people of the Tsegi Phase villages could be mobilized and their activities coordinated to perform secular as well as religious activities for the benefit of the community. A number of examples of this type of behavior are indicated by the data. The founding of Betatakin is a prime example of effort on behalf of the community. Dendrochronological analyses show that tree-cutting at Betatakin was a communal rather than an individual or household activity (Dean

1969: 80). The construction of large community structures such as the galleries at Betatakin and Batwoman House, the scaffold at Scaffold House, and the retaining wall and southwest "street" at Kiet Siel required the coordinated efforts of large groups of people. Unfortunately, there is no evidence pertinent to the nature of the political organization of these villages. However, it may be inferred that the secular leadership was thoroughly bound up with the religious organization and that there probably were no full-time leadership specialists. Burial data, if there were any, might be expected to indicate the existence of status differences among the inhabitants of a particular village, but this is another problem that must be attacked through the excavation of a site or sites other than those considered here.

Data from Betatakin and Kiet Siel indicate that the strength of village integration varied among the Tsegi Phase communities (Dean 1969: 148-50). A number of differences between the two sites are significant in this regard: Betatakin rooms are uniformly rectangular (Fig. 13) as opposed to the formal variety of Kiet Siel rooms (Fig. 14); Betatakin masonry is good, while that at Kiet Siel is generally poor; the occurrence of jacal walls at Betatakin is regular, at Kiet Siel variable; interior living room features are highly standardized at Betatakin, heterogeneous at Kiet Siel; the two Betatakin kivas are more similar to each other than are any two of the six kivas associated with Kiet Siel; tree-cutting was a communal activity at Betatakin, an individual undertaking at Kiet Siel. The homogeneity of Betatakin architecture probably reflects a greater degree of intravillage cooperation and the existence of stronger bonds of social integration than prevailed at Kiet Siel. Betatakin was the more tightly integrated of the two, probably because it was a unified community throughout its history, whereas Kiet Siel was a frequently changing assemblage of historically unrelated households or fragments of other communities.

It is not likely that Tsegi Phase villages were organized into multivillage units. There are no great kivas, no structural or formalized spatial relationships among sites, and no evidence of intervillage cooperative activities. The people of some of the smaller sites may have been integrated into the social and ceremonial organization of larger nearby villages, but these are examples of nonlocalized communities and not of formal relationships between independent villages. This type of situation is probably analogous to the relationship between Oraibi and its Moenkopi colony before 1900 (Mindeleff 1900: 648-50; Titiev 1944: 95). Despite the lack of intervillage structural relationships, the Tsegi Phase villages were probably linked into a loosely defined "community" by a network of informal ties based on trade, interpersonal relations, intermarriage, and contiguity; however, it is unlikely that these elements were institutionalized into defined inter-village ties at the community level of organization.

Many late Pueblo III Kayenta Branch sites near Navajo Mountain exhibit a community pattern quite different from that of the contemporaneous Tsegi Phase sites (Ambler, Lindsay, and Stein 1964; Hobler 1964; Lindsay et al. 1968). These sites consist of masonry surface rooms or pithouses oriented around a large plaza that contains one or more kivas, a community pattern that conforms closely to the definition of a habitation unit. Presumably, the plaza sites represent a localized lineage type of organization (Aikens 1966a: 56), which contrasts with the nonlocalized lineage and clan organization inferred for the Tsegi Phase room cluster sites. On Segazlin Mesa at the foot of Navajo Mountain, a number of small, late Pueblo III sites, each made up of several courtyard complexes, were apparently organized into a larger community (Lindsay in Jennings 1966: 58), a situation that may represent the transition between localized and nonlocalized lineages (Aikens 1966a: 41). The persistence of independent lineage organization in the Navajo Mountain area at the same time that nonlocalized lineages existed in the Tsegi area may be a result of more stable environmental and demographic conditions in the former locality.

To summarize, the available evidence gives rise to the following hypotheses relative to some aspects of Tsegi Phase social organization. The basic structural unit of the village was the matrilocal extended family household, which, as the only localized subvillage social unit, occupied a room cluster. The households were probably grouped into matrilineal lineages and clans, neither of which was localized within the village. The freedom of the households to move from one village to another made it impossible for clans to maintain any degree of localization, since their composition at any one village changed relatively rapidly. By themselves, lineage and clan organizations would tend to segment rather than unify the village, and other organizational principles probably crosscut those of the lineage and clan to strengthen village integration. It is possible that ceremonial sodalities whose membership crosscut that of the kinship units served to bind the village into a system of overlapping ceremonial rights and obligations deemed necessary to the well-being of the community as a whole. It is doubtful that each village was integrated by any sort of village-wide ceremonial system. There appears to have been no formalized intervillage social organization.

IMPLICATIONS

The results of the Betatakin and Kiet Siel dating projects, especially insofar as they bear on the reconstruction of Tsegi Phase village organization, have important implications for the study of prehistoric social systems. First, of course, is the demonstration of the contributions that refined chronological controls can make to the understanding of behavioral aspect of prehistoric social units identified on the basis of other types of archaeological data. We have seen the way in which the chronological analyses of rooms and groups of rooms at Betatakin and Kiet Siel were crucial to the demonstration of the fundamental position of the room cluster, and by extension the household, in Tsegi Phase village structure. Precise control of the temporal factor adds a second dimension to the analyses of the patterned distributions of artifacts and features within a site. The Betatakin and Kiet Siel studies were necessarily limited to the temporal, spatial, and associational distributions of architectural features, since nearly all the artifacts had long ago been removed from the sites; however, the potential of chronological analyses of this type combined with studies of the nonrandom distributions of artifacts and stylistic elements as a basis for sociological inferences is obvious. Such combined analyses, of course, would demand a rather special type of site—a well-preserved undisturbed cliff dwelling or a thoroughly burned open site in which datable tree species were commonly used for construction purposes.

The Tsegi Phase data provide archaeological documentation of a phenomenon that has often been noted by ethnographers (Mindeleff 1900: 643-44; Titiev 1944: 96-97) but rarely noticed by archaeologists. That is the high degree of mobility exhibited by the supposedly sedentary Pueblo farmers. In the Tsegi area, the latter half of the thirteenth century was characterized by the rapid movement of large numbers of people. In a period of 50 years, approximately 700 people moved into Tsegi Canyon, founded a number of villages, and then departed. Despite this state of flux, there was no detectable breakdown in Kayenta culture. Ceramic technology and artistry reached a peak, and community size achieved a maximum as relatively mobile household units were integrated without apparent difficulty into the social systems of the villages. This situation belies the usual assumption that Pueblo societies were rigidly structured sedentary units rooted in one spot until forced by direst necessity to move. Probably all Pueblo societies, prehistoric and historic, were capable of maintaining some sort of social cohesion and organization under the stress of moving from one place to another, and the fact that they moved does not necessarily imply the disruption of the sociocultural system.

A major contribution of the Tsegi data is the indication of the magnitude of the changes that can occur in a short period of time: Betatakin, a relatively large village, was founded, peopled, and abandoned within a period of no more than 33 years; the history of Kiet Siel spanned a maximum of 50 years; and some sites—such as Scaffold House, Lolomaki, Batwoman House, and Twin Caves Pueblo—were occupied for no more than 25 years. Anderson's (1966) demonstration of a significant change in the pottery-type-frequency composition of the ceramic assemblage at Kiet Siel that took place within a period of fewer than 5 years is a good example of the types of change that can occur in a very brief time.

Any attempt to reconstruct extinct sociocultural systems from archaeological data must take into account the temporal variable. No society is absolutely static and unchanging over a period of years, even in the absence of social or physical environmental pressures that might trigger cultural changes of an adaptive nature. Even in a society that has achieved a stable and productive adjustment to a particular environment, the processes of culture change operate within the limits established by the adaptive situation. Individual variation in behavior, the selection of alternative ways of doing certain things, innovations in style or techniques of craft production, and the spread of such innovations to other members of the society and to different communities are but a few of a number of processes that over a period of years may cause changes that can be perceived in archaeological contexts. Changes of this sort, which reflect the passage of time but have little or no adaptive or social significance, may produce patterned distributions of cultural elements within a site or among different sites. Refined chronological controls are crucial to distinguishing these two types of patterning from one another. A different kind of problem caused by culture change through time is that one type of sociocultural organization may evolve into another during the occupation of a particular site, and, in the absence of a controlled intrasite chronology, the two types of structure may inadvertently be lumped and considered to be one (Hill 1966: 12).

Nonrandom distributions of cultural elements within a site may be products of the effects of any one or combinations of a number of factors, among which are sampling error, chance, functional differences, social differences, and temporal differences. Sampling techniques can offset the effects of the first two of these factors, but only evidence from the site itself can enable the effects of the last three factors to be differentiated from one another. The temporal factor is an important variable that must be accorded consideration equal to that given to other possible variables. A couple of examples might be introduced at this point to illustrate situations in which, in the absence of good chronological controls, changes through time might be attributed to functional or social differences. First, it is possible to envision a situation in which significantly different localized clusters of elements represent functionally similar activities that were carried on at different times rather than functionally different activities that were performed simultaneously. Second, the 1272-75 immigration into Kiet Siel, which produced a number of changes in the village, suggests a hypothetical but not improbable example of such a situation. If room by room analyses of the distributions of ceramic types and design elements were possible, they might very well show two significant clusterings, one cluster associated with rooms built before 1271, the other associated with rooms constructed during the 1272-75 period. If the temporal distributions of these rooms were not known, the archaeologist might be tempted to impute functional or social differences to these clusters. Knowledge that the two clusters represent rooms with different but overlapping temporal distributions would suggest an alternative hypothesis. Such clusters of ceramic attributes could very well have been produced by the presence in the earlier group of rooms and the absence in the later rooms of pottery type frequencies and design elements that were generally characteristic of the early part of the Tsegi Phase throughout the canyon and not just at Kiet Siel. In short, such clustering could have been a result solely of changes through time that took place among all the Tsegi Phase communities and not a result of the presence at Kiet Siel of two different social units each with its own microtradition of ceramic production and design. Precise chronological controls may be extremely important in generating hypotheses relative to the nature of significant differences in the distributions of cultural elements that are indicated by other types of analysis.

Good dating controls are crucial to the study of intrasite and intersite interaction and variability. For example, knowing that residence units defined by clustering of cultural elements within a site are actually contemporaneous is vital to any attempt to comprehend the social organization of the site in question. One cannot deal with the interaction of such residence units unless he is reasonably certain that they existed at the same time. By the same token, one is not justified in hypothesizing about the interaction of groups of people that inhabited different sites unless he can demonstrate that the sites were occupied simultaneously. Knowing that Kiet Siel was occupied for at least 17 years before Betatakin was founded enabled Anderson (1966) to restrict his comparison of the ceramics of the two sites to samples that were absolutely contemporaneous. Had he not been able to do this, he might have reached some erroneous conclusions regarding the differences between the two ceramic assemblages. The same type of situation could have arisen had he been comparing inferred aspects of the social organization of the two villages.

The significance of the results of the Tsegi Phase analyses for the description and explanation of prehistoric sociocultural systems is twofold. First, the archaeologist must be aware that recognizable changes in the cultural elements that are recovered from archaeological contexts can occur in very short periods of time, and therefore that lack of variation through time cannot be made an a priori assumption in the analysis of even a short-lived site. Second, contemporaneity cannot be assumed, even for different parts of a single site that was apparently occupied for only a short time. If sociological inferences are to be drawn from the nonrandom distributions of cultural elements within a site, it must be shown, by means of whatever evidence is available, that the site actually represents a synchronous event. Unfortunately, independent chronological controls as good as those for the Tsegi Phase are rarely available, and the archaeologist must operate on the basis of the best evidence at hand. However, he must be aware of the possibility that he is not dealing with a synchronous event and be alert to any evidence relative to the temporal relationships among the various subunits within his site. Control of the temporal variable is especially important for the study of prehistoric social organization, for change through time as well as patterned behavior can affect the distributive patterning of cultural elements throughout a site or a region.

NOTE

1. Various aspects of the work upon which this paper is based were supported by the Southwest Regional Office of the U.S. National Park Service, the Arizona State Museum, and the National Science Foundation (grants GS-247 and GS-908 to the Laboratory of Tree-Ring Research); the assistance of these institutions is gratefully acknowledged. This paper is based on a doctoral dissertation submitted to the faculty of the Department of Anthropology at the University of Arizona, and I am indebted to my dissertation committee—Emil W. Haury, Raymond H. Thompson, and Bryant Bannister—for innumerable suggestions for improving the dissertation. William J. Robinson read the manuscript and offered valuable comments. Finally, I am deeply indebted to my fellow participants in the School of American Research seminar whose comments sharpened my awareness of the conceptual basis for the reconstruction of extinct sociocultural systems and opened for me vast new vistas for this type of research. None of the individuals or groups mentioned above should in any way be held responsible for the shortcomings of this paper, since I have not followed their suggestions in all cases.

The Postmigration Culture:
A Base for Archaeological Inference[1]

DOUGLAS W. SCHWARTZ

School of American Research

A review of the ethnographic migration literature, covering sedentary agricultural groups varying in technological level from primitive subsistence-farming to modern peasant-subsistence commercial types, has suggested cross-culturally recurrent consequences of migration that are important to archaeological data collection and inference. This paper examines those consequences and their implications for collecting archaeological data pertinent to a prehistoric migration. The results of the ethnographic review cover only those parts of culture that currently lend themselves to archaeological examination: forces prompting the migration, community configuration, technology, economy, social organization, and religion. Several categories, including land tenure, ethnocentricity, and role change, exhibited a tendency toward cross-cultural regularity but have not been included here, since the present level of approaches to archaeological inference makes it difficult to work with them. For each of the postmigration changes that might have occurred in these cultural categories, a series of archaeological test expectations has been compiled which will be used to examine the presence or absence of the change in a specific archaeological situation: Unkar Delta, a 300-acre alluvial deposit at the bottom of the Grand Canyon.

Migration, as opposed to range expansion or seasonal movement, is defined here as a geographical movement of individuals or groups over a significant distance. Such a movement is relatively permanent and the old territory is abandoned by the migrating group. A significant distance may be considered to be enough distance to be disjunctive with the old territory, with an area that is unoccupied between the old and new territories, and with this intervening area perhaps being ecologically unfavorable for occupation. By *relatively permanent* is meant that the movement is nonseasonal or nonperiodic. In referring to the abandonment of the old territory, it is recognized that a group will frequently retain ritual and emotional ties to a homeland; and if only part of a population migrates, property and territorial rights may be retained. However, it is conceived that in a migration the former territory is not utilized to its former extent by the group that actually migrates, and this group will not exercise direct control over the old territory.

THE ETHNOGRAPHIC LITERATURE REVIEW

This review was intended to reveal the alternative directions of culture-change that might be encountered in dealing with a migration situation. All the topics that have been included—reasons for movement, total community configuration, economics, technology, social organization, and religion—not only appear to change in limited directions but are susceptible to study in the present archaeological case. Each of these topics will be discussed with reference to ethnographic examples as a base from which more intelligent questions can be asked to better design the archaeological field work and laboratory analyses.

REASONS FOR MOVEMENT

Migrations are frequently the result of a perceived threat to the way of life of the community. While not all communities so threatened move, witness those at the base of active volcanoes, if free land or better living conditions are available, a migration frequently results. Perhaps the most common cause of community movement is economic, as exemplified by the move of the Homestead community from the south plains of western Texas and Oklahoma to New Mexico, due on the one hand to drought and depression in the home area, and on the other to the availability of land in New Mexico under the Homestead Act (Vogt 1955). Other examples of economic motivation include the Basque move to Idaho (Edlefsen 1950); the Escalante Mormons in Utah (Nelson 1952); the Orton Mormon community in Alberta, Canada (Dawson 1936); and the East Indians who moved to Fiji because of economic depression in their home area (Mayer 1961).

A related cause is overpopulation, a frequent motivator in the movement of primitive peoples. Examples of this include the highland Quechua of Peru who have been moving inland to the selva-montaña region for the past 100 years, with an intensification of movement during the last 6 years because of overpopulation and economic depression (Stewart 1965). A second example is the Toba-Bataks who moved to the coastal lowlands of East Sumatra from the Meat Valley to the west, between 1950 and 1956, because of overpopulation in their home area and the availability of level, fertile land on former plantations in eastern Sumatra (Cunningham 1958). Overpopulation has also motivated several Pacific Islands groups to emigrate to new homes, including the migrations of Tikopians to the Russell Islands (Larson 1966) and Gilbertese to the Solomon Islands (Knudson 1964).

A threat to core values such as religion is also a frequent cause of migration, as it was for: the Latvian settlers of Varpa who moved to Brazil as a result of a split in the Baptist Church (Augelli 1958); the Doukhobors who moved from Russia to Canada (Dawson 1936); several of the Mormon groups (Nelson 1952, Dawson 1936); and the Oren village of Israel which was founded by immigrants from Morocco who had fled because of their persecution as Jews (Weingrod 1962).

Factionalism, frequently in the face of internal change, is another important cause of migration, as in the classic Hopi case at Oraibi (Titiev 1944), although in this case the result was more of a range expansion. However, the Oraibi situation also clearly illustrates the overlap in causes possible in population movement, where economic failure, overpopulation, and factionalism due to change may all be involved.

POSTMIGRATION CULTURE
Total Community Configuration

The second area which emerges from the ethnographic literature review and suggests cross-cultural regularity in postmigration situations is the development of total community configuration. This is best seen in chronological perspective. Three stages of postmigration community configuration emerged from the literature: pioneering phase, consolidation phase, and stabilization phase. Furthermore, in the first two of these phases, both a pull toward factionalism and a pull toward solidarity were frequently evidenced. A summary of this sequence is presented first, followed by a more detailed examination of each:

1. *Pioneering Phase.* For the initial two to four years following a migration, the community is likely to be directing its efforts toward physical survival; the first shelters are built, fields are prepared, and the first crops are planted. During the pioneering phase the total group is likely to be characterized by stronger solidarity and greater ethnocentricity than was the case in their premigration situation. On the other hand, some families or groups may develop by disagreements with the main body, some to the point of abandoning the new settlement.

2. *Consolidation Phase.* Generally after the first or second good harvest, more permanent shelters are constructed and the first community structures are added. Also, at this time, the development and crystallization of formal and informal social institutions and associations are likely to occur. Factions are also likely to arise during the consolidation phase; in some cases, these will split from the new community as a group, or they may simply continue to exist within the new community.

3. *Stabilization Phase.* Eventually, depending on the degree of change from the original settlement, the effects of the migration pass, and the community settles down to develop along lines not directly related to the move.

Pioneering Solidarity. With the movement of a community into a new area, a greater degree of group solidarity among the community's members may develop, particularly in areas involving contact with new social groups. This change was noted in: the Mennonite communities (Dawson 1936: 113); the Basque enclave in Idaho (Edlefsen 1950); the Varpa who had feelings of ethnic superiority over the local Brazilians (Augelli 1958: 378-79); the Toba-Batak immigrants who developed strong feelings of superiority over the resident groups in eastern Sumatra (Cunningham 1958: 132-36); the East Indians who developed feelings of group superiority and encouraged little or no contact with the local Fijians (Mayer 1961: 182); the Gilbertese settlers who state frequently that "understanding has not yet come to the Solomon Islanders" (Knudson 1964: 205); the Tikopians who felt extremely hostile toward the resident Russell Islanders (Larson 1966: 52-54); and the Homestead community members who developed strong in-group feelings, were suspicious of outsiders, and encouraged little contact with neighboring Mormons, Spanish Americans, or Pueblo Indians (Vogt 1955: 126, 134).

Frequently during the pioneering phase, there tends to be a much greater degree of group cooperation than in the premigration society. Examples of this are common in the literature: in the Mennonite group, cooperation manifested itself in construction and farm work (Dawson 1936: 111); early group cooperation was present among the Doukhobors (Dawson 1936: 30, 42); the Homestead community in the early years after settlement was characterized by cooperation among neighbors (Vogt 1955: 70, 154); the Varpa group lived on a communal basis during the first year of settlement (Augelli 1958: 370); the Quechua Indians brought with them their tradition of cooperative work associations, but these were extended into social as well as economic affairs (Stewart 1965: 153); the Oren community was characterized by cooperation, although more on a kin than a community level, as was the Gilbertese community (Knudson 1964: 225); and, finally, the Mormon groups, especially at Escalante and Ephraim, were characterized by intense cooperation during the first years of settlement (Nelson 1952: 85-86, 137).

Dawson (1936: 377) has hypothesized that "cooperative endeavor prevails to some extent in all pioneering communities," although he qualifies this statement by noting that this cooperation is "spasmodic and uncertain," especially in those situations in which individual families from different communities come together to form a new community. Judging from a case described by White (1965) among a group of transplanted Ellice Islanders in Fiji, group identification and cooperation are also less strong among people who emigrate to a new home primarily for material gain rather than to escape a threat.

Pioneering Dissension. Not all the individuals in a postmigration com-

179

munity are solidly behind the move, however, and the new conditions may pose individual problems to which they cannot adjust. Therefore, during the first year or two of a new settlement, it is common for one or two small groups or families to break away from the settlement and return to the home area, or migrate to another area. In Hotevilla, for example, in the first few months after the move, a group of moderate hostiles returned to Oraibi, while later another group split to settle the village of Kitotomovi, while still others migrated to Moenkopi (Titiev 1944: 93). In eastern Sumatra, the early response of some migrants was discouragement, and return to the Meat Valley resulted. Others moved away to settle new areas, but the majority stayed in the new settlement (Cunningham 1958: 111). Other examples of initial dissension are: in the Oren settlement (Weingrod 1962: 122); the Mennonite community (Dawson 1936: 147-48); the Doukhobor migration (Dawson 1936: 19); and the Orton village, which some left because of discouragement (Dawson 1936: 218).

Consolidation Solidarity. In some migration situations, group solidarity continues even after the needs of the initial settlement have been met. This solidarity may go so far as to influence the development of a rigid social order where there are strong sanctions against deviation from the social norms and change. The Hotevilla case is an excellent example, where there occurred a strong adherence to Hopi traditions and a resistance to outside contact, cultural deviance, and change (Thompson 1950: 82). Even when change is necessitated by the new environment, there is often an attempt to retain the old ways, as in the Tikopian colony where deviations from the norm were explained as "temporary adjustments" (Larson 1966: 178). In the Mennonite example, the church precepts were strongly enforced with strict adherence to traditional norms (Dawson 1936: 114, 159-60). As Dawson (1936: xii-xiv) has hypothesized, this is the case with other sectarian communities: "In the sect a spontaneous enthusiasm for an ideal way of life unites the members regardless of how divergent the original backgrounds. In time, the purposes of the sect become defined in a way of life which prescribes for every member what he should unalterably do in the most intimate affairs."

In some cases, such as the Gilbertese, there is a strong feeling that they are no longer bound by the norms which had formerly channeled their behavior, and they are consequently more receptive to culture change as a group (Knudson 1964: 159, 161).

Consolidation Factionalism. Nevertheless, while Dawson's suggestion of an "ideal way of life" may characterize a few immigration sects, it does not seem to hold true for all, particularly those made up of families from different communities. Hammond's analysis of the migrating sect characterizes it as generally involving schisms, defections, and internal chaos (Hammond 1963: 275-83). The Homestead community is an example of this process, as it was characterized by factionalism, seen in the proliferation of churches and in general individualism (Vogt 1955: 161, 169, 170-71). However, this development may have resulted in part from the value orientation of individualism possessed by the Homesteaders before the migration (Vogt and O'Dea 1953: 653). Cunningham (1958: 128-37) has indicated that currently the East Sumatra case has passed beyond the stage of pioneering solidarity, and the political organization has gone in the direction of internal division and confusion. Similarly, the communal base of the first year of the Varpa settlement was followed by a breakup of the colony into separate farms (Augelli 1958: 370). Also, a number of factions developed in the church over differing interpretations, yet the church is still the main source of community unity (Augelli 1958: 370-84). In the Ephraim Mormon community, "the communal institutions of the pioneer period were short-lived and appear therefore to have been the result of the compelling forces of the pioneer era," for after the initial communal efforts, a pattern of competition arose (Nelson 1952: 137). The Doukhobor settlement initially was planned as communistic, but schisms developed, and there was a gradual weakening of the adherence to the sect's principles. Consequently, the communal living plan changed toward small clusters of several families that seemed to work more successfully (Dawson 1936: 83).

Other sources of factionalism can be found in: the Norwegian sect (Hammond 1963: 275); among the Mennonites (Dawson 1936: 147-49); and in the Oren community which became splintered into various factions as a result of political differences (Weingrod 1962: 122-23). In Nukufero, the Tikopian colony in the Russells, differences in community policy often occurred between individuals. However, these differences were subordinated to maintaining kinship ties and economic cohesion (Larson 1966: 177). In Kioa, the Ellice colony, generational factionalism arose because a great premium was placed on the ability to deal with the new physical and social environment and younger men were assuming positions of authority not formerly possible (White 1965: 164).

Although, in many cases, these factions resulted in the establishment of new villages or new communities, in some cases they simply resulted in a more complex social organization within the community. This is exemplified among the Pueblos where factionalism seems to be characteristic. Dozier (1966b: 172-85) in his analysis of Santa Clara factionalism suggests that the basic ingredient for the rise of dissenting groups is the highly authoritarian nature of Pueblo society. He suggests that, in prehistoric times, nonconforming individuals were either evicted or moved voluntarily and founded new villages. Only rarely did the pueblo itself disappear. He suggests that the persistence of the pueblos may be partly explained by this skimming off of malcontents, leaving the main village's population oriented more along traditional lines and restricted to those who valued communal living.

Stabilization Phase. Eventually, depending on the degree of change from the original settlement, the effects of the migration pass, and the community settles down to develop along lines not directly related to the move.

Technological and Economic Change

The amount of economic and technological change resulting from a migration seems to depend to a large extent on the differences between the original and the new physical environments. When a move takes place within the same environment, the traditional economy usually continues: Hopi (Titiev 1944); range expansion of Toba-Bataks within the Meat Valley (Cunningham 1958); Chan Kom (Redfield and Rojas 1934: 27); and Nukufero (Larson 1966: 8-9).

If a community moves into a new environment, technological and economic changes usually result. In the Homestead community, for example, a shift occurred from cotton and wheat farming to the cultivation of pinto beans. Piñon nut collection was added, based on techniques learned from the Navajo (Vogt 1955: 43-44, 175). The Quechua changed from a highland farming economy to one of tropical agriculture in the montaña region. Their new farming techniques were learned from montaña haciendas, where many worked during the first one or two years after the migration. Agricultural and building techniques were also borrowed from local Indians (Stewart 1965: 148, 152-53). The Toba-Batak move to eastern Sumatra involved a change in environment, but a continuation of traditional rice cultivation was possible even though changes were required in technique for the cultivation of the level and more extensive plots (Cunningham 1958: 138-39, 121-22). The Titiana community was also able to retain its economic emphasis on the production of copra, although the heavier rainfall in the Solomons forced them to substitute hot-air drying of the material for sun drying (Knudson 1964: 186).

The Indians who moved to Fiji encountered a change in environment resulting in their cultivation of sugarcane in the valleys around the coasts of large islands, in contrast to the local Fijians who grew copra and bananas in the interior. The Indians learned their new farming techniques at the local plantations, where they were indentured workers, during the first two to five years (Mayer 1961: 12, 38). The settlement of Varpa in Brazil took the Latvians to a new environment requiring different crops and agricultural techniques. Although most of the immigrants were peasant farmers in Latvia before the migration, they had to learn new farming techniques, in part from their non-Latvian neighbors (Augelli 1958: 368-71). The Moroccans who settled the Oren community of Israel moved into a new environment resulting in a radical economic change (Weingrod 1962: 121, 125).

As has been noted in several cases above, generally where technological change occurred, new tools or techniques were usually borrowed from frequently dominant neighboring groups, even in situations where there tended to be little social interaction between the migrating group and the local settlements.

After a migration, there may be a temporary or permanent loss or decline of certain nonutilitarian crafts. Although there are not enough data to construct a general pattern, some examples can be cited. The Toba-Batak women stopped weaving after their migration to East Sumatra because of a lack of time and the traditional materials. New houses also lacked traditional design (Cunningham 1958: 121, 116). Among the Fiji-Indians, some craft specialties were lost because of a lack of time, incentives, and need (Mayer 1961: 158-59).

Social Effects of Migration

Changes in three areas of social structure following a migration were present in many of the newly established communities reviewed: (1) social stratification, (2) traditional social units, and (3) authority patterns. These occurred both singly and in combination.

Social Stratification. Migration may have an initial equalizing tendency within the society. In the new Canadian settlement of the Doukhobors, for example, there was an initial emphasis on socioeconomic equality among the settlers (Dawson 1936: 44). In the Indian communities of Fiji, there was a decrease in emphasis on caste differences from the pre-migration situation (Mayer 1961: 142-43). At Homestead, there was no rigid social class stratification (Vogt 1955: 168). At Oren in Israel, an initial leveling of social distinctions was noted by Weingrod (1962: 125). However, in certain migrating groups with strongly developed social distinctions before migration and less social displacement after migration, the social class structure of the home area may be continued, as in the Meat Valley (Cunningham 1958: 34, 55) and Varpa (Augelli 1958: 380) examples. In Nukufero, the premigration class system was maintained, and, although class differences were being obscured, it was believed that they would be reinstated once the community was settled (Larson 1966).

Change in Social Units. Units of social interaction may be modified as a result of migration, although it is difficult to make any generalizations as to the type of unit which may become significant. Some cases may at least provide an exemplification of the range. The nuclear family in a household may become more important as a socioeconomic unit with larger forms of social grouping decreasing in importance, as with the Toba-Bataks (Cunningham 1958: 81, 140-43). Extended kin relationships may become more important as a means of widening obligations and responsibilities in a new settlement, as with the Fiji-Indians (Mayer 1961: 37, 176), the Tikopians at Nukufero (Larson 1966: 149), and the Moroccans at Oren (Weingrod 1962: 126). A social unit with broad membership, such as a church, may become important as a means of integrating the new settlement, as with the Varpa (Augelli 1958: 379) and the Fiji-Indians (Mayer 1961: 96).

However, traditional forms of social interaction may also continue to be of the same significance as before the migration. This is generally found in migrations involving short-distance moves of fairly homogeneous populations within the same ecological niche, such as the migration within the Meat Valley of the Toba-Bataks (Cunningham 1958: 139-43), the Mormon villages (Nelson 1952: 101, 227, 243, 257), the Mennonites (Dawson 1936: 112), and the Gilbertese communities in the Sydney Islands (Knudson 1964: 167).

Authority. Both strong and weak authority patterns are found in postmigration situations. Strong authority patterns tend to occur in new settlements which are:

1. The result of well-organized migrations of cohesive social groups, of a whole community, or of part of a community, in which the traditional authority patterns and institutions are brought intact to the new settlement—for example, the Hopi pueblo of Hotevilla (Titiev 1944: 207), and the Toba-Batak range-expansion within the Valley of Meat (Cunningham 1958: 137).

2. The results of the careful planning of a religious organization with strong central authority, as among the Mennonites (Dawson 1936: 112), the Mormon villages (Nelson 1952: 261), the French-Canadians (Dawson 1936: 342), and the German-Catholics in Canada (Dawson 1936: 290).

Weak authority patterns may be found in new settlements resulting from migration of families or groups which were not previously living in the same community, as among the Toba-Bataks moving into East Sumatra (Cunningham 1958: 119, 120, 138), the Moroccan settlement at Oren (Weingrod 1962: 123), and the Norwegian Sloopers (Hammond 1963: 279). Among the Ellice Islanders on Fiji, who had migrated sporadically from the same community primarily to satisfy personal ambitions, authority patterns were also weak (White 1965: 167).

Religion

Three generalizations concerning change in religion as a consequence of migration emerged from the literature survey. It should be understood that while one or more of these occurred in each of the cases examined there is no indication that they are independent variables and therefore may or may not occur together:

1. During the early years following a migration, a simplification of the religious system may take place.

2. Religion may become more important following the migration.

3. Religion may serve as a vehicle for factionalism after the initial period of settlement.

Simplification. With the rigors of life in a new area, religion is likely to be affected by: a loss of certain ceremonies, failure to replace certain ceremonial paraphernalia, a general reduction in complexity (Fernea and Kennedy 1966), and a lack of personnel for ceremonial offices. At Bakavi, after 27 years of settlement, Titiev (1944: 213) found that the ceremonial system was still fragmentary, with a lack of traditional officers and paraphernalia. In the movement of the Toba-Bataks to East Sumatra, although religion was important after migration, certain ceremonies, such as those associated with housebuilding and family burial, declined (Cunningham 1958: 109). At the Indian communities on Fiji, religious gatherings were important occasions for social purposes, but there was a decrease in ritual (Mayer 1961: 96).

Increasing Importance of Religion. Following a migration, religion may become an important focus for community unity in the new settlement. Although the ceremonial-religious features may not necessarily become more important, it may be that the religious system becomes more secular and broadens its purpose and function. In the Mormon villages, for example, the church remained strong both in its ceremonial aspects and as a community unifier (Nelson 1952: 101, 227, 243, 257). In the Latvian Varpa settlement, religion was a binding force in the colony and became the most important focus of group activity (Augelli 1958: 379). Of course, when a religious sect is the active organizer of a migration, as in the Doukhobor (Dawson 1936: 318, 320) cases, there is strong religious participation from the early days of the settlement.

Religion as a Vehicle for Factionalism after the Period of Initial Settlement. The Latvian Varpa settlement is an excellent example of this situation in which there was a rapid split in the church over the interpretations of the tenets of the faith. So many lay preachers developed as a result that the community could not support them as full-time specialists (Augelli 1958: 379). Among the Fiji-Indians, there was a proliferation of religious sects and associations (Mayer 1961: 9), as was similarly the case in the Homestead (Vogt 1955: 161) and Toba-Batak communities (Cunningham 1958: 140). In the Ellice community of Kioa, the church opened up a new channel by which the older and more conservative members of the group could assert themselves in the face of culture-change after the traditional forms of authority became restricted (White 1965: 107).

SUMMARY

The review of several ethnographic migration situations suggests that cross-cultural regularities or limited possibilities as a consequence of migration can be identified. Furthermore, the analysis indicates that in the areas of migration motivation, economy, technology, social organization, religion, and total community configuration—rather definite consequences—emerged; and a limited range of consequences could be identified, though this range was clearly not so wide as the number of cases studied. In addition, a rough correlation seems to exist between the type of migration and the consequences.

Although no claims to strong identification of clearly cross-cultural consequences are made, it does seem reasonable, on the basis of the review, that correlations can be identified between specific types of migrations with specific changes in the postmigration culture. If this is true, then the archaeological analysis of migration, from the standpoint of these limited possibilities, should reveal a great deal more about the culture than would be expected from a standard archaeological analysis stressing cultural descriptions.

ARCHAEOLOGICAL DATA EXPECTATIONS

The ethnographic review of postmigration culture was originally made as background for a better understanding of an archaeological migration observed on Unkar Delta in the Grand Canyon of northern Arizona (Schwartz 1965). It was assumed that to understand more about this archaeological situation than simply the time it occurred and the description of the material culture remains, questions about the nonmaterial aspects of the culture would have to be formulated on the basis of ethnographic information.

The types of archaeological data expectations deemed necessary to validate the changes observed in the ethnographic cases are presented below. Since the data necessary to test the hypotheses have yet to be collected, this section of the paper should be considered as an example of a possible operational approach to the method of using this type of ethnographic material in archaeological research.

Motivation

The most frequent cause of migration is an economic threat to the way of life of the community. Evidence gathered from the Unkar sites during the 1967 field season suggests that two processes were operating relevant to this proposition: climate change within the canyon and a population buildup on the north rim of the canyon. To further examine the first factor, additional pollen work is needed on the late major occupation sites in the canyon. This will indicate more precisely the nature of the climate change and help determine whether it was constant during the total occupation period or whether there was an even greater amount of available moisture during the later major occupation. Pollen samples will also be collected from contemporaneous sites on the north rim, to examine the nature of the changes in that area and obtain a clearer picture of its total ecological configuration.

There is a general indication from Hall's survey material (1942) that a population buildup was occurring on the north rim prior to the time of the Unkar migration. To confirm this hypothesis, Hall's rather intensive survey data will be reexamined, utilizing the more refined ceramic chronology that has become available in the quarter-century since the publication of his report. The area encompassed by Hall's work, the Walhalla Glades of the north rim, has well-defined boundaries, so the population concentration there can also be analyzed in terms of its "carrying capacity." Hill (1963: 114) has discussed this process, noting that many primitive societies, upon seeing their resources dwindle under the pressure of increasing population, move to a new locale before the situation becomes critical. Combining the additional pollen data from the north rim and the canyon with a reanalysis of Hall's work, it should be possible to understand both the factors which encouraged the potential migrants to look elsewhere and those which attracted the migrants to the canyon.

Total Community Configuration

Migrations seem to have a significant impact on the initial organization of the total community, although the nature of this impact is altered with the passage of time. During the immediate postmigration period, a pioneering phase has been identified. Ethnographically, it is characterized by: a major effort directed toward physical survival in the new environment, strong group solidarity, and cooperation. With the passage of time, the new way of life consolidates, although in some cases factions may arise. Finally, a period of stabilization is reached when the effects of the migration pass and the community begins to develop along lines not directly related to the move.

188

Postmigration Culture: Base for Archaeological Inference

Basic to the examination of these possible directions of culture-change is the development of precise chronological site control. This will be accomplished by combining information from additional excavations, especially from the late major occupation sites, yielding ceramic, architectural, palynological, radiocarbon, and lithic data. Ceramic data from the survey and radiocarbon dates from the initial excavations have already suggested a gross temporal outline, but this must be refined with further data. Finer temporal divisions and perhaps site-by-site seriation may be possible with additional pollen work and architectural data. Once the sites are placed in a tight temporal framework, information will be available to answer many of the questions regarding the immediate and lingering consequences of migration on the total community structure.

Pioneering Phase. With good chronological site control, many of the changes relating to total community configuration can be examined. For the pioneering phase, the degree of effort directed toward physical survival may be studied by determining whether those sites with basic utilitarian functions, such as living units and agricultural terraces, were constructed first. Nonutilitarian items such as beads, pendants, and highly decorated pottery might also be expected to occur at a lower frequency during the pioneering phase but should increase during the later part of the occupation. Tool types will be analyzed to determine whether those most directly related to physical survival are more frequent than those more generally associated with the manufacture of nonutilitarian arts and crafts. The same tools will be examined to determine whether there was a difference in the workmanship standards in the early period as opposed to those at the later sites. In summary, the presence of a pioneering orientation, comparable to that found in the ethnographic cases studied, should be manifested by: (1) the presence of utility-oriented constructions, (2) a lower frequency of nonutilitarian artifacts, (3) a lower frequency and quality of decorated pottery, (4) cruder artifacts, and (5) tools more closely related to utilitarian activities.

With data available upon completion of excavation at late major occupation sites, it should also be possible to compare the degree of variability in architecture, artifact styles, and ceramic designs. Greater group solidarity should be evidenced in the early sites by a narrower range of variability. Examination of the plans of north rim sites made by Hall (1942) will be used as a general premigration control to obtain comparative data as to the nature of these sites. Finally, greater group cooperation

189

may be reflected in the construction of larger and better-planned dwellings in the early postmigration sites. From present evidence, this seems to be the case, but it cannot be confirmed without additional chronological and architectural information from the unexcavated early major occupation sites.

Finally, the yearly permanence of the initial settlement will be further examined. Although data collected during the first field season were adequate to hypothesize a nonseasonal occupancy, confirmation requires further evidence. The major approach will be through pollen analysis. A year-round pollen rain study will be made of the inner canyon area to establish the nature of the total sequence. This will then be compared to a microstratigraphic analysis of pollen occurring in both early and late occupation sites. Seasonal occupation should appear as a discontinuous pollen sequence, while a permanent occupation should leave evidence of a steady pollen rain comparable to that of the contemporary collection.

Consolidation Phase. A few years after a migration has occurred, when the initial survival requirements have been fulfilled, a satisfactory adaptation to the new environment has been made, the strict interest in utility declines, and new technological developments are discernible. At this point, the community is likely to develop in one of two directions: either community solidarity continues or tensions may arise producing factions.

Archaeological data bearing on the development of a consolidation phase may be relatively easy to identify, but those dealing with factionalism are somewhat more difficult to discover. With the fulfillments of the primary survival requirements, an increase in nonutilitarian arts, crafts, and architecture is to be expected. The workmanship of artifacts may improve in quality, and the amount of decorated pottery may increase in frequency.

If the consolidation phase on Unkar Delta were characterized by a continuation of a solidarity orientation, then traits characteristic of this orientation during the pioneering phase would be expected to continue. However, if factionalism developed, the archaeological record will have to be examined closely to differentiate this from other processes that may be in operation.

It has been suggested in the culture-history reconstruction that, following the initial period of construction, the number of sites increased significantly in number while the size of the individual sites decreased. This increase in number may have been the result of one process or a combination of three processes: normal population growth, additional migrants, or factionalism. A normal population growth, as the result of an increasing adaptation to the canyon environment, should be manifested archaeologically by an uninterrupted sequence of cultural change suggesting no intrusion of additional migrants. The use of purely local materials in the manufacture of ceramics is an example. Furthermore, an index of artifact homogeneity should suggest an internal population growth and cultural development.

Population growth as the result of additional immigration from the north rim should be apparent by the appearance of nonlocal material in the manufacture of pottery and other artifact types. A detailed petrographic analysis of the pottery will be made and compared with source materials from the delta and the north rim to provide data on which to draw conclusions on this problem and the previous problem.

If the expansion in the number of sites was the result of local population growth but was triggered by factionalism, it is assumed that the factions would develop style differences. Therefore, if material in the later sites shows a higher rate of variability and perhaps even some distinct trait clusters, but no use of foreign elements in the ceramics, the assumption of factionalism will be more supportable than if a normal curve of variability is revealed.

Changes in Social Organization

The problem of factionalism in the postmigration culture has already been discussed, but at least two other changes in the social organization occurring as a result of the migration will be investigated. The ethnographic review has suggested that during the early years of a postmigration community, an equalizing tendency occurs in the social stratification and/ or differentiation. This hypothesis will be examined by analyzing room size and function. The assumption will be made that uniformity of size in rooms having similar function would suggest a higher degree of social equality than would a high degree of variance. An even distribution of cultural materials among rooms of a large site, or between small sites of the same time period, would also suggest a greater degree of social equality than would an uneven distribution. A comparison of both changes in the frequency of room size and in artifact occurrence will also be made between early and late major occupation sites to examine possible changes in social stratification between time periods comparable to the pioneering and consolidation phases.

Changes in social units following a migration are also suggested by the literature review. Two directions are indicated: either the nuclear family becomes most important, or larger kin groupings are emphasized. An analysis of ceramics within and between rooms and sites will be the main direction of emphasis for this problem. Longacre (1964a) has applied a technique of pottery analysis using ceramic design that provides a model for application to this type of problem. He has suggested that certain recurrent ceramic design elements may indicate whether a society was kin-oriented. He has suggested that groups develop idiosyncrasies of design over time, so that by isolating the designs and tracing their distribution, the important social unit can be distinguished. If the design, for example, is confined to a small area of the site, or to one site in a cluster, the possibility of kin-orientation increases. If, on the other hand, the design is widespread, but still within a limited geographical district, the affiliation may well be larger than kin.

Economic and Technological Changes

Several indications of technological change have already been discussed, especially with regard to the lower frequency of nonutilitarian tool types and decorative items during the initial phases of the migration. In addition, adaptations to a new environment should trigger economic readjustments that would be reflected in other technological changes. The material collected by Hall (1942) on the north rim will be used to provide a base for such a comparison. It is to be expected, for example, that an increase in agricultural tools over hunting implements should occur as a result of a more favorable agricultural environment. Some new tool types may also be expected as a result of the move to a quite different life zone.

A society's religion seems to be affected in one way or a combination of ways following a migration: (1) it may become simplified; (2) it may increase in importance; or (3) it may serve as a vehicle of factionalism. The results of the 1967 field work clearly indicated that, far from becoming simplified, religion was most important on the delta, evidenced by the large kiva (Un 2) built at the same time as, or soon after, the initial living structures. Additional excavation is required, however, to determine what happened at the time the later major occupation sites were built. If religious buildings, specifically additional kivas, were built at that time and the initial kiva was abandoned before the total settlement, and if other evidence for factionalism is apparent, then it may be hypothesized that, after its early importance, religion indeed became a vehicle for factionalism.

CONCLUSION

This paper has attempted to show that the postmigration community as a type exhibits certain cultural regularities of change, the knowledge of which can generate inferences about prehistoric cultures. The demonstrable cross-cultural validity of these regularities provides the substance for this conclusion. Perhaps more important, however, this approach suggests that there may be other dynamic or sequential cultural types (in addition to those which have been the subject of acculturation studies) which also may exhibit cross-cultural regularities helpful to the archaeologist in attempting to understand nonmaterial aspects of prehistoric societies. Other examples of "dynamic" or "sequential" culture types might be the dying community or the expanding farming village. Only a greater awareness on the part of the archaeologist that he must dig deeply not only into the ground and into the ethnographic literature but also into additional conceptual realms will demonstrate the validity of those possibilities.

NOTE

1. This paper was initiated as background for National Science Foundation sponsored projects GS 1519, 1792, and 2068. This support is gratefully acknowledged.

Explanation
As an Afterthought
and As a Goal[1]

PAUL S. MARTIN

Department of Anthropology,
Chicago Natural History Museum

The papers that I am about to discuss are a remarkable collection. They are perceptive, well written, and brilliant. They represent a singular departure from traditional approaches to archaeology. The participants should feel a sense of accomplishment because their essays represent a major step in the creation of an archaeology whose effort is dedicated to the use of prehistory in finding and testing explanations of cultural process.

Many may not realize the changes that these essays illustrate. They mark a metamorphosis, a reversal, a vision. Compare their contents with those which have appeared in *American Antiquity* over the last 25 years. To make my point more specific, let me mention a few titles:

1. "A problematic example of Peruvian resist-dyeing"
2. "A decorated bone rattle from Mexico"
3. "Further notes on clay human figurines in the Western United States"

Explanation as an Afterthought and as a Goal

What has happened? I think that I am not overdramatizing when I say that a revolution has taken place in archaeological thinking, philosophy, methodology, and goals. Archaeology in the spirit of these papers is anthropology and explanation. I salute the authors.

CHANGED GOALS

One salient point in the papers impressed me, and that was the shift in goals. The papers do not dwell on traits, artifacts, the history of traits, or taxonomy. They are not written in terms of "brown ware people" or "gray ware people"; they do not equate difference in social organization with differences in traits. Archaeology is explicitly viewed as anthropology and social organization is viewed as social organization. The goals are the discovery of cultural regularities, the formulation of laws of cultural dynamics, the search for trends in and causes of human behavior, and, finally, the attainment of sufficient sophistication to make predictions with a high degree of probability.

JEFFREY S. DEAN

Dean has presented an arresting and scholarly paper—perhaps the best available analysis of interpueblo and intrapueblo growth. Tree-ring dates are used not just to place Kiet Siel and Betatakin in a temporal context but to examine the evolution of social organization at these sites. Dean provides important data bearing on two alternative explanations of pueblo lineages, those of Titiev and Eggan. His analysis indicates that these two pueblos were the result of the amalgamation of different groups at different points in time and thus tends to support Eggan's explanation of lineages. At the intersite level, the movement of ideas and peoples in the Tsegi region and the relation of these movements to events in the Southwest as a whole are thoroughly explored.

JAMES N. HILL

Hill's essay on *Theory and Method* represents the ultimate in contemporary archaeological conceptions and imagination. He emphasizes that clearly stated hypotheses and the testing or demonstration of them are lacking in many research designs and publications. Inferences are frequently resorted to, but little effort has been made to support or reject such ideas by means of independent but relevant data. Many archaeologists are interested in *making* inferences but fail to understand that demonstration is an important adjunct to theory.

I cannot praise enough Hill's remarks about the stultifying effect of pursuing the elusive concept of "norms" that each "culture" is supposed to manifest. It reminds me of the medieval medical concept of "miasma," a noxious, although invisible and unidentifiable, vapor that was supposed to account for malaria and other dread diseases. Although nonexistent and imaginary, like phlogiston, *miasma* was uncritically accepted for generations. I hope his criticism of the normative approach will help dissipate it, along with such fantasies as "typical behavior," and "diagnostic traits." Such crotchets muddy the waters and retard methodological and theoretical advances, since they are not observable, measurable, or subject to statistical manipulation or verification. Probably no single idea other than the normative approach has been so responsible for concealing the true nature of human data—archaeological or contemporary. I refer to the fact that variability is the rule in human societies. The idea that culture consists of shared ideas and behavior is nonsense of the first magnitude, as Hill demonstrates.

The discussion of "general methodological considerations" is a brilliant exposition concerning the fundamental nature of demonstration. Without demonstration we do not advance our knowledge one iota. As Hill points out, an untested hypothesis indicates a mind content to admit that there is nothing new to learn about the past.

But perhaps best of all, Hill's essay serves as an effective foil to a totally inductive approach to the study of the past. His statements about the logic of science and its application to archaeology place new emphasis on the hypothetico-deductive approach. This, if followed, assumes a conclusion, a law; it is a rigorous method that will guide research design and bring fruitful conclusions. The inductive approach holds that archaeological inferences are to be evaluated by means of the education and experience of the investigator. This implies a kind of mystical property that permits the investigator to identify himself in some occult manner with his artifacts which, when conditions are correct, will speak to him and give up their secrets.

I am not quarreling with the inductive approach, although I am unable to adapt to it. My principal criticism is that it is *not* the way of contemporary science. It is not a method susceptible to rigorous testing, and, therefore, I find it fallible.

In brief, Hill represents the best in the new generation of anthropologists; his ideas indicate the revolution that has taken place in archaeology in the last decade.

WILLIAM D. LIPE

Lipe's paper demonstrates how inferences concerning social organization can be supported with survey data. I found his discussion of the Anasazi periphery interesting and indicative of how a cultural tradition changes in response to the changing environment encountered in moving from the Anasazi heartland to southern Utah.

WILLIAM A. LONGACRE

Longacre's essay undertakes to provide an underpinning for the problem we had set ourselves: *the reconstruction of prehistoric Pueblo social organization*. His review highlights our heritage as archaeologists and points out how difficult it has been on the one hand, to build on past knowledge, and on the other hand to free ourselves from seeking facts as an end in itself, from concern with culture-history, from fatuous obsession with culture traits, and from unstructured research.

Longacre's perceptive analysis shows that ever since 1960 a shift in goals has taken place—a shift from unsupported inferences and an emphasis on analyses of contemporary Puebloan social systems as keys to the secrets of ancient social institutions to an emphasis on basic research directed toward an understanding of the nature of culture, culture processes, and human behavior of the past.

As Longacre concludes, archaeologists no longer merely dig for things, traits, or treasure. Before putting a shovel in the ground, they have created propositions or hypotheses that guide their work and indicate what data are necessary for demonstrating or rejecting their ideas.

To these trends, I would add one more. I think that we will soon develop hypotheses concerning past culture processes and human behavior that will be applicable to contemporary problems of our society. At first glance, this may seem impossible, but I am convinced that our present paradigm and methodologies will make this possible. This idea was foreshadowed in a symposium devoted to the Southwest held in Tucson in 1953 (Martin 1954).

DOUGLAS W. SCHWARTZ

Schwartz's essay represents a perceptive approach to one of the oldest concerns of Southwestern archaeologists—migrations. An extensive review of the available ethnographic literature bearing on migrations of peoples provided Schwartz with a basis for formulating a rigorous research design for the analysis of migrations. From this anthropological analysis, he deduces the specific evidence that would confirm or refute the hypotheses constituting the model in specific archaeological contexts. The result is a sophisticated approach for interpreting and studying prehistoric migrations by analyzing observed empirical data and matching them with the expectations derived from a model. Schwartz analyzes not by collecting data and trying to find for them an ethnographic model but by using ethnography as a basis for specifying what data will be relevant to his analysis before the analysis begins, and as a basis for interpreting the absence as well as the presence of excavated data.

R. GWINN VIVIAN

Vivian's paper is full of ideas and possibilities, and I hope he will soon publish a major analysis of social organization and water control in the Southwest. Among other things, Vivian controls his subject and data and demonstrates a remarkable insight into a situation that has been entirely overlooked by three generations of explorers and archaeologists. Vivian's work is an example of how a change in paradigm results in the researcher's seeing things where others saw nothing before. He and his father found water control systems where others saw nothing or mistook what they saw for villages—and this in an area which has been explored countless times in the past 50 years.

I was fascinated by his suggestion that the differences in towns and villages argue for two different social organizations adapted to different circumstances. I think that archaeologists working throughout the Southwest will soon begin to find similar phenomena in their areas.

It is difficult for me to understand how the villagers could have raised crops dependent on rainfall, whereas the town had to resort to water control through irrigation, and so on. Is it not conceivable that one could advance hypotheses that would account for the observed differences in village pattern, wealth, and trade goods in terms of incipient urbanism? Might it not be possible that the inhabitants of the canyon shared economic resources and that the towns were centers of redistribution and trade?

It may soon be shown that the Southwest contained substantially more social stratification than our analyses in the past have suggested and that the approach to truly urban adaptations was much closer than we have believed. At least I would hope that many research projects organized to test these hypotheses will result from Vivian's work.

CHANGED METHODS

To attain the goals of these authors, we will need substantial improvements in our methodology. It is not enough to be interested in new data and new ways of using old data. If we are to use the old in new ways, then we must convince many archaeologists that there is a basis for extending the use of our data in the methods that we are using in our analyses. We must learn to employ more rigorous methods of research—methods which characterize scientific inquiry—physical, biological, or social.

What do I mean by improvements?

First of all, I shall mention vision. We must develop vastly different conceptual organizations. We must see a sunrise not from a geocentric point of view but from a heliocentric one. Sometimes we do not see an object or system because we do not know how to see it. Hence, we must invent new ways of thinking about facts, as Hill and Vivian have done.

Second, I emphasize that archaeology is or can be a science when it establishes general laws concerning the behavior of observed events or objects with which we are concerned.

Third, we must realize that unstructured collecting of data produces a morass and does not lead to patterns of explanation. This inductive approach is not fruitful because it assumes that facts will speak for themselves and this they will not do. A collection of facts cannot be called a science any more than a pile of bricks can be called a house. Facts are pertinent only when they are used in testing the validity of a hypothesis. Hypotheses are deductively formulated to give direction to scientific investigation. Such hypotheses determine what data are to be collected. The main point is that hypotheses must be tested by independent but relevant data. The fruitful approach lies in the system of logic in which deduction and induction interplay.

These papers go as far as any that I have seen in meeting standards such as those which I have described, especially Hill's. Nevertheless, I feel that there are areas in which we can all improve. But what concerns me most is how these papers will be received. A few years ago most of them would have been dismissed as speculation. I think that the authors have demonstrated that their inferences are sound and far beyond the level of speculation. With closer attention to deductive scientific methods, the transition from conjecture to tested hypotheses would be even more complete. Now my greatest worry is that other archaeologists will view these works not as a spur to formulating their own explanations and testing their own hypotheses but as a kind of Bible to which they bring their data for interpretation after they have been collected.

I can best explain this fear in terms of Schwartz's paper—in no way intended as criticism of Schwartz. It is conceivable that some readers will want to use Schwartz's evidence as a means of interpreting their data rather than as a means of formulating their own hypotheses before collecting data. This is the heritage of a traditional archaeology that has pursued explanation as an afterthought rather than a justification for doing the work.

Neither should Schwartz's interest in migrations be regarded as the only possible use of archaeological data. Too often in the past have we moved people about almost like chessmen without scrutinizing the evidence and looking for other and perhaps simpler explanations.

Ethnography rightfully plays an important part in the interpretation of excavated materials. But we should not hold the expectation that archaeological and ethnographic evidence will always coincide. We are archaeologists because we believe that our data present unique opportunities for analyzing social processes of the past, especially changes and developments that span a long time interval.

Thus, our interest is in formulating hypotheses concerning the nature of migration to arrive at laws that govern the causality, the how and why of migrations in general. Migrations and the reasons for them vary, and we should try to discover their uniqueness and their similarities. By the same token, we can surely conceive of migrations as a kind of change. Hence we can use the situation that brings about migrations to test hypotheses and formulate laws of change. I think we must adopt this approach. Explanations must be our final goal.

NOTE

1. Parts of this paper were prepared with the assistance of a colleague, Dr. Fred T. Plog, University of California at Los Angeles.

Making Inferences
From the Present
to the Past

EDWARD P. DOZIER

Department of Anthropology,
University of Arizona

The following comments regarding inferences about the past from the present are offered entirely from the perspective of the ethnologist or social anthropologist. While I have in mind what I think the archaeologist wants to know to make his own inferences—not being an archaeologist I do not know if I have anticipated his needs correctly, nor even that I have provided useful information.

I assume at the outset that we are in accord with Dean's statement (pp. 143-44): "The most useful analogies in dealing with archaeologically observed results of patterned behavior are those made with functioning sociocultural systems or subsystems rather than with the units of which such systems are composed." In the light of this statement, the possible inferences I comment about are "systems" not "elements" or "traits," although the inferences may derive from a particular material item or items. An example might be: The discovery of a wall painting depicting a number of masked human figures in a room different from other rooms (in size, shape, and so forth) in a Southwestern village site would strongly suggest the existence of an esoteric men's organization. From this inference, increasingly less reliable inferences might be made, provided that we bear in mind the speculative nature of our inferences. In this latter category would come statements such as: (1) The paintings suggest a men's organization and so, by analogy to ethnologic Pueblos, a separation of the sexes at certain times of the year, (2) That particular prehistoric society has anxiety about the weather—again by analogy to ethnologic Pueblos, particularly to the western Pueblos where the kachina cult is the dominant ceremonial organization and where the environment is perhaps the most inhospitable for farmers. The inference in this case also assumes—again through analogy to ethnologic Pueblos—that an association (sodality) of masked ceremonial performers is involved with weather control—particularly the petition for rain.

In the examples above, it will be noted that the inferences are about "systems" rather than specific items. Also, it will be noted that the first statement has the most reliability; thereafter the statements tend to become more and more speculative. Or put in a different way: The more inclusive or grosser statement of analogy is the most obvious and, therefore, the most plausible. For example, there will probably be general agreement that compact, apartment-like village sites are correlated with highly structured social organizations. But, from this point on, more specific statements about the nature of the sociocultural organization—even though we are still concerned about patterned or system generalizations—have increasingly less reliability. The inferences I make in this paper—which are disappointingly few—will be of the kind I have indicated above.

In making inferences, we need to be guided by a number of premises.

First, it is important to have the temporal factor in mind. The shorter the time gap between a prehistoric site and the living[1] site, the more likely that the inference will be a reliable one (compare Dean, this volume).

Second, and this must be related to the first premise, the sociocultural level of the prehistoric and ethnologic group must be matched—at least roughly. For example, analogies between band-level societies and tribal ones may be made only with caution, as there is great disparity between such societies in terms of sociocultural organizations.

Third, the second premise above refers to a typology based on sociocultural integration; in addition it is important to compare societies having the same type of subsistence economy: hunting-gathering with hunting-gathering ones, agricultural with agricultural ones, and so forth.

Fourth, inferences about societies widely separated in space can be made only with extreme caution. For example, a Western African matrilineal clan is quite a different kind of an organization from a Hopi matrilineal clan. If an archaeologist infers the existence of matrilineal clans in a Southwestern site by evidence that he believes is convincing, inferences about the characteristics of that clan ought to be made by analogy to Hopi, Zuni, or Acoma pueblos rather than with analogy to the attributes of Western African clan organizations. This may seem to be an obviously ridiculous precautionary premise, but in recent years too much emphasis has been placed on shared correspondences across groups of the same level of sociocultural integration. While it is important to remember the importance of sociocultural integration levels represented in an area (see premise two), it is also advisable to know that classifications of this type are still in their infancy. The initial work on inferences with analogy to ethnologic groups should be restricted to contiguous areas where the history, prehistory, and distribution of sociocultural and linguistic groups are fairly well known.

Fifth, in making inferences, language affiliation should be given low priority. Two examples will suffice: Hano is typically Hopi in social organization (with minor differences), yet it speaks a language mutually intelligible with the Eastern Tewa whose society is quite different; the Navajo and Kiowa Apache illustrate a similar pair where language is close, but not the social systems. Therefore, it would be foolish to say, for example, that ceremonial moieties are a Tewa characteristic (not true of Hano) or that curing chants with dry paintings are an Apachean characteristic (not true of Kiowa Apache). These are examples from ethnologic groups but a lesson to archaeologists and historically minded anthropologists not to impute languages (either language families or stocks) to specific prehistoric sites or prehistoric regions.

The *sixth* and final premise: Some measure of how conservative the ethnologic culture has been over time should be established, insofar as possible. Such knowledge would give the anthropologist a basis of reliability for his inferences. The importance of this last premise may be illustrated by reference to the Pueblos on one hand and the Yaquis on the other (Spicer 1961; Chapters 2 and 3). I believe that the ethnologic

Making Inferences from the Present to the Past

Pueblos are better than the Yaquis as mirrors of the nature of the prehistoric social organizations in adjacent sites. This is because we have historical knowledge that the impact of Spanish rule did not modify the Pueblos as profoundly as the Yaquis. Descriptions of the Pueblos by Antonio de Espejo and Castaño de Sosa in 1582 and 1591, can be used with only slight changes to stand for valid comments on the Pueblos in 1900. Occasional statements where characteristics of Pueblo sociopolitical organizations are mentioned by these explorers and colonial officials indicate that the organizations typical of the Pueblos today were present then. It is unlikely that this conservatism is a phenomenon of the oppressive Spanish contact. The coercive techniques of Spanish cultural agents certainly brought about the patterns of reticence so typical of the Pueblos in discussing indigenous sociocultural organizations, but the conservatism of these Pueblos cannot be attributed to Spanish conquest and oppression. The same conservatism exists, for example, among the Hopi and Zuni Pueblo Indians who did not experience the forceful policies of Spanish civil and church authorities.

As a contrastive acculturative situation, the Yaqui absorbed an enormous amount of European-type social structures from Spanish cultural agents in the seventeenth century. Such structures may have combined with indigenous Yaqui patterns, but the amalgam is so thoroughly mixed that it is impossible to recognize the provenience of the items that make up the systems. What may have been indigenous institutions are impossible to trace—all Yaqui sociocultural systems have a European cast—more appropriately a medieval European aspect. It is highly unlikely that any of these organizations existed in the prehistoric past of the Yaqui. While Yaqui culture also became conservative later, obviously because of adverse historical circumstances, what was retained and guarded against change in succeeding centuries was the earlier amalgam achieved in the seventeenth century.

SOURCES OF INFORMATION ON THE EARLY HISTORY OF PUEBLO SOCIETY AND CULTURE

Rather reliable reports, both ethnological and historical, give us confidence in postulating what prehistoric Pueblo society and culture might have been like. We have good studies of the Pueblos going back almost a century. Such studies begin with Fewkes, the Mindeleffs, Stephen, and Voth among the Hopi, and Cushing with the Zuni. Unfortunately, no comparable work on the Keresan and Tanoan Pueblos was performed until Parsons began her investigations at Laguna Pueblo in 1916. Bandelier worked at Cochiti and other Rio Grande Pueblos in the early 1890s, but his reports are of a general nature; they are wanting in ethnographic detail. Parsons' work, covering a span of almost 25 years, is the most reliable and the most voluminous of Pueblo studies. Parsons' investigations and later those of Leslie White, Esther Goldfrank, Florence Hawley Ellis, and Charles Lange have given us most of our information about the Keresan Pueblos. Florence Hawley Ellis (Hawley 1950b; Ellis 1959) and Lange (1958) have presented the general features of Keresan Pueblo culture drawing from their own work and those of others. Among the Tanoans, Parsons' work is most extensive, although Harrington, Trager, and my own studies on the Tewa have contributed to the ethnographic literature. Still no single Pueblo community among the Keresan and Tanoan Pueblos has received the attention accorded the Hopi and Zuni Pueblos. We believe that the reason for this discrepancy in ethnographic coverage is historical. The western Pueblos have been most receptive to study, because being remote from Spanish colonial administration they did not suffer as much from Spanish oppression and have not developed the resistance patterns to White intruders so characteristic of the eastern Pueblos. Hopi society and culture have been studied by Lowie, Parsons, the Beagleholes, Titiev, Eggan, and many others; for Zuni a few among the many include Kroeber, Parsons, Bunzel, Benedict, and Li An-Che. It is apparent why the characteristics reported for Hopi and Zuni were indiscriminately considered "Pueblo" even though such traits may not have characterized other Pueblo communities.

In addition to the ethnographic literature, there are reliable descriptions of Pueblo life in early Spanish historical documents and somewhat less extensive materials from the Mexican and early American periods. The earliest reports are those of the "entradas" or exploring ventures from Coronado's expeditions, 1540-42, to that of de Sosa, 1591-92. Oñate's colonization of the Pueblo region in 1598 produced another series of reports describing the relations of the colonists and the Pueblos. Some of the most important of these sources are the following: *Revised Memorial of Alonzo de Benavides, 1634* (Hodge, Hammond, and Rey, eds. 1945); *Revolt of the Pueblo Indians of New Mexico and Otermin's Attempted*

Making Inferences from the Present to the Past

Reconquest 1680-82 (Hackett and Shelby 1942); *Bishop Tamaron's Visitation of New Mexico, 1790* (Adams, ed. 1954); and *The Missions of New Mexico, 1776* (Adams and Chavez, eds. 1956). An exemplary analysis of life in Spain's most northern province involving colonists and Pueblo Indians is contained in the works of Scholes (1930, 1935, 1942). Scholes' research and interpretation give a moving picture of the impact of Spanish civil and church policy on the Pueblos.

The early nineteenth century—the transition period from Spanish to Mexican rule—is comparatively meager in documentary sources. The reports of three prominent citizens of New Mexico during this period, however, give us a view of this troubled era. These are contained in *Three New Mexico Chronicles: The Exposición of Don Pedro Bautista Pino, 1812; the Ojeada of Lic. Antonio Barreiro, 1832; and the Additions of José Augustín de Escudero, 1849* (Carroll and Haggard 1942).

For the early American period a number of accounts by early frontiersmen and traders give us glimpses of Pueblo Indian life. Those of Josiah Gregg (Thwaites 1905) and Davis (1938) have the most information about the Pueblos. During the second half of the nineteenth century, the writings of Bancroft (1889) and John C. Bourke's journal (Bloom 1935-38) of his travels among the Pueblos, give us a good grasp of the externals of Pueblo life. Bourke's journal contains rather detailed information about Pueblo architecture and the daily life of the Indians.

OUTLINE OF PUEBLO SOCIAL ORGANIZATION

This section provides an outline of Pueblo social organization which any anthropologist interested in making inferences about the characteristic social and cultural features of Pueblo culture must bear in mind.

The social organization of the western Pueblos, that is, of Hopi, Zuni, Hano, Acoma, and Laguna, has been sketched by Eggan in admirable fashion.

> ... [The western Pueblo] type of social structure is characterized by a kinship system of "Crow type" organized in terms of the lineage principle; a household organization based on the lineage and clan and, in some cases, the phratry group; an associational structure organized around the ceremony and its symbols, with relationships to lineage, clan, and household; and a theocratic system of social control.

There is a further relationship of the social system to the world of nature through the extension of social patterns to natural phenomena (Eggan 1950: 291).

Most Hopi and Zuni ceremonies involve the men's kachina organization—each kiva has a troop.

With the Jemez Pueblo excepted, the Tanoan-speaking Pueblos in the northern Rio Grande Valley have a social organization of quite another type. Despite considerable minor variations among specific Pueblos, the social system of all Tanoan Pueblos is similar. Its kinship system is of the bilateral type—the terms are descriptive and arranged bilaterally. The household or residence unit is either of the nuclear type or else extended to include two or three older relatives on one or both sides of the parents. Beyond the residence unit is a bilaterally extended unit—a bilateral descent group. The unit was important, especially in the past, in group tasks such as planting, harvesting, and so forth. Other related structures include three types of sodalities or associations: (1) those with governmental and religious functions associated with the dual divisions (called moieties in the ethnographic literature), (2) medicine associations embodying curing and exorcising practices, and (3) associations with special functions, such as those for war, hunting, and clowning. In addition, Tanoan village communities have a kachina cult or some vestige of an organization concerned with supernatural beings vaguely connected with ancestral spirits common among all other Pueblos. None of these related structures are kinship units. Moiety membership is required of all, ar moiety affiliation is usually with the father's moiety but may be changed a marriage or for other reasons. Kachina membership is village-wide for men, and membership is confirmed by invitation at the time of puberty. Medicine and special-function associations are voluntary but are most often joined to rid oneself of an illness.

The eastern Keresan and Jemez, on the other hand, exhibit affinity to a social structure of the general western Pueblo type described above. Terms are classificatory, but the patterns of organization vary in some Keresan villages between an old system fitted to a lineage principle (White 1942: 159; Eggan 1950: 207-08; Mickey 1956) and one where usages are arranged on a "bilateral" pattern. The three types of sodalities or associations related above are present as well, although there is a greater number of medicine associations. Curing appears to receive greater emphasis among Keresans, while among Tanoans warfare and hunting associations are correspondingly stressed. The clan is weak in functions among the Keresans as compared to the western Pueblos, being relegated mainly to marriage control. But some Pueblos indicate what may have been formerly more characteristic of the clan's role in Keresan society. In Zia, for example, the village chief comes from a specific clan. In Zia, also, clans conduct initiation ceremonies, and the leaders of certain religious societies come from specific clans (Hawley 1950b: 506-07).

POINTS ABOUT MAKING INFERENCES CONCERNING PREHISTORIC PUEBLO SOCIAL ORGANIZATION

The kinds of social structures found among the Pueblos today appear to be extremely old. Since conditions of life did not drastically change until recently, the Pueblos would appear to mirror the past rather well. The moves from subsistence farming to a credit system and then to a cash economy with wage work all came about in the second and third decades of this century. Hence the old social structures were still functioning when the basic ethnographic studies of the Pueblos were made. It is not out of order, therefore, to suggest that probably all of the structures now found in the Pueblos existed in prehistoric times. Even factional disputes and migrations and the kinds of social structures which ensue from such disruptions of Pueblo life can by analogy be inferred from the ethnologic Pueblos. Schwartz's paper in this volume on the postmigration culture is timely and relevant to processes evident in the ethnological literature of the Pueblos.

If the kinds of social structures found in living Pueblos were present in prehistoric times, the important problem is how to establish with reasonable certainty the presence of one type of social structure as against a number of other possible ones in a given site. The discovery of ceremonial buildings, that is, architectural structures used for purposes other than food storage or residence, is important. But here we have a wide range of inferences to make about the kinds of social structures that might be associated with them.

Kiva-like buildings are perhaps the most common type of nondwelling structures found in prehistoric Pueblo sites. In the archaeological literature, I believe kivas are most often associated with esoteric and secret ceremonial rites. The functions of the kiva among historic Pueblos does not quite fit this characterization. In the recent past and at present, the kiva was, and is, a kind of theatre open to the entire pueblo and to Indian visitors as well. At other times, the kiva functioned as a dormitory for single men, widowers, or men separated from their wives. Or, during the day, especially in winter, it operated as a workshop. There is no reason to assume that the kiva was used in a different fashion in the past. This knowledge is important in making inferences. Kivas might tell us about a men's organization, dramatic performances given for a lay public, and the existence of certain types of crafts manufactured by men, but they are not likely to reveal evidences of associations (sodalities) or clans (lineages), as the religious activities associated with these structures are carried on and housed in rooms within the residential house-blocks—at least among the historic Pueblos.

A dual (moiety) kiva system (as among the Rio Grande Keresan Pueblos) does not necessarily indicate a strong dual division system. For example, dual oppositions permeate the whole societal makeup of the Tewa Pueblos, yet they do not have a two-kiva system. A single large kiva as a sociopolitical integrator of a village does seem to hold up by analogy to the ethnologic Tewa Pueblos, however. Each of the governmental-ceremonial moieties has a smaller building within the block of residential houses where the ceremonial paraphernalia is kept, but for pueblo-wide activities, the large single kiva is used by both moieties. The idea also seems sound that in prehistoric times the large kiva may have acted similarly to integrate multivillage units. Apparently, none of the ethnologic Pueblos (after the prehistoric Classic Pueblo period) reached a point of sociocultural complexity to attempt sociopolitical integration on a multivillage basis. Vivian's paper is provocative for inferences about larger political integration—that is beyond the village level. The study of irrigation canals, their pattern of distribution, and their possible use can be a way of revealing multivillage cooperation and the inference of a larger sociopolitical integration.

How about the identity and distinction of kinship structures from non-kinship units in prehistoric sites? The nuclear family is probably the easiest unit to identify, but since the unit is universal, information about its existence in prehistoric sites is of little value. Were it possible to ascertain that it is a *basic* social unit, then such information would be valuable. But nowhere among the ethnologic Pueblos is the nuclear family unit an isolated structure; it is always a part of a larger extended family or perhaps part of a larger localized unit, such as a lineage or a bilateral descent group. Some kinship unit larger than the nuclear family, in all likelihood, was also the case among the prehistoric sedentary Pueblos. Unless we can find scattered settlement patterns of small one-room units, I cannot believe that the prehistoric Pueblos lived in independent units smaller than the extended family. Some evidence is afforded this belief by Lipe's work among the Anasazi groups of the Red Rock Plateau (Utah) reported in this volume. Lipe contends that the extended family-based household of the western Pueblo type was maintained throughout the period of occupation among this group of dispersed sedentary agriculturalists.

Our problem is to recognize the larger kinship extensions (beyond the nuclear family) and then to distinguish them from nonkinship sodalities or associations. Kinship units among the ethnological Pueblos are matrilineally structured extended families, lineages, clans, and phratries, and bilaterally structured extended families and descent groups. The "moiety" is not a kinship grouping among the Tewa Pueblos; it simply divides the population of the Pueblo in half for various purposes, primarily ceremonial and recreational.

There are other dual divisions among the Tewa, dividing the population in a different way and resulting in different kinds of membership. While a child initially joins the moiety organizations of his father, membership may be changed at will later on. The dual divisions of the Tewa, therefore, are not kinship groupings. The most important dual division organization involved in supervising governmental and ceremonial activities is also referred to in the literature as a "moiety." These are the moieties dividing the population into "Summer" and "Winter" people, with a chief priest presiding over each moiety (his position is for life). There are other dual divisions for relay races, warfare, and shinny games. In addition, there is a north-south division of a Pueblo for other types of ceremonial events. Within each of the governmental-ceremonial moieties is a sodality or association with a small membership; it is from this group that the governmental-ceremonial priest or "cacique" is selected, one for each moiety.

In addition to the governmental-ceremonial associations or sodalities, the Tewa (and most of the Pueblos) have nonkinship associations for various specific functions, such as war, curing, hunting, clowning, and the like.

A clan (more properly a clan segment or lineage) within each western Pueblo village has a woman head, but her brother, nephew, or some other close male clan relative performs the actual ritual activities. The lineage has a room where the clan's ceremonial paraphernalia is stored and where on ritual occasions the male head erects his altar, displaying in the altar the ceremonial possessions of the clan. The altar varies in size, but is usually two or three feet square and is sometimes defined by a line of white corn meal. Within the altar are a variety of objects. In some altars a kind of lattice work of boards (slat altar) is placed in back. The floor of the altar contains odd-shaped figurines, pottery vessels, and the like. Centrally located in the array of items is the clan fetish (Hopi wuya), an ear of corn wrapped in feathers and tied with a piece of woven cotton cloth or cord. Since clans "own" or are in charge of nonkinship associations among the western Pueblos, the clan paraphernalia and altar also represent the association, although on the occasion of a ritual given by a specific association the special wuya of that association may occupy the prominent position within the altar.

Among the eastern Keresans and the Tanoans, the head of an association has a similar collection of ceremonial paraphernalia. This collection is stored in a special room, usually a back room, in the home of the head association member. While there is considerable variation in the appearance of clan and association altars and in the items displayed, they have a general resemblance. It would be impossible, therefore, to distinguish a clan or association altar even among the living Pueblos. Unless other information is available, it would be impossible to predict in a given site from altar paraphernalia alone whether the site represents a pueblo organized along unilineal kinship structures or in terms of nonkinship units.

Other approaches to the determination of kinship versus nonkinship units and unilineal versus nonunilineal organization of kin may be more appropriate. Hill's statement (p. 13) that most of our inferences about prehistoric social organization are hypotheses rather than tested demonstrations is well taken. We need more studies of the kind pioneered by Deetz (1965), Hill (1970), and Longacre (1964a). Analysis of pottery remains and other evidence of craft work in archaeological sites combined with the social structures of adjacent ethnological groups are important in giving us a more realistic picture of the nature of prehistoric social organization for specific sites.

Making Inferences from the Present to the Past

NOTE

1. More properly "ethnologic site"—a historical group for which a good descriptive study exists, although the group may no longer exist as a viable, functioning society. For variety I have used "living" and "ethnologic" group or site interchangeably in this paper.

Comments

DAVID F. ABERLE

Department of Sociology and Anthropology,
University of British Columbia

An ethnologist who is asked in a short period of time to comment on two archaeological symposia (Aberle 1968: 353-59) may be entitled to wonder whether he is regarded as a soft touch for amiable remarks. I shall begin with a few and then provide some critical comments.

These papers are remarkable for their freshness and vigor. Their range of interests—in economic, political, and kinship systems; in change and migration; in ecological determinants of community location and patterns of resource exploitation; and in ecological change and its effects on Pueblo migration and community integration—commends them to ethnologists with ecological and evolutionary orientations. Underlying all of them is evidence that the writers have in mind a new synthesis of Pueblo prehistory, although that is not yet at hand. The effort to formulate hypotheses for exploration, and where possible to gather the data for testing them, also makes them of unusual interest. It is pleasant to think that the future will bring more work of this quality.

Comments

Nevertheless, there are a few problems. If I pass over the papers of Longacre, Lipe, and Vivian without comment, it is not for lack of appreciation of their qualities, but because there are no specific points that provoke criticism. If the other papers are criticized, the disagreements are not crucial to their main thrust, with which I agree.

The first problem in Hill's paper lies in his use of the term "theory." He has written one of a number of statements by the "new archaeologists" in which strong views are expressed about the importance of theory, and in which Hempel and other philosophers of science are quoted or cited to justify the methodological approach they propose. Anthropologists, including me (Aberle 1960, 1968: 353n.), use the term "theory" very loosely. We will undoubtedly continue to use the term loosely. But once the philosophers of science are brought in, those who do so must abide by the consequences.

As I understand Hempel, a theory is a proposition or a set of propositions that links several empirical (experimental) laws and explains their regularities and that ordinarily provides predictions or "postdictions" of additional regularities not contained in the original empirical laws (Hempel 1966: 70-75; Nagel 1961: especially 79-105 seems to take a similar position). There are few, if any, empirical laws in anthropology; that is, general propositions that state regular relationships between phenomena with sufficient precision to predict the behavior of previously unexamined instances of these classes of phenomena. Finding few in anthropology in general, I am not surprised to find that Hill's paper contains no empirical laws. But if there are no laws to be linked by theory, then there can be no theory. Hence it is premature is most areas of anthropology to call for theory.

Instead, when Hill speaks of theory, it would be better to use words like "hypothesis" in some cases and "assumption" in others. The change would not affect his argument, but it would result in more modest claims for anthropology in general and archaeology specifically. This is fitting in a field with so little in the way of empirical laws as anthropology.

Hill's drift from Hempel's use of "theory" toward the everyday use of the term is evident in the two "theoretical tenets" that he advances (both of which would appear to me to be better termed as "assumptions": (1) "cultures are complex behavioral systems," and (2) "cultural systems (including social organization) are *adaptive*." These are assumptions that I accept, but I cannot think of the empirical laws that have been united by either of these propositions. Hence they seem to be assumptions, since they are not theories (for reasons just stated), hypotheses (because there seems no way to disprove them), or laws (because they do not state relationships between variables).

Quarreling about labels is usually not too fruitful; yet Hill's use of the term "normative theory" seems to me to raise a second problem with his paper. The label appears to have been first used by Binford (1965) as a compact way of designating a series of polemical targets. "Normative theory" for Binford includes views that assume that culture is best viewed as a set of norms, rather than viewing it as including material elements, as an energy-harnessing device, and as having a systemic character. The label is also used for a view of culture as "shared behavior" as contrasted with a view that has regard for the variability inherent in the very operation of cultural systems. Finally, and perhaps here I misunderstand Hill in his interpretation of the term "normative theory," the label seems to be used for views that norms are important. He says:

> Analyses of social organization require attention to intrasite and intra-region variability, and a concern for this does not follow from the premise that culture consists of shared ideas and behavior. This kind of "normative" view simply obscures the fact that there are a large number of *different* groups and statuses within a society, and the people involved in them are often *not* participating in the same kinds of behavior. . . . Artifacts do not necessarily represent norms or shared ideas; they represent functional contexts in society—activities and social segments (p. 18).

It would seem best to separate the various strands of argument that have been united by the term "normative theory." For what Hill needs to claim is less than he seems to claim. The essential features of his argument are as follows: (1) culture is systemic; (2) it is an energy-harnessing system that articulates a human population with its environment; (3) by virtue of the nature of the productive activities and the social organization of production, there will be nonrandom variation within settlements as a result of (a) different practices in different family or larger kinship groupings, (b) differential locus of various activities, (c) status differentiation, if any, and (d) other reasons; (4) in an archaeological site, these differences appear in nonrandom variability of artifacts, styles, leavings, and so forth. So, (5) it is insufficient for purposes of archaeological analysis to "type" a site and let it go at that.

Comments

The further issue suggested by the label, however, is a fight about norms, which can proliferate disputes endlessly: do people "have" norms, is culture "made up of" norms, do norms "determine" behavior, and so on. Hill's nonrandom variation can often be interpreted as representing the "tradition" of some family group in a community—in other words, as having a normative element. Spaulding's approach to artifact typing suggests that he views the results of typological work by statistical methods as discovering norms: he speaks of attributes as "minimal units of meaningful behavior" (1960: 442) and apparently regards a high degree of attribute clustering as equivalent to what is often called "rigidly stylized" (1960: 445). To move, then, from treating the site as homogeneous to treating it as heterogeneous is not to move from norms to no norms, but from broader to narrower norms. This statement leaves completely open the question whether norms "govern" behavior. It says only that prehistoric peoples had norms, in which respect they resemble us. So there would be advantages in finding some phrase other than "normative theory" to fight the battle of intrasite variability.

The third problem raised by Hill's paper is the issue of ethnographic analogies. He says:

> The number of testable propositions that can be generated and tested is almost infinite, and it should be possible to expand our knowledge of prehistoric social organization almost indefinitely. This expansion of knowledge will not *depend* on ethnographic information, even though such information is the most immediate and useful source of ideas for generating propositions. . . . Those methodological approaches regarding ethnographic analogies as *answers* should be abandoned (p. 27; italics are Hill's).

If by this Hill means that no simple and mechanical reading back from specific cultures as totalities to specific sites is advisable, there can be no objection to this. Thus, if we find that Hopi sodalities contain people from several clans who meet in one kiva, we would be ill-advised to assume that past kivas are necessarily the sites of sodalities with multiclan membership. (Dean's paper is very cautious on this score.) If Hill means that one should not use simple analogy without asking what further evidence would justify the application of the analogy, this also seems a reasonable position (see Binford 1967a). But the general dependence of archaeology on ethnological data seems obvious.

In fact, the remainder of Hill's paper and certain sections of Dean's,

Lipe's, Schwartz's, and Vivian's show the archaeologist's dependence on the ethnographic record. Furthermore, they show that the archaeologist's work could be greatly improved if the ethnographic record were better and that he is dependent on his understanding of live cultures, an understanding mediated by his particular version of ethnological "theory." His work will run into difficulties where he lacks our ethnographic observations, and it will run into further difficulties if his grasp of modern ethnological approaches is defective, if he selects inappropriate approaches, or if those approaches are, as sadly is often the case, themselves defective.

Indeed, Hill points out that if ethnographers had done more work on the material correlates of social organization, the archaeologists would be better off.

Dean's very interesting paper seems to me to run into minor difficulties because he is overconcerned about whether clans and lineages are dispersed or localized. This concern seems to spring directly from his close attention to the principal ethnographers of the Hopi, who, it seems to me, have led him a little astray. Both Eggan (1950) and Titiev (1944) use the term "clan" to refer both to the organized members of a named, exogamic, stipulated descent group in a particular village and to the members of a named, exogamic, stipulated descent category spread over several villages, which is not organized. More to the point, in a given village the members of a particular clan have a male head and a female head, a clan house, a fetish (or several), and sometimes a kiva and the control of offices in a particular ceremonial sodality. They regard themselves as related to members of other units with the same name in other villages. At this point, let me introduce my own terminology and call the local unit a *subclan* and the overall, unorganized category a *clan*. A subclan is composed of one or more lineages, and the women of these lineages are to be found residing in one or more households in a given village. The households of a lineage, if there are two or more, and the households of the women of a subclan may be dispersed within the village or localized (to judge from Titiev 1944: 50, 54).

The clans are united in phratries, which are exogamous, unorganized, stipulated categories. I say "the clans" rather than "the subclans," because the phratry plan is uniform for the various Hopi villages, even though no one village has all the known clans represented among its subclans. Within a village the subclans of a phratry are regarded as symbolically united or complementary but may in fact be rivalrous (see Titiev 1944).

Comments

Eggan and Titiev, like Steward (1955), Murdock (1949), Driver (1956), Gough (1961), and Aberle (1961), among others, are inclined to see matrilocal residence as the seedbed of matrilineal descent groups, and to see local descent groups (lineages or groups like today's subclans) preceding the development of dispersed clans cutting across a number of communities. This has driven Dean to a concern to discover the point at which localized descent groups gave way to dispersed ones. He does not seem to allow sufficiently for the possibility that one can have both: a localized segment of a clan making up a community or a segment of a community, *and* a dispersed descent group uniting members of several communities as well. Furthermore, he seems to follow Eggan, who follows Steward, in assuming that the dispersed clan was a late arrival among the ancestors of the Hopi.

Yet once unilocal residence has given rise to a dogma of descent, that dogma can be used for two different purposes: to unite individuals *within* a local organized unit for such purposes as cooperation, corporate resource control, and ritual, or to unite members of *different* local units. In a kinship-based society with no authority above the community level, hospitality and protection are exceedingly important. They are afforded in the ordinary case by clanship. One can find societies, indeed, where common clanship is far more important as a basis for *intercommunity* relationships than is common subclanship as a basis for *intracommunity* organization. (Goodenough [1963] has suggested ways in which clans might arise *without* matrilocal residence, but here we will assume the priority of matrilocal residence.)

How does this relate to Dean's construction? In the Kayenta area, agriculture became important in late Basketmaker III, in the ninth century A.D., and "monolineage communities" emerge during Pueblo I, in the tenth to twelfth centuries. "If ever the ancestral Hopi household, lineage, and clan were coterminous and localized, it was during this period," says Dean (p. 149). It is reasonable, however, to suggest an emendation of his phrasing: "If ever the ancestral Hopi household, lineage, and *subclan* were coterminous and localized, it was during this period." One would expect, that is, that a nonlocalized clan would either have emerged at an earlier period (quite possibly along with subclans or shortly after localized clans), or that it did so now. It is not possible for me to guess when such a dispersed unit may have emerged, but I would expect it to emerge very rapidly once there was a dogma of descent because of its utility for intercommunity relationships. I am strengthened in this view by the observation that the clan names among the Keresans, the Zuni, and the Hopi have many parallels and some differences (see Eggan 1950). Equations of this sort, common in many parts of the world, ordinarily permit cross-ethnic hospitality to be extended and to serve as devices for protection and trade. The differences among these systems suggest either a long period of mutual accommodation of different systems, or the early diffusion of a common system with subsequent differentiation. (Clan names can spread, but they don't always, and kinship forms can diffuse in kinship-based societies, [with due respect to Murdock].)

Given a dispersed clan, a monolineage community moving as a unit could establish relations with neighboring units by affinity or consanguinity, and a multilineage community could integrate new subclans or integrate into its existing subclans new extended or nuclear families. This position is consistent with Eggan's view that newcomers among the Hopi "arrived as communities or fragments of communities such as household groups. . ." (Eggan 1950: 130). It is even consistent with Eggan's statement that they did not arrive "as lineages and clans as such" (ibid.), but I would argue that the clan in my sense would never "arrive" as such, being a dispersed unit. As for "lineages" arriving as such, I am not sure what Eggan had in mind. A lineage composed of men and women matrilineally affiliated and with a matrilocal form of residence cannot be a unit of movement, nor can a subclan. Only if a whole community moves can its lineages move as such; it is true, of course, that the movement of two or more households *might* result in *some* lineages moving more or less intact, but not moving as such. This would be more likely if households, lineages, or subclans practiced cross-cousin marriage, which is assumed for the ancestors of the Hopi or the Hopi themselves in the past (cf. Eggan 1950: 121; Titiev 1938).

The reasons for not imputing dispersed clans to the ancestors of the Hopi during or before the Tsegi phase, whether by Eggan, by Steward, or by Dean are not clear to me. Dean says that Eggan believes that "lineage and clan organization were not highly developed among Kayenta Branch peoples until they arrived in the Hopi area in the fourteenth century. . ." (p. 164). I find Eggan not so explicit as this (cf. 1950: 130), but Dean's is a reasonable interpretation of Eggan's meaning. What has happened, however, is that Steward used archaeology and ethnology to arrive at a reconstruction of Pueblo prehistory; Eggan accepted it and applied it to the

Comments

Hopi; and now Dean accepts it and applies it backward once again to the Tsegi phase. All of them, in my opinion, have confounded two issues: a relatively tightly organized subclan and the date of its emergence, and a dispersed, unorganized clan and the date of its emergence.

It is conceivable that the dispersed clan was quite early, and that within such a dispersed clan system, the subclan in various areas went through various phases and even cycles: monolineage communities; small, localized units within a village; larger, dispersed units within a village; and so forth, with, for various reasons, relatively tight and relatively loose organization of the subclan.

While there is no reason to place much weight on my reconstruction (particularly since dispersed clans may well not have archaeological correlates), there is also no reason to base one's approach on a reconstruction that puts the clan system so late, because dispersed clans are a widepread phenomenon and one not dependent on a high level of productivity.

This points to a relatively trivial revision of Dean's statement: "Since these processes of integration [of households] already seem to be in operation by the beginning of the Tsegi Phase, I would go so far as to propose that nonlocalized lineage and clan organization may have developed during that virtually unknown period between 1150 and 1250, after the breakdown of the independent habitation unit communities" (p. 164). I would change this to read, "nonlocalized clan organization must have existed by the time Betatakin and Kiet Siel were built and may well have existed for a considerable period before that time."

My point is that the shift from "monolineage communities" to larger ones and the pattern of clusters and sequence of building in these ruins strongly suggests the existence of dispersed clans at this time (with subclans being constituted within each community, in all probability), but the presence of "monolineage communities" cannot be used to infer the absence of dispersed clans.

This brings us, finally, to the problem of the monolineage community itself. Its plan, with a kiva in each habitation unit, does suggest a fairly highly structured local group. If we assume that this is a patrilocal unit with no dogma of descent or a patrilineal one, no particular problem arises. If, however, we assume that it is matrilocal, there are problems. Schneider has said, "Isolated communities (or smaller groups) consisting of matrilineal core and in-marrying spouses are extremely difficult to maintain" (1961: 27; italics omitted). The reasons for this have to do with the ties between the men and the women of a matrilineal descent group (ibid.). I have found statistical support for this proposition (Aberle 1961: 715-16). Matrilineal, matrilocal systems can operate most easily either in communities composed of more than one descent group or in monolineage communities that are very close together (for example, the Yao; Mitchell 1951, 1956: esp. 143-44, and Gough 1961: 559-60). It would be worthwhile to know the distances between the habitation units of the Pueblo I period of the Tsegi Phase.

The "monolineage community" raises the problem of the dispersed clan again. It is easy to conceive of a culture with a matrilocal bias and no dogma of descent forming small communities. (We are assuming matrilocality; evidence for the assumption is not at hand.) But a well-structured community of relatively fixed plan, with a kiva, does, as Dean says, suggest a fairly organized group. If a group with a matrilocal bias (or rule of residence) and with these features of local organization is found, it seems reasonable to impute a dogma of descent. And it seems quite possible that such units did have a subclan-fetish-kiva complex, extrapolating backward from Hopi. But how likely is it that every such unit constituted a distinct and separate unilineal descent group, unaffiliated by dispersed clan ties with other like units? I suggest that it is very likely that if these units were matrilocal, they already had a dispersed clan system as well as a subclan identical with the habitation unit.

All of this is highly hypothetical, but then, so is much of Dean's, Eggan's, and Steward's reconstruction. Mine, however, would take advantage of evidence that a great many societies follow a ground plan that includes both dispersed, unorganized and localized, organized units in a clan system; a reconstruction should not ignore this possibility.

With respect to Schwartz's paper, the principal problem seems to be the analogy between the kinds of communities he has examined ethnologically and the community he wishes to examine archaeologically. By and large, he has studied communities in complex societies, the causes of whose movements and the nature of whose external relations before and after the move stem at least in part from the relationships of those communities to the complex societies in which they are embedded. This applies, unless I am mistaken, even to the Tikopians and Marshallese, whose relocation was carried out by their administrators, though with their consent, and whose subsequent relations with new populations was conditioned by the fact that all parties were administered peoples. The result seems to me to involve the confounding of two kinds of variables: those that result from the material facts of pioneering and those that result from external social relationships. If a group of people found a new community where there was none before, they will necessarily spend a good deal of their initial time and energy in building the community. Otherwise, they will be forced to leave, or they will die. This applies alike to Puebloans and Hutterites. If a group of people form an isolated community of Puebloans, in minimal contact with non-Puebloans, they do not, however, have the same kind of problem in external relations that the people of Hotevilla and Bakabi had earlier in the twentieth century or that Hutterites have today. Various features of religious emphasis, factionalism, and so forth, seem to stem from external relations, in part, in the cases Schwartz has studied. If the effects of pioneering and the effects of external relations are not separated, one would expect that he might have some difficulty in formulating adequate hypotheses, in validating those he formulated, or in accounting for failures of validation.

Most of these matters, however, are minor, reparable in most instances by changes of phrasing. These papers manage an extraordinarily fine-grained analysis and provide unusually interesting reconstructions, even if a good deal needs to be done to confirm a number of details. The papers reveal a potential, partly already realized, for understanding the historical transformation of a series of culture types adapting to a changing environment over time. Such an understanding should enormously increase our knowledge about Southwestern culture in particular and cultural processes in general. Ethnology normally works with short spans of time: a visit of a summer, 1 year, or 2 years; a restudy after 10, 20, or 30 years. Ethnohistory begins to produce spans of a few hundred years. The proposed methods, attached to the problems these archaeologists are interested in, provide us with analyses of sequences of more than 2000 years of Puebloan history. And archaeology will always have one strength that ethnology lacks: the ability to study change over long periods of time. The future for such studies looks bright.

References

ABERLE, DAVID F.
1960   "The Influences of Linguistics on Early Culture and Personality Theory," *Essays in the Science of Culture in Honor of Leslie A. White*, ed. by Gertrude Dole and Robert L. Carneiro (New York: Thomas Y. Crowell Company), pp. 1-29.
1961   "Matrilineal Descent in Cross-Cultural Perspective," *Matrilineal Kinship*, ed. by David M. Schneider and Kathleen Gough (Berkeley and Los Angeles: University of California Press), pp. 655-727.
1968   "Comments," *New Perspectives in Archaeology*, ed. by S. R. Binford and L. R. Binford (Chicago: Aldine Publishing Company), pp. 353-59.

ADAMS, ELEANOR B. (ed.)
1954   *Bishop Tamaron's Visitation of New Mexico, 1760*, Historical Society of New Mexico, Publications in History, vol. 15. (Albuquerque: University of New Mexico Press).

ADAMS, ELEANOR AND FRAY ANGELICO CHAVEZ (eds.)
1956   *The Missions of New Mexico, 1776* (Albuquerque: University of New Mexico Press).

ADAMS, WILLIAM Y. AND NETTIE K. ADAMS
1959   *An Inventory of Prehistoric Sites on the Lower San Juan River, Utah*, Museum of Northern Arizona Bulletin, no. 31 (Flagstaff: the museum).

AIKENS, C. MELVIN
1966a   *Virgin-Kayenta Cultural Relationships*, University of Utah Anthropological Papers, no. 79 (Salt Lake City: University of Utah Press).
1966b   *Fremont-Promentory-Plains Relationships in Northern Utah*, University of Utah Anthropological Papers, no. 82 (Salt Lake City: University of Utah Press).

AMBLER, J. RICHARD, ALEXANDER J. LINDSAY, JR., AND MARY ANNE STEIN
1964   *Survey and Excavations on Cummings Mesa, Arizona and Utah, 1960-1961*, Museum of Northern Arizona Bulletin, no. 39, Glen Canyon Series, no. 5 (Flagstaff: the museum).

ANDERSON, KEITH M.
1966   "Tsegi Phase Technology: A Test Case for Intraphase Culture Process," paper presented at the 31st Annual Meeting of the Society for American Archaeology, Reno, Nev.

ARENSBERG, CONRAD
1961 "The Community as Object and as Sample," *American Anthropologist*, vol. 63, pp. 241-64.

ASCHER, ROBERT
1961 "Analogy in Archaeological Interpretation," *Southwestern Journal of Anthropology*, vol. 17, pp. 317-25.

AUGUELLI, JOHN P.
1958 "The Latvians of Varpa," *Geographical Review*, vol. 48, pp. 365-87.

BAERREIS, D. A. AND R. A. BRYSON
1965 "Climatic Episodes and the Dating of Mississippian Cultures," *The Wisconsin Archeologist*, vol. 46, pp. 206-20.

BANCROFT, H. H.
1889 *The Works of Hubert Howe Bancroft, History of Arizona and New Mexico 1530-1888*, vol. 17 (San Francisco: The History Company).

BANDELIER, ADOLF F.
1881 *Report of the Ruins of the Pueblo of Pecos, Papers of the Archaeological Institute of America, American Series*, vol. 1, no. 2. (Boston: A. Williams and Company).
1892 *Final Report of Investigations among the Indians of the Southwestern United States, Carried out Mainly in the Years from 1880 to 1885*, part II, *Papers of the Archaeological Institute of America, American Series IV*, (Cambridge: John Wilson and Son, University Press).

BANNISTER, BRYANT
1966 "Tree-Ring Dating of the Archaeological Sites in the Chaco Canyon Region, New Mexico," *Southwestern Monuments Association, Technical Series*, vol. 6, part II (Globe, Ariz.: the association), pp. 116-201.

BEAGLEHOLE, E., AND PEARL BEAGLEHOLE
1935 *Hopi of the Second Mesa, American Anthropological Association Memoir*, no. 44. (Menasha, Wis.: the association).

BEALS, RALPH L., GEORGE W. BRAINERD, AND WATSON SMITH
1945 *Archaeological Studies in Northeast Arizona, University of California Publications in American Archaeology and Ethnology*, vol. 44, no. 1 (Berkeley and Los Angeles: University of California Press).

BENEDICT, RUTH
1935 *Zuni Mythology*, two vols. (New York: Columbia University Press).

BINFORD, LEWIS R.
1962 "Archaeology as Anthropology," *American Antiquity*, vol. 28, no. 2, pp. 217-25.
1964 "A Consideration of Archaeological Research Design," *American Antiquity*, vol. 29, no. 4, pp. 425-41.
1965 "Archaeological Systematics and the Study of Culture Process," *American Antiquity*, vol. 31, no. 2, part 1, pp. 203-10.
1967a "Smudge Pits and Hide Smoking: The Use of Analogy in Archaeological Reasoning," *American Antiquity*, vol. 32, no. 1, pp. 1-12.
1967b "Methodological Considerations of the Archaeological Use of Ethnographic Data," *Man the Hunter: Proceedings of a Symposium Sponsored by the Wenner-Gren Foundation for Anthropological Research*, ed. by Richard B. Lee and Irven DeVore (Chicago: Aldine Publishing Company), pp. 268-73.

References

1968   "Archeological Perspectives," *New Perspectives in Archeology*, ed. by S. R. Binford and L. R. Binford (Chicago: Aldine Publishing Company), pp. 5-32.

BINFORD, LEWIS R. AND S. R. BINFORD
1966   "A Preliminary Analysis of Functional Variability in the Mousterian of Levallois Facies," *Recent Studies in Paleoanthropology*, American Anthropologist, vol. 68, no. 2, part 2, pp. 238-95.

BINFORD, S. R. AND L. R. BINFORD (eds.)
1968   *New Perspectives in Archeology* (Chicago: Aldine Publishing Company).

BLOOM, L. B.
1935-38   "Bourke on the Southwest," *New Mexico Historical Review*, vol. 10, pp. 271-322; vol. 11, pp. 217-82; vol. 12, pp. 41-77; vol. 13, pp. 192-238.

BLUHM, ELAINE A.
1957   "Patterns of Settlement in the Southwestern United States, A.D. 500-1250," unpublished doctoral dissertation, Department of Anthropology, University of Chicago.
1960   "Mogollon Settlement Patterns in Pine Lawn Valley, New Mexico," *American Antiquity*, vol. 25, no. 4, pp. 538-46.

BRANDES, RAY
1960   "Archaeological Awareness of the Southwest as Illustrated in Literature to 1890," *Arizona and the West*, vol. 2, no. 1, pp. 6-25.

BRETERNITZ, DAVID A.
1957a   "1956 Excavations Near Flagstaff," part I, *Plateau*, vol. 30, no. 1, pp. 22-30.
1957b   "1956 Excavations near Flagstaff," part II, *Plateau*, vol. 30, no. 2, pp. 43-54.

BREW, JOHN OTIS
1946   "The Use and Abuse of Taxonomy," *Archaeology of Alkali Ridge, Southeastern Utah, Papers of the Peabody Museum of American Archaeology and Ethnology, Harvard University*, vol. 21 (Cambridge: the museum), pp. 44-66.

BULLARD, WILLIAM ROTCH, JR.
1962   *The Cerro Colorado Site and Pithouse Architecture in the Southwestern United States Prior to A.D. 900, Papers of the Peabody Museum of American Archaeology and Ethnology, Harvard University*, vol. 44, no. 2 (Cambridge: the museum).

BUNZEL, RUTH L.
1929   *The Pueblo Potter: A Study of Creative Imagination in Primitive Art* (New York: Columbia University Press).
1932   "Introduction to Zuni Ceremonialism," *Bureau of American Ethnology Annual Report*, no. 47 (Washington, D.C.: U.S. Government Printing Office). pp. 467-544.

CARROL, H. BAILEY AND J. V. HAGGARD
1942   *Three New Mexico Chronicles: The Exposición of Don Pedro Bautista Pino, 1812; the Ojeada of Lic. Antonio Barreiro, 1832; and the additions of José Augustín de Escudero, 1849* (Albuquerque: The Quivera Society).

CHAMBERLIN, T. C.
1965   "Method of Multiple Working Hypotheses," *Science*, vol. 148, pp. 754-59.

CHANG, KWANG-CHIH
1958   "Study of the Neolithic Social Groupings: Examples from the New World," *American Anthropologist*, vol. 60, no. 2, part 1, pp. 298-334.

227

1967 "Major Aspects of the Interrelationship of Archaeology and Ethnology," *Current Anthropology*, vol. 8, no. 3, pp. 227-34.

COLTON, HAROLD S.
1932a "A Possible Hopi Tradition of the Eruption of Sunset Crater," *Museum Notes*, vol. 5, no. 4 (Flagstaff: Museum of Northern Arizona), pp. 23-30.
1932b *A Survey of Prehistoric Sites in the Region of Flagstaff, Arizona*, Bureau of American Ethnology Bulletin, no. 104 (Washington, D.C.: U.S. Government Printing Office).
1933 "Wupatki, the Tall House," *Museum Notes*, vol. 5, no. 11 (Flagstaff: Museum of Northern Arizona), pp. 61-64.
1936 "The Rise and Fall of the Prehistoric Population of Northern Arizona," *Science*, vol. 84, pp. 337-43.
1939 "Prehistoric Culture Units and their Relationships in Northern Arizona," *Museum of Northern Arizona Bulletin*, no. 17 (Flagstaff: the museum).

COOLEY, MAURICE E.
1962 "Late Pleistocene and Recent Erosion and Alluviation in Parts of the Colorado River System, Arizona and Utah," *Geological Survey Research 1962: Short Papers in Geology, Hydrology, and Topography, Articles 1-59*, United States Geological Survey Professional Paper, no. 450-B (Washington: U.S. Government Printing Office), pp. 48-50.

CUMMINGS, BYRON
1910 *The Ancient Inhabitants of the San Juan Valley*, Bulletin of the University of Utah, vol. 3, no. 3, part 2, (Salt Lake City: University of Utah Press).
1953 *First Inhabitants of Arizona and the Southwest* (Tucson, Ariz.: Cummings Publication Council).

CUNNINGHAM, CLARK E.
1958 *The Postwar Migration of the Toka-Bataks to East Sumatra*, Yale University Southeast Asia Studies (New Haven: Yale University Press).

CUSHING, F. H.
1890 "Preliminary Notes on the Origin, Working Hypotheses, and Primary Researches of the Hemingway Southwestern Expedition," *Proceedings of the Seventh International Congress of Americanists* (Berlin: the congress), pp. 151-93.
1896 "Outlines of Zuni Creation Myths," *13th Annual Report of the Bureau of American Ethnology* (Washington, D.C.: U.S. Government Printing Office), pp. 325-447.

DANSON, EDWARD B.
1957 *An Archaeological Survey of West Central New Mexico and East Central Arizona*, Papers of the Peabody Museum, Harvard University, vol. 44, no. 1 (Cambridge: the museum).

DAVIS, W. W. H.
1938 *El Gringo, or New Mexico and her People* (Santa Fe: Rydal Press).

DAWSON, CARL A.
1936 *Group Settlement: Ethnic Communities in Western Canada* (Toronto: The Macmillan Co. of Canada, Ltd.).

DAY, K. C.
1963 "Moqui Canyon and Castle Wash Survey," F. W. Sharrock, K. C. Day, and

228

References

D. S. Dibble, 1961 *Excavations, Glen Canyon Area*, app. II, *University of Utah Anthropological Papers*, no. 63 (Salt Lake City: University of Utah Press), pp. 237-305.

DEAN, JEFFREY S.

1966 "The Pueblo Abandonment of Tsegi Canyon, Northeastern Arizona," paper presented at the 31st Annual Meeting of the Society for American Archaeology, Reno, Nev.

1969 *Chronological Analysis of Tsegi Phase Sites in Northeastern Arizona*, Papers of the Laboratory of Tree-Ring Research, no. 3 (Tucson: University of Arizona Press).

DEETZ, JAMES D. F.

1960 "An Archaeological Approach to Kinship Change in Eighteenth Century Arikara Culture," unpublished doctoral dissertation, Harvard University.

1965 *The Dynamics of Stylistic Change in Arikara Ceramics, Illinois Studies in Anthropology*, no. 4 (Urbana: University of Illinois Press).

DiPESO, CHARLES C.

1958 *The Reeve Ruin of Southeastern Arizona*, Amerind Foundation Publication no. 8 (Dragoon, Ariz.: the foundation).

DITTERT, A. E., JR., J. HESTER, AND F. W. EDDY

1961 *An Archaeological Survey of the Navajo Reservoir District, Monographs of the School of American Research and the Museum of New Mexico*, no. 23 (Santa Fe: School of American Research).

DOLE, GERTRUDE E. AND ROBERT L. CARNEIRO (eds.)

1960 *Essays in the Science of Culture in Honor of Leslie A. White* (New York: Thomas Y. Crowell Company).

DOZIER, EDWARD P.

1954 *The Hopi-Tewa of Arizona, University of California Publications in American Archaeology and Ethnology*, vol. 44 (Berkeley and Los Angeles: University of California Press).

1960 "The Pueblos of the South-Western United States," *The Journal of the Royal Anthropological Institute of Great Britain and Ireland*, vol. 90, part 1 (London: the institute), pp. 146-60.

1965 "Southwestern Social Units and Archaeology," *American Antiquity*, vol. 31, no. 1, pp. 38-47.

1966a *Hano: A Tewa Community in Arizona* (New York: Holt, Rinehart and Winston, Inc.).

1966b "Factionalism at Santa Clara Pueblo," *Ethnology*, vol. 5, no. 2, pp. 172-85.

DRIVER, HAROLD E.

1956 "An Integration of Functional, Evolutionary, and Historical Theory by Means of Correlations," *Indiana University Publications in Anthropology and Linguistics, Memoir of the International Journal of Linguistics*, no. 12 (Baltimore: Waverly Press, Inc., pp. 1-35.

DUTTON, BERTHA P.

1938 *Leyit Kin, a Small House Ruin, Chaco Canyon, New Mexico, University of New Mexico Bulletin, Monograph Series*, vol. 1, no. 6 (Albuquerque: University of New Mexico Press).

References

EDLEFSEN, JOHN B.
1950 "Enclavement among Southwest Idaho Basques," *Social Forces*, vol. 29, no. 2, pp. 155-58.

EGGAN, FRED
1950 *Social Organization of the Western Pueblos* (Chicago: University of Chicago Press).
1952 "The Ethnological Cultures and their Archaeological Backgrounds," *Archaeology of Eastern United States*, ed. by James B. Griffin (Chicago: University of Chicago Press), pp. 35-45.
1966 *The American Indian, Perspectives for the Study of Social Change* (Chicago: Aldine Publishing Company).

ELLIS, FLORENCE HAWLEY
1951 "Pueblo Social Organization and Southwestern Archaeology," *American Antiquity*, vol. 17, no. 2, pp. 148-51.
1959 "An Outline of Laguna Pueblo History and Social Organization," *Southwestern Journal of Anthropology*, vol. 15, no. 4, pp. 325-47.
1964 *A Reconstruction of the Basic Jemez Pattern of Social Organization with Comparisons to Other Tanoan Social Structures*, University of New Mexico Publications in Anthropology, no. 11 (Albuquerque: University of New Mexico Press).

EULER, ROBERT C.
1964 "Southern Paiute Archaeology," *American Antiquity*, vol. 29, no. 3, pp. 379-81.

FERNEA, ROBERT A. AND JOHN G. KENNEDY
1966 "Initial Adaptations to Resettlement: A New Life for Egyptian Nubians," *Current Anthropology*, vol. 7, no. 3, pp. 349-54.

FEWKES, JESSE WALTER
1896 "The Prehistoric Culture of Tusayan," *American Anthropologist*, vol. 9, pp. 151-74.
1898 "Archaeological Expedition to Arizona in 1895," *17th Annual Report of the Bureau of American Ethnology* (Washington, D.C.: U.S. Government Printing Office), pp. 529-636.
1900 "Tusayan Migration Myths," *19th Annual Report of the Bureau of American Ethnology* (Washington, D.C.: U.S. Government Printing Office), pp. 573-633.
1904 "Two Summers' Work in the Pueblo Ruins," *22nd Annual Report of the Bureau of American Ethnology* (Washington, D.C.: U.S. Government Printing Office), pp. 173-95.
1909 *Antiquities of the Mesa Verde National Park: Spruce-Tree House*, Bureau of American Ethnology Bulletin, no. 41 (Washington, D.C.: U.S. Government Printing Office).
1911a *Preliminary Report on a Visit to the Navaho National Monument, Arizona*, Bureau of American Ethnology Bulletin, no. 50 (Washington, D.C.: U.S. Government Printing Office).
1911b *Antiquities of the Mesa Verde National Park, Cliff Palace*, Bureau of American Ethnology Bulletin, no. 51 (Washington, D.C.: U.S. Government Printing Office).
1917 "A Prehistoric Mesa Verde Pueblo and Its People," *Annual Report of the Smithsonian Institution, 1916* (Washington, D.C.: the institution), pp. 461-88.

References

1919 Prehistoric Villages, Castles, and Towns of Southwestern Colorado, Bureau of American Ethnology Bulletin, no. 70 (Washington, D.C.: U.S. Government Printing Office).

1922 "Ancestor Worship of the Hopi Indians," Smithsonian Institution, Annual Report, 1921 (Washington, D.C.: U.S. Government Printing Office), pp. 485-506.

FORDE, C. DARYELL
1931 "Hopi Agriculture and Land Ownership," Journal of the Royal Anthropological Institute of Great Britain and Ireland, vol. 61 (London: the institute), pp. 357-405.

FREEMAN, LESLIE G., JR. AND JAMES A. BROWN
1964 "Statistical Analysis of Carter Ranch Pottery," Paul S. Martin, John B. Rinaldo, William A. Longacre, Leslie G. Freeman, Jr., James A. Brown, Richard H. Hevly, and M. E. Cooley, Chapters in the Prehistory of Eastern Arizona, II, Fieldiana: Anthropology, vol. 55 (Chicago: Chicago Natural History Museum), pp. 126-54.

FRITTS, H. D., D. G. SMITH, AND M. A. STOKES
1965 "The Biological Model for Paleoclimatic Interpretation of Mesa Verde Tree-Ring Series," Contributions of the Wetherill Mesa Archeological Project, ed. by Douglas Osborne, memoir no. 19 (Salt Lake City: Society for American Archaeology), pp. 101-21.

FRITZ, JOHN M.
1968 "Archaeological Epistemology: Two Views," unpublished master's thesis, University of Chicago.

FRITZ, JOHN M. AND FRED T. PLOG
1968 "The Nature of Archaeological Explanation," paper presented at the 33rd Annual Meeting of the Society for American Archaeology, Santa Fe, N.M.

GALINAT, W. C. AND J. H. GUNNERSON
1963 "Spread of Eight-Rowed Maize from the Prehistoric Southwest," Botanical Museum Leaflet, vol. 20, no. 5 (Cambridge: Harvard University), pp. 117-60.

GLADWIN, WINIFRED AND HAROLD S. GLADWIN
1934 A Method for Designation of Cultures and their Variations, Medallion Papers, no. 15 (Globe, Ariz.: Gila Pueblo).

GOLDFRANK, ESTHER
1927 The Social and Ceremonial Organization of Cochiti, Memoirs of the American Anthropological Association, vol .33.

GOODENOUGH, WARD H.
1963 "Review of Matrilineal Kinship," ed. by David M. Schneider and Kathleen Gough, American Anthropologist, vol. 65, pp. 923-28.

GOUGH, KATHLEEN
1961 "Variation in Matrilineal Systems," Matrilineal Kinship, ed. by David M. Schneider and Kathleen Gough (Berkeley and Los Angeles: University of California Press), pp. 445-652.

GREENBERG, JOSEPH
1968 "Anthropology: The Field," International Encyclopedia of the Social Sciences, vol. I, ed. by David L. Sills (New York: The Macmillan Co. and The Free Press), pp. 304-13.

231

References

GREGORY, H. E.
1938   The San Juan Country, U.S. Geological Survey Professional Paper, no. 188 (Washington, D.C.: U.S. Government Printing Office).

HACK, JOHN T.
1942   The Changing Physical Environment of the Hopi Indians of Arizona, Papers of the Peabody Museum of American Archaeology and Ethnology, Harvard University, vol. 35, no. 1, Reports of the Awatovi Expedition, no. 1 (Cambridge: the museum).
1945   "Recent Geology of the Tsegi Canyon," Ralph L. Beals, George W. Brainerd, and Watson Smith, Archaeological Studies in Northeast Arizona, app. I, University of California Publications in American Archaeology and Ethnology, vol. 44, no. 1 (Berkeley and Los Angeles: University of California Press), pp. 151-58.

HACKETT, W. W. AND C. C. SHELBY
1942   Revolt of the Pueblo Indians of New Mexico and Otermin's Attempted Reconquest, 1680-82, Coronado Historical Series, vols. 8 and 9.

HALL, EDWARD T., JR.
1942   Archaeological Survey of Walhalla Glades, Museum of Northern Arizona Bulletin, no. 20 (Flagstaff: the museum).

HAMMOND, PHILIP E.
1963   "The Migrating Sect: An Illustration from Early Norwegian Immigration," Social Forces, vol. 4, pp. 275-83.

HARGRAVE, LYNDON L.
1931   "First Mesa," Museum Notes, vol. 3, no. 8 (Flagstaff: Museum of Northern Arizona), pp. 1-7.

HARRINGTON, JOHN P.
1907-08   "Ethnogeography of the Tewa Indians," 29th Annual Report of the Bureau of American Ethnology (Washington, D.C.: U.S. Government Printing Office), pp. 29-618.

HAURY, EMIL W.
1956   "Speculations on Prehistoric Settlement Patterns in the Southwest," Prehistoric Settlement Patterns in the New World, ed. by G. R. Willey, Viking Fund Publications in Anthropology, no. 23 (New York: Wenner-Gren Foundation for Anthropological Research, Inc.). pp. 3-10.

HAWLEY, FLORENCE M.
1934   The Significance of the Dated Prehistory of Chetro Ketl, Chaco Canyon, New Mexico, University of New Mexico Bulletin, Monograph Series, vol. 1, no. 1 (Albuquerque: University of New Mexico Press).
1937a   "Pueblo Social Organization as a Lead to Pueblo History," American Anthropologist, vol. 39, no. 3, part 1, pp. 504-22.
1937b   "The Place of Tseh So in the Chaco Culture Pattern," Tseh So, a Small House Ruin, Chaco Canyon, New Mexico, University of New Mexico Bulletin, Anthropological Series, vol. 2, no. 2 (Albuquerque: University of New Mexico Press), pp. 115-19.
1950a   "Big Kivas, Little Kivas, and Moiety Houses in Historical Reconstruction," Southwestern Journal of Anthropology, vol. 6, pp. 286-302.
1950b   "Keresan Patterns of Kinship and Social Organization," American Anthropologist, vol. 52, pp. 499-512.

References

HAYES, ALDEN C.
1964   The Archeological Survey of Wetherill Mesa, Mesa Verde National Park, Colorado, National Park Service Archeological Research Series, no. 7a (Washington, D.C.: U.S. Government Printing Office).

HEMPEL, CARL G.
1966   Philosophy of Natural Science (Englewood Cliffs, N.J.: Prentice-Hall, Inc.).

HEROLD, JOYCE
1961   Prehistoric Settlement and Physical Environment in the Mesa Verde Area, University of Utah Anthropological Papers, no. 53 (Salt Lake City: University of Utah Press).

HEVLY, RICHARD H.
1964   "Paleoecology of Laguna Salada," Paul S. Martin, John B. Rinaldo, William A. Longacre, Leslie G. Freeman, Jr., James A. Brown, Richard H. Hevly, and M. E. Cooley, Chapters in the Prehistory of Eastern Arizona, II, Fieldiana: Anthropology, vol. 55 (Chicago: Chicago Natural History Museum), pp. 171-87.

HEWETT, EDGAR L.
1905   "A General View of the Archaeology of the Pueblo Region," Annual Report of the Smithsonian Institution, 1904 (Washington, D.C.: the institution), pp. 583-605.
1908   Les Communautés Anciennes dans le Désert Américain (Geneva: Librairie Kundig).

HIBBEN, FRANK C.
1937   "The Site and the Excavations," Tseh So, a Small House Ruin, Chaco Canyon, New Mexico, University of New Mexico Bulletin, Anthropological Series, vol. 2, no. 2 (Albuquerque: University of New Mexico Press), pp. 67-84.

HILL, JAMES N.
1963   "A Processual Analysis of Non-seasonal Population Movement in Man and Other Terrestrial Mammals," unpublished master's thesis, University of Chicago.
1966   "A Prehistoric Community in Eastern Arizona," Southwestern Journal of Anthropology, vol. 22, no. 1, pp. 9-30.
1967   "Structure, Function, and Change at Broken K Pueblo," Paul S. Martin, William A. Longacre, and James N. Hill, Chapters in the Prehistory of Eastern Arizona, III, Fieldiana: Anthropology, vol. 57 (Chicago: Chicago Natural History Museum), pp. 158-67.
1968   "Broken K Pueblo: Patterns of Form and Function," New Perspectives in Archeology, ed. by S. R. Binford and L. R. Binford (Chicago: Aldine Publishing Company), pp. 103-42.
1970   Broken K Pueblo: Prehistoric Social Organization in the American Southwest (Tucson: University of Arizona Press).

HILL, JAMES N. AND RICHARD H. HEVLY
1968   "Pollen at Broken K Pueblo: Some New Interpretations," American Antiquity, vol. 33, no. 2, pp. 200-10.

HOBLER, PHILIP M.
1964   "The Late Survival of Pithouse Architecture in the Kayenta Anasazi Area," unpublished master's thesis, University of Arizona, Tucson.

233

References

HODGE, F. W., G. P. HAMMOND, AND AGAPITO REY (eds.)
1945 Revised Memorial of Alonzo de Benavides, 1634, Colorado Cuarto Centennial Publications, 1540-1940, vol. 4 (Albuquerque: University of New Mexico Press).

HOLE, FRANK AND ROBERT F. HEIZER
1965 An Introduction to Prehistoric Archeology (New York: Holt, Rinehart and Winston, Inc.).

HOLSINGER, S. J.
1901 Report on Prehistoric Ruins of Chaco Canyon National Monument, General Land Office Manuscript (Washington, D.C.: National Archives).

JENNINGS, JESSE D.
1956 "The American Southwest: A Problem in Cultural Isolation," Seminars in Archaeology: 1955, ed. by Jesse D. Jennings and Robert Wauchope, memoir no. 11 (Salt Lake City: Society for American Archaeology), pp. 60-127.
1963 Anthropology and the World of Science, Bulletin of the University of Utah, vol. 54, no. 18 (Salt Lake City: University of Utah Press).
1966 Glen Canyon: A Summary, University of Utah Anthropological Papers, no. 81 (Salt Lake City: University of Utah Press).

JUDD, NEIL M.
1959 Pueblo del Arroyo, Chaco Canyon, New Mexico, Smithsonian Miscellaneous Collections, vol. 138, no. 1 (Washington, D.C.: Smithsonian Institution).
1964 The Architecture of Pueblo Bonito, Smithsonian Miscellaneous Collections, vol. 147, no. 1 (Washington, D.C.: Smithsonian Institution).

KAPLAN, ABRAHAM
1964 The Conduct of Inquiry (San Francisco: Chandler Publishing Company).

KELLY, I. T.
1964 Southern Paiute Ethnography, University of Utah Anthropological Papers, no. 69 (Salt Lake City: University of Utah Press).

KIDDER, ALFRED V.
1962 An Introduction to the Study of Southwestern Archaeology (New Haven: Yale University Press).

KIDDER, ALFRED V. AND SAMUEL J. GUERNSEY
1919 Archaeological Explorations in Northeastern Arizona, Bureau of American Ethnology Bulletin, no. 65 (Washington, D.C.: U.S. Government Printing Office).

KLUCKHOHN, CLYDE
1940 "The Conceptual Structure in Middle American Studies," The Maya and their Neighbors, ed. by C. L. Hay, R. L. Linton, S. K. Lothrop, H. L. Shapiro, and G. C. Vaillant (New York: D. Appleton-Century Co.), pp. 41-51.

KLUCKHOHN, CLYDE AND PAUL REITER (eds.)
1939 Preliminary Report on the 1937 Excavations, Bc50-51, Chaco Canyon, New Mexico, University of New Mexico Bulletin, Anthropological Series, vol. 3, no. 2 (Albuquerque: University of New Mexico Press).

KNUDSON, KENNETH E.
1964 Titiana: A Gilbertese Community in the Solomon Islands, Field Studies in the Project for the Comparative Study of Culture Change and Stability in Displaced Communities in the Pacific, Homer G. Barnett, director (Eugene: University of Oregon).

References

KROEBER, ALFRED L.
1917 "Zuni Kin and Clan," *Anthropological Papers of the American Museum of Natural History*, vol. 28, part 2 (New York: the musuem), pp. 39-205.
1928 "Native Culture of the Southwest," *University of California Publications in American Archaeology and Ethnology*, vol. 23, no. 9 (Berkeley and Los Angeles: University of California Press), pp. 374-98.

LANCE, J. F.
1963 "Alluvial Stratigraphy in Lake and Moqui Canyons," F. W. Sharrock, K. C. Day, and D. S. Dibble, *1961 Excavations, Glen Canyon Area*, app. IV, *University of Utah Anthropological Papers*, no. 63 (Salt Lake City: University of Utah Press), pp. 347-76.

LANGE, CHARLES
1958 "The Keresan Component of Southwestern Pueblo Culture," *Southwestern Journal of Anthropology*, vol. 14, pp. 34-50.

LANGE, C. H. AND C. L. RILEY
1966 *The Southwestern Journals of A. F. Bandelier, 1880-1882* (Albuquerque: University of New Mexico Press).

LARSON, ERIC H.
1966 *Nukufero: A Tikopian Colony in the Russell Islands, Field Studies in the Project for the Comparative Study of Cultural Change and Stability in Displaced Communities in the Pacific*, Homer G. Barnett, director (Eugene: University of Oregon).

LI, AN-CHE
1937 "Zuni: Some Observations and Queries," *American Anthropologist*, vol. 39, pp. 62-76.

LINDSAY, ALEXANDER J., JR.
1961 "The Beaver Creek Agricultural Community on the San Juan River, Utah," *American Antiquity*, vol. 27, no. 2, pp. 174-87.

LINDSAY, ALEXANDER J., JR., AND J. RICHARD AMBLER
1963 "Recent Contributions and Research Problems in Kayenta Anasazi Prehistory," *Plateau*, vol. 35, no. 3, pp. 86-92.

LINDSAY, ALEXANDER J., JR., J. RICHARD AMBLER, MARY ANNE STEIN, AND PHILIP M. HOBLER
1968 *Survey and Excavations North and East of Navajo Mountain, Utah, 1959-1962*, Museum of Northern Arizona, Flagstaff.

LIPE, W. D.
1967 *Anasazi Culture and Its Relationship to the Environment in the Red Rock Plateau Region, Southeastern Utah* (Ann Arbor, Mich.: University Microfilms).

LISTER, R. H.
1959 "The Glen Canyon Right Bank Survey," D. D. Fowler et al., *The Glen Canyon Archeological Survey, University of Utah Anthropological Papers*, no. 39, part 1 (Salt Lake City: University of Utah Press), pp. 27-161.

LONG, PAUL V., JR.
1966 *Archaeological Excavations in Lower Glen Canyon, Utah, 1959-1960*, Museum of Northern Arizona Bulletin, no. 42 (Flagstaff: the musuem).

LONGACRE, WILLIAM A.
1963 "Archaeology as Anthropology: A Case Study," unpublished doctoral dissertation, Department of Anthropology, University of Chicago.

References

1964a "Archeology as Anthropology: A Case Study," *Science*, vol. 144, pp. 1454-55.
1964b "Sociological Implications of the Ceramic Analysis," Paul S. Martin, John B. Rinaldo, William A. Longacre, Leslie G. Freeman, Jr., James A. Brown, Richard H. Hevly, and M. E. Cooley, *Chapters in the Prehistory of Eastern Arizona, II, Fieldiana: Anthropology*, vol. 55 (Chicago: Chicago Natural History Musuem), pp. 155-70.
1964c "A Synthesis of Upper Little Colorado Prehistory, Eastern Arizona," Paul S. Martin, John B. Rinaldo, William A. Longacre, Leslie G. Freeman, Jr., James A. Brown, Richard H. Hevly, and M. E. Cooley, *Chapters in the Prehistory of Eastern Arizona, II, Fieldiana: Anthropology*, vol. 55 (Chicago: Chicago Natural History Museum), pp. 201-15.
1966 "Changing Patterns of Social Integration: A Prehistoric Example from the American Southwest," *American Anthropologist*, vol. 68, no. 1, pp. 94-102.
1968 "Some Aspects of Prehistoric Society in East-Central Arizona," *New Perspectives in Archeology*, ed. by S. R. Binford and L. R. Binford (Chicago: Aldine Publishing Company), pp. 89-102.

LOWIE, ROBERT H.
1929 *Hopi Kinship, Anthropological Papers of the American Museum of Natural History*, vol. 30, part 7 (New York: the museum).

MacNITT, FRANK
1957 *Richard Wetherill: Anasazi* (Albuquerque: University of New Mexico Press).

MacWHITE, EOIN
1956 "On the Interpretation of Archeological Evidence in Historical and Sociological Terms," *American Anthropologist*, vol. 58, no. 1, pp. 3-25.

MARTIN, PAUL S.
1954 "Comments," *American Anthropologist*, vol. 56, no. 4, part 1 (August), pp. 570-02.
1967 "Paleo-anthropological Research and Computers," *Computers in Humanistic Research*, ed. by E. A. Bowles (Englewood Cliffs, N.J.: Prentice-Hall, Inc.), pp. 40-46.

MARTIN, PAUL S., WILLIAM A. LONGACRE, AND JAMES N. HILL
1967 *Chapters in the Prehistory of Eastern Arizona, III, Fieldiana: Anthropology*, vol. 57 (Chicago: Chicago Natural History Museum).

MARTIN, PAUL S., AND JOHN B. RINALDO
1950 *Sites of the Reserve Phase, Pine Lawn Valley, Western New Mexico, Fieldiana: Anthropology*, vol. 38, no. 3 (Chicago: Chicago Natural History Museum).

MARTIN, PAUL S., JOHN B. RINALDO, WILLIAM A. LONGACRE, CONSTANCE CRONIN, LESLIE G. FREEMAN, JR., AND JAMES SCHOENWETTER
1962 *Chapters in the Prehistory of Eastern Arizona, I, Fieldiana: Anthropology*, vol. 53 (Chicago: Chicago Natural History Museum).

MARTIN, PAUL S., JOHN B. RINALDO, WILLIAM A. LONGACRE, LESLIE G. FREEMAN, JR., JAMES A. BROWN, RICHARD H. HEVLY, AND M. E. COOLEY
1964 *Chapters in the Prehistory of Eastern Arizona, II, Fieldiana: Anthropology*, vol. 55, (Chicago: Chicago Natural History Museum).

References

MAYER, ADRIAN C.

1961 *Peasants in the Pacific: A Study of Fiji Indian Rural Society* (Berkeley and Los Angeles: University of California Press).

McFEAT, TOM F. S.

1960 "Some Social and Spatial Aspects of Innovation at Zuni," *Anthropologica*, vol. 11, no. 1, pp. 1-30.

McGREGOR, JOHN C.

1965 *Southwestern Archaeology* (Urbana: University of Illinois Press).

MICKEY, BARBARA

1956 "Acoma Kinship Terms," *Southwestern Journal of Anthropology*, vol. 12, pp. 249-56.

MINDELEFF, COSMOS

1896 "Aboriginal Remains in the Verde Valley," *13th Annual Report of the Bureau of American Ethnology* (Washington, D.C.: U.S. Government Printing Office), pp. 185-258.

1897 "The Cliff Ruins of Canyon de Chelley, Arizona," *16th Annual Report of the Bureau of American Ethnology* (Washington, D.C.: U.S. Government Printing Office), pp. 79-198.

1898 "Origin of the Cliff Dwellings," *Bulletin of the American Geological Society*, vol. 30, no. 2, pp. 111-23.

1900 "Localization of Tusayan Clans," *19th Annual Report of the Bureau of American Ethnology* (Washington, D.C.: U.S. Government Printing Office), pp. 635-53.

MINDELEFF, VICTOR

1891 "A Study of Pueblo Architecture: Tusayan and Cibola," *8th Annual Report of the Bureau of American Ethnology* (Washington, D.C.: U.S. Government Printing Office), pp. 12-228.

MITCHELL, J. CLYDE

1951 "The Yao of Southern Nyasaland," *Seven Tribes of British Central Africa*, ed. by Elizabeth Colson and Max Gluckman (London: Oxford University Press), pp. 292-353.

1956 *The Yao Village, a Study in the Social Structure of a Nyasaland Tribe* (Manchester: Manchester University Press).

MORGAN, LEWIS HENRY

1965 *Houses and House-Life of the American Aborigines* (Chicago: University of Chicago Press).

MORRIS, EARL H.

1939 *Archaeological Studies in the La Plata District, Carnegie Institution of Washington Publications*, no. 519 (Washington, D.C.: the institution).

MURDOCK, GEORGE P.

1949 *Social Structure* (New York: The Macmillan Co.)

NAGEL, ERNEST

1961 *The Structure of Science: Problems in the Logic of Scientific Explanation* (New York: Harcourt, Brace & World, Inc.)

NAROLL, RAOUL

1962 "Floor Area and Settlement Population," *American Antiquity*, vol. 27, no. 4, pp. 587-89.

NELSON, LOWRY

1952   *The Mormon Village* (Salt Lake City: University of Utah Press).

NEQUATEWA, EDMUND

1943   "Some Hopi Recipes for the Preparation of Wild Plant Foods," *Plateau*, vol.
16, no. 1, pp. 79-198.

PARSONS, ELSIE CLEWS

1925   *The Pueblo of Jemez, Papers of the Southwestern Expedition,* Department of
Archaeology, Phillips Academy, no. 3 (New Haven: Yale University Press).

1929   *The Social Organization of the Tewa of New Mexico,* American Anthropological Association Memoirs, no. 36.

1936   *Hopi Journal of Alexander M. Stephen, Columbia University Contributions to
Anthropology,* vols. 23 and 24 (New York: Columbia University Press).

1939   *Pueblo Indian Religion,* two vols. (Chicago: University of Chicago Press).

PLATT, JOHN R.

1964   "Strong Inference," *Science,* vol. 146, no. 3642, pp. 347-53.

PLOG, FRED T.

1968   "Archeological Surveys: A New Perspective," unpublished master's thesis, University of Chicago.

REAGAN, ALFRED B.

1920   "Who Made the Kayenta-National Monument Ruins?" *American Anthropologist,* vol. 22, no. 4, pp. 387-88.

REDFIELD, ROBERT AND ALFONSO ROJAS

1934   *Chan Kom, A Maya Village* (Washington, D.C.: Carnegie Institution).

REED, ERIK K.

1950   "Eastern-Central Arizona Archaeology in Relation to the Western Pueblos,"
Southwestern Journal of Anthropology, vol. 6, pp. 120-38.

1956   "Types of Village Plan Layouts in the Southwest," *Prehistoric Settlement Patterns in the New World,* ed. by G. R. Willey, *Viking Fund Publications in
Anthropology,* no. 23 (New York: Wenner-Gren Foundation for Anthropological Research, Inc.), pp. 11-17.

ROBERTS, FRANK H. H., JR.

1931   *The Ruins at Kiatuthlana, Eastern Arizona,* Bureau of American Ethnology
Bulletin, no. 100. (Washington, D.C.: U.S. Government Printing Office).

ROHN, ARTHUR H.

1963   "Prehistoric Soil and Water Conservation on Chapin Mesa," *American Antiquity,* vol. 28, no. 4, pp. 441-55.

1965   "Postulation of Socio-Economic Groups from Archaeological Evidence," *Con-
tributions of the Wetherill Mesa Archeological Project,* assembled by Douglas
Osborne, memoir no. 19, *American Antiquity,* vol. 31, no. 2, part 2 (Salt Lake
City: Society for American Archaeology), pp. 65-69.

ROUSE, IRVING

1953   "The Strategy of Archaeology," *Anthropology Today,* ed. by A. L. Kroeber
(Chicago: University of Chicago Press), pp. 57-76.

SACKETT, JAMES R.

1966   "Quantitative Analysis of Upper Paleolithic Stone Tools," *Recent Studies in
Paleoanthropology, American Anthropologist,* vol. 68, no. 2, part 2, pp. 356-94.

References

SAHLINS, MARSHALL D.
1964 "Culture and Environment: The Study of Cultural Ecology," *Horizons of An-thropology*, ed. by Sol Tax (Chicago: University of Chicago Press), pp. 132-47.

SCHNEIDER, DAVID M.
1961 "Introduction: The Distinctive Features of Matrilineal Descent Groups," *Matri-lineal Kinship*, ed. by David M. Schneider and Kathleen Gough (Berkeley and Los Angeles: University of California Press), pp. 1-29.

SCHNEIDER, DAVID M. AND KATHLEEN GOUGH (eds.)
1961 *Matrilineal Kinship* (Berkeley and Los Angeles: University of California Press).

SCHOENWETTER, JAMES
1962 "The Pollen Analysis of Eighteen Archaeological Sites in Arizona and New Mexico," Paul S. Martin, John B. Rinaldo, William A. Longacre, Constance Cronin, Leslie G. Freeman, Jr., and James Schoenwetter, *Chapters in the Pre-history of Eastern Arizona, I, Fieldiana: Anthropology*, vol. 53 (Chicago: Chicago Natural History Museum), pp. 168-209.
1967 "Pollen Survey of the Chuska Valley," Arthur H. Harris, James Schoenwetter, and A. H. Warren, *An Archaeological Survey of the Chuska Valley and the Chaco Plateau, New Mexico, Part I: Natural Science Studies, Musuem of New Mexico Research Records*, no. 4 (Santa Fe: Museum of New Mexico Press), pp. 72-103.

SCHOENWETTER, JAMES AND FRANK W. EDDY
1964 *Alluvial and Palynological Reconstruction of Environments, Navajo Reservoir District, Museum of New Mexico Papers in Anthropology*, no. 13 (Santa Fe: Museum of New Mexico Press).

SCHOLES, FRANCE V.
1930 "The Supply Service of the New Mexico Missions in the Seventeenth Century," *New Mexico Historical Review*, vol. 5, pp. 93-115, 186-98.
1935 "Civil Government and Society in the Seventeenth Century," *New Mexico Historical Review*, vol. 10, pp. 71-111.
1942 *Troublous Times in New Mexico 1659-70, Historical Society of New Mexico, Publications in History*, vol. 2.

SCHULMAN, E.
1956 *Dendroclimatic Changes in Semiarid America* (Tucson: University of Arizona Press).

SCHWARTZ, DOUGLAS W.
1960 "Archaeological Investigations in the Shinumo Area of Grand Canyon, Ari-zona," *Plateau*, vol. 32, no. 3, pp. 61-67.
1965 "Nankoweap to Unkar: An Archaeological Survey of the Upper Grand Canyon," *American Antiquity*, vol. 30, no. 3, pp. 278-96.
1966 "A Historical Analysis and Synthesis of Grand Canyon Archaeology," *American Antiquity*, vol. 31, no. 4, pp. 469-84.

SEARS, WILLIAM H.
1961 "The Study of Social and Religious Systems in North American Archaeology," *Current Anthropology*, vol. 2, no. 3, pp. 223-31.

SERVICE, ELMAN R.
1962 *Primitive Social Organization: An Evolutionary Perspective, Random House Studies in Anthropology* (New York: Random House).

References

SHARROCK, F. W., K. M. ANDERSON, D. D. FOWLER, AND D. S. DIBBLE
1961   1960 Excavations, Glen Canyon Area, University of Utah Anthropological Papers, no. 52 (Salt Lake City: University of Utah Press).

SHARROCK, F. W., K. C. DAY, AND D. S. DIBBLE
1963   1961 Excavations, Glen Canyon Area, University of Utah Anthropological Papers, no. 63 (Salt Lake City: University of Utah Press).

SHARROCK, F. W., D. S. DIBBLE, AND K. M. ANDERSON
1961   "The Creeping Dune Irrigation Site in Glen Canyon, Utah," American Antiquity, vol. 27, no. 2, pp. 188-202.

SIEGEL, SIDNEY
1965   Non-parametric Statistics for the Behavioral Sciences (New York: McGraw-Hill Book Co.).

SIMMONS, L. W.
1942   Sun Chief (New Haven: Yale University Press).

SMITH, M. A.
1955   "The Limitations of Inference in Archaeology," The Archaeological Newsletter, vol. 6, no. 1, pp. 1-7.

SMITH, WATSON
1952   Excavations in Big Hawk Valley, Wupatki National Monument, Arizona, Museum of Northern Arizona Bulletin, no. 24 (Flagstaff: the museum).

SPAULDING, ALBERT C.
1953   "Statistical Techniques for the Discovery of Artifact Types," American Antiquity, vol. 18, no. 4, pp. 305-13.
1960   "The Dimensions of Archaeology," Essays in the Science of Culture in Honor of Leslie A. White, ed. by Gertrude E. Dole and Robert L. Carneiro (New York: Thomas Y. Crowell Company), pp. 437-56.

SPICER, EDWARD H. (ed.)
1961   Perspectives in American Indian Culture Change (Chicago: University of Chicago Press).

STEEN, CHARLIE R.
1949   "Archaeological Survey, Citadel District," D. S. King, Nalakihu, Museum of Northern Arizona Bulletin, no. 23 (Flagstaff: the musuem), pp. 158-62.

STEWARD, JULIAN H.
1937   "Ecological Aspects of Southwestern Society," Anthropos, vol. 32, pp. 87-104.
1938   Basin-Plateau Aboriginal Sociopolitical Groups, Bureau of American Ethnology Bulletin, no. 120 (Washington, D.C.: U.S. Government Printing Office).
1941   Archeological Reconnaissance of Southern Utah, Bureau of American Ethnology Bulletin, no. 128, Anthropological Paper, no. 18 (Washington, D.C.: U.S. Government Printing Office).
1955   Theory of Culture Change: The Methodology of Multilinear Evolution (Urbana: University of Illinois Press).

STEWART, G. R.
1940   "Conservation in Pueblo Agriculture: I, Primitive Practices; II, Present-day Flood Water Irrigation," Scientific Monthly, vol. 51, nos. 3 and 4, pp. 201-20, 329-40.

STEWART, G. R. AND MAURICE DONNELLY
1943   "Soil and Water Economy in the Pueblo Southwest: I, Field Studies at Mesa

References

Verde and Northern Arizona; II, Evaluation of Primitive Methods of Conservation," *Scientific Monthly*, vol. 56, nos. 1 and 2, pp. 31-44, 134-44.

STEWART, N. R.
1965 "Migration and Settlement in the Peruvian Montaña," *Geographical Review*, vol. 55, pp. 143-57.

STRONG, WILLIAM DUNCAN
1927 "An Analysis of Southwestern Society," *American Anthropologist*, vol. 29, no. 1, pp. 1-61.

SUPPES, PATRICK
1967 "What is Scientific Theory," *Philosophy of Science Today*, ed. by Sidney Morgenbesser (New York: Basic Books, Inc.), pp. 55-67.

SWEENEY, C. L. AND R. C. EULER
1964 "Southern Paiute Archaeology in the Glen Canyon Drainage: A Preliminary Report," *Nevada State Museum Anthropological Papers*, no. 9 (Carson City: The Museum), pp. 5-9.

TAYLOR, WALTER W.
1948 *A Study of Archeology*, American Anthropological Association Memoir, No. 69, vol. 50, no. 3, part 2.
1954 "Southwestern Archeology, Its History and Theory," *American Anthropologist*, vol. 56, no. 4, part 1, pp. 561-75.

THOMPSON, LAURA
1950 *Culture in Crisis* (New York: Harper and Brothers).

THOMPSON, RAYMOND H.
1956 "The Subjective Element in Archaeological Inference," *Southwestern Journal of Anthropology*, vol. 12, no. 3, pp. 327-32.
1958 *Modern Yucatecan Maya Pottery Making*, memoir no. 15, American Antiquity, vol. 23, part 2. (Salt Lake City: Society for American Archaeology).

THWAITES, R. G. (ed.)
1905 *Josiah Gregg's Commerce of the Prairies, 1831-39; Early Western Travels 1748-1846*, vols. 19 and 20, part 2 (Cleveland: The A. H. Clark Company).

TITIEV, MISCHA
1938 "The Problem of Cross-Cousin Marriage among the Hopi," *American Anthropologist*, vol. 40, pp. 105-111.
1943 "The Influence of Common Residence on the Unilateral Classification of Kindred," *American Anthropologist*, vol. 45, no. 2, pp. 511-30.
1944 *Old Oraibi: A Study of the Hopi Indians of Third Mesa*, Papers of the Peabody Museum of American Archaeology and Ethnology, Harvard University, vol. 22, no. 1 (Cambridge: the museum).

TRAGER, GEORGE L.
1942 "The Comparative Phonology of the Tiwa Languages," *Studies in Linguistics*, vol. 1, pp. 1-10.

TRAGER, GEORGE L. AND EDITH CROWELL TRAGER
1959 "Kiowa and Tanoan," *American Anthropologist*, vol. 61, pp. 1078-83.

TURNER, C. G.
1963 *Petrographs of the Glen Canyon Region*, Museum of Northern Arizona Bulletin, no. 38 (Flagstaff: the museum).

241

TURNER, C. G. AND M. E. COOLEY

1960 "Prehistoric Use of Stone from the Glen Canyon Region," *Plateau*, vol. 33, pp. 46-53.

VIVIAN, R. GORDON

1959 *The Hubbard Site and Other Tri-Wall Structures in New Mexico and Colorado*, National Park Service Research Series, no. 5 (Washington, D.C.: U.S. Government Printing Office).

1965 *The Three-C Site, an Early Pueblo II Ruin in Chaco Canyon, New Mexico*, University of New Mexico Publications in Anthropology, no. 13 (Albuquerque: University of New Mexico Press).

VIVIAN, R. GORDON AND TOM W. MATHEWS

1966 *Kin Kletso, a Pueblo III Community in Chaco Canyon, New Mexico*, Southwestern Monuments Association Technical Series, vol. 6, part 1 (Globe, Ariz.: the association).

VIVIAN, R. GORDON AND PAUL REITER

1960 *The Great Kivas of Chaco Canyon and their Relationships*, Monograph of the School of American Research and the Museum of New Mexico, no. 22 (Santa Fe: School of American Research).

VOGT, EVON A.

1955 *Modern Homesteaders* (Cambridge, Mass.: Belknap Press and Harvard University Press).

VOGT, EVON A. AND THOMAS O'DEA

1953 "A Comparative Study of the Role of Values in Social Action in Two Southwestern Communities," *American Sociological Review*, vol. 18, pp. 645-54.

WEINGROD, ALEX

1962 "Reciprocal Change: A Case Study of a Moroccan Immigrant Village in Israel," *American Anthropologist*, vol. 64, pp. 115-31.

WENDORF, FRED

1956 "Some Distributions of Settlement Patterns in the Pueblo Southwest," *Prehistoric Settlement Patterns in the New World*, ed. by G. R. Willey, Viking Fund Publications in Anthropology no. 23 (New York: Wenner-Gren Foundation for Anthropological Research, Inc.), pp. 18-25.

WHITE, G. M.

1965 *Kioa: An Ellice Community in Fiji*, Field Studies in the Project for the Comparative Study of Cultural Change and Stability in Displaced Communities in the Pacific, Homer G. Barnett, director (Eugene: University of Oregon).

WHITE, LESLIE A.

1942 *The Pueblo of Santa Ana, New Mexico*, American Anthropological Association Memoir, no. 60, (Menasha, Wisc.: the association).

1949 *The Science of Culture: A Study of Man and Civilization* (New York: Grove Press, Inc.).

1954 Reviews of *The Nature of Culture* by A. L. Kroeber and *Culture: A Critical Review of Concepts and Definitions* by A. L. Kroeber and Clyde Kluckhohn, *American Anthropologist*, vol. 56, no. 3, pp. 461-68.

1962 *The Pueblo of Sia, New Mexico*, Bureau of American Ethnology Bulletin, no. 184 (Washington, D.C.: U.S. Government Printing Office).

References

WHITING, ALFRED F.
1939 Ethnobotany of the Hopi, Museum of Northern Arizona Bulletin, no. 15 (Flagstaff, Ariz.: the museum).
WILLEY, GORDON R.
1966 An Introduction to American Archaeology, vol. I, North and Middle America (Englewood Cliffs, N.J.: Prentice-Hall, Inc.)
WILLEY, GORDON R. AND PHILIP PHILLIPS
1958 Method and Theory in American Archaeology (Chicago: University of Chicago Press).
WILSON, E. BRIGHT
1952 An Introduction to Scientific Research (New York: McGraw-Hill Book Co., Inc.).

Index

achieved status, 45-48
Acoma, 48
Adams, Nettie L., 119
Adams, William Y., 119
age, as basis for status, 46-48
Anderson, Keith M., 171, 173
archaeological data, limitations, 11-13, 48-56, 84
archaeological structure of site, 19-20
Arizona State Museum, 69
artifacts, determining use, 50
ascribed status, 45-48
Athabascan raiders, 3
avunculocal residence, 39

Bandelier, Adolf F., 3, 77, 206
Bannister, Bryant, 64, 174
Bc 50 and 51, 60, 62, 63
Bc 59, 62, 63, 68
bear clan (Hopi), 46
"behavioral meaning," 20, 44, 143
Bernheimer expedition, 98
Betatakin, 141, 142, 143, 152, 157, 158-59, 165, 167, 170, 171, 173, 195; history of the community, 158-59
bilocal residence, 39, 54, 81
Binford, Lewis R., 216
Broken K Pueblo, 27, 45, 48
Bullard, William R., Jr., 141

canals, Anasazi area, 77
canals, Chaco Canyon, 72, 73-74, 75
Carter Ranch site, 37-38, 41, 47
Casas Grandes (Mexico), 48
ceremonial annex, 155, 167
ceremonial association rooms, 32
ceremonial rooms, 23-24, 30, 34, 35, 36, 43-45, 47, 130, 154-155. See also Kiva

Chaco Canyon, physiography, 61
Chang, Kwang-Chih, 129, 144, 145, 149, 157
Chetro Ketl, 65, 66, 67, 68, 69, 72, 73, 74
clan, 2, 3, 4, 44, 79, 149, 164, 166, 167, 169, 211-12, 218
clan-house, 31, 166, 167
Colton, Harold S., 141
community, defined, 86
community types: Chaco Canyon, 62, 66-68, 69, 75, 78; Tsegi Canyon, 157
consolidation phase, 178, 190-91
cultural process, 9, 197
"Cushing-Fewkes" era, 1, 2
Cushing, F. H., 2

dams, Chaco Canyon, 72
Dean, Jeffrey S., 114, 139, 195, 202, 203, 217, 219, 222
deduction, viii, 55, 196, 199, 200
Deetz, James, 212
demonstration, 13, 20-21
DiPeso, Charles C., 48
doorways, 35, 40, 79, 81
Dozier, Edward P., 43, 44, 80, 81, 157, 163, 164, 165, 182
dual division, 34, 36, 44, 55, 57, 80-83, 166, 210
duolocal residence, 39
Dutton, Bertha, 60

economic reciprocity, 45
Eggan, Fred, 7-8, 55, 81, 144, 163, 164, 195, 207-08, 218, 219, 220, 222
ethnographic analogy, 2, 3, 4, 6, 9, 12, 25, 27, 30, 50-51, 130, 143-44, 163, 165, 203, 217

ethnography, 28
extended family household unit, 35, 163

farming terraces, Chaco Canyon, 69
Fewkes, J. W., 2, 3
Field Museum of Natural History, 59
Fritz, John M., 56

Glen Canyon, population fluctuations, 112-14, 122-23
Glen Canyon Project: aims, 86; phases established, 87; sites, 87
great kivas, Chaco Canyon, 64, 66, 68, 82
Grebinger, Paul, 83
grid borders, Chaco Canyon, 69-70

habitation unit, defined, 141
Hall, Edward T., Jr., 188, 189, 192
Hano, 36
Haury, Emil W., 174
Hawley, Florence (Ellis), 60, 65
Hempel, Carl G., 215
Hewett, Edgar L., 4
"hidden data," 49-50
Hill, James N., 9, 78, 83, 142, 188, 195-97, 212, 215-18
Hopi, 2, 3, 4, 21, 23-24, 31, 42, 45-46, 57, 99, 100, 129, 137-38, 144, 149, 163, 165, 166, 177, 180, 182, 185, 204-05, 208, 218-19, 220; prehistoric background, 144
Horsefly Hollow Phase: ceramics, 125-26; dating, 122; site locations, 123-24; types of sites, 124-30
Hungo Pavi, 65, 67, 72
hypothesis testing, viii, 6, 13-14, 21-27, 33-34, 140, 195

induction, viii, 196, 199
inferences, evaluation, 51

Jennings, Jesse D., 86, 87, 121, 122
Judd, Neil M., 64, 67

kachina society, 32, 42-44, 208
Kayenta Branch, 141, 144, 145, 220; development, 147-51
Kayenta-Mesa Verde relationships, 133-36
Kiet Siel, 141, 142, 143, 152, 157, 159, 161, 163, 165, 168, 170, 171, 172, 173, 195; history of community, 159-61
Kin Bineola, 64, 65, 67, 68, 72
Kin Kletso, 60
Kin Klizhin, 67, 72, 73
Kin Nahasbas, 67, 72

Kin Ya-a, 67, 72, 73
kiva, archaeological significance, 4, 34, 35, 36, 43-45, 192-93, 209-10; features, 111
kiva styles in Chaco Canyon, 62, 66, 68, 166. See also great kivas
kivas, Kayenta Branch, 148, 154-55
kivas, Tsegi Phase, 165. See also Kivas, Kayenta Branch
Klethla Phase: dating, 112; site locations, 114-16; types of sites, 116-21
Kluckhohn, Clyde, 6, 60

Laboratory of Tree-Ring Research, 174
legends. See myths
Lindsay, Alexander J., Jr., 137
lineage-like units, 35, 210-11
lineage, localized, 79-80, 149, 164, 165, 169
Lipe, William D., 197
living rooms, 29, 34
Long, Paul V., 119
Longacre, William A., 37-38, 45, 47, 83, 119, 192, 197, 212

Martin, Paul S., 7, 9, 10
Mathews, Thomas W., 60
matrilocal residence, 4, 9, 38-39, 164, 219
McElmo Phase, 60
Mesa Verde, 114, 166
methods, archaeological, 199-201
migration, defined, 176; reasons for, 176-77
Mindeleff, Cosmos, 3
Mindeleff, Victor, 3
mobility of population, Tsegi Canyon, 170
moiety house, 31-32
Morgan, Lewis H., 4
Mug House, 166
myths, 2, 3, 6, 9

Naroll, Raoul, 102
National Science Foundation, 69, 174, 193
Navajo Reservoir District, 76-77, 151
neolocal residence, 39
New Alto, 73
norms, 17-18, 33, 49, 52, 196, 216-17
nuclear family household unit, 35, 57, 81, 82, 119, 163, 184, 210

Old Alto, 66, 67, 73
"Old Bonitian," 64
oral history. See myths

Index

Original Pueblo concept, 2

Paiute, 97, 100, 104
patrilocal residence, 39
Peñasco Blanco, 64, 65, 67, 72, 73
pioneering phase, 178, 189-90
plaza, 31
Plog, Fred T., 56, 201
political-economic status, 46
pollen, 27, 57, 75, 151, 188, 190
population patterns, Colorado Plateau, 150-51
postmarital residence, 4, 37-42, 163
postmigration phases, 178-82
Pueblo Alto, 72, 73, 74, 75
Pueblo Bonito, 34, 60, 64, 65, 66, 67, 68, 72, 73, 74, 75, 81
Pueblo del Arroyo, 63, 66, 67, 68, 72, 73, 74, 75
Pueblo Pintado, 67, 68, 72, 73

Red Rock Plateau: abandonment, 136-37; growing season, 92; physiography, 88-93; seasonal occupation, 119-22
reservoirs, Chaco Canyon, 73
residence: See avunculocal, bilocal, duo-local, matrilocal, neolocal, patrilocal, uxorilocal, virilocal
residence unit, 15, 19, 33-37, 45, 46, 117, 131, 149, 173
Rinaldo, John B., 7
Rinconada, 67
Roberts, Frank H. H., 65
Robinson, William J., 174
Rohn, Arthur H., 141
rooms: cluster, Tsegi Phase, 155-57, 159; function, 9, 153-57; variability, 29-33, 191. See also storage rooms

salvage archaeology, philosophy, 86
sampling, 17, 53-54, 88, 104, 142
Schneider, David, 221
Schoenwetter, James, 75-77
School of American Research, vii
Schroeder, Mrs. Ella, ix
Schulman, E., 114, 139
Schwartz, Douglas W., viii, 198, 222-23
Schwartz, Mrs. Douglas, ix
seminar focus, vii
Service, Elman, 15, 144
settlement pattern, 8
sex, as basis for status, 46-48
"Shiwian," 2
sites, typology, 111-12

social organization, definition, 15-16
social unit, archaeological evidence, 34-37
sodalities, 4, 15, 42-45, 46, 165, 167, 169
solstice ceremony (Hopi), 46
Soyal ceremony (Hopi), 46
Spaulding, Albert, 217
stabilization phase, 178
Staley, Greg, 83
statuses, 16, 45-48
status reflected in burial data, 46-48
Steward, Julian H., 6-7, 8, 144, 145, 219, 220, 222
storage rooms, 29-30, 34, 79-80. See also rooms
style (as test implication), 35, 36, 41, 57, 79-80, 81-82, 172
subclan, 218

task unit, 15, 28-33
Taylor, Walter W., 1, 2, 5, 6
temporal change, 37, 82
test implications, 23-27, 30-33, 35-37, 38-39, 43-45, 79-80, 81-83, 150
Thompson, Raymond H., 174
Three-C site, 62, 65
"Time-Space Revolution," 5
Titiev, Mischa, 144, 186, 195, 218
tower kivas, Chaco Canyon, 68
traits, 5-6, 17, 52, 192
Tsegi Canyon, physiography, 145-47
Tsegi Phase: dates, 141; population, 152, 164; room types, 153-57; settlement pattern, 153
Turner, C. G., 138
typology, 53

Una Vida, 64, 65, 67, 72
U.S. National Park Service, 83, 86, 174
uxorilocal residence, 13, 37-42, 47, 54-55, 57, 79-80, 164

village layout, 34
virilocal residence, 39, 41, 42, 54
Vivian, Pat, 83
Vivian, R. Gordon, 60, 69, 83
Vivian, R. Gwinn, 198-99

water control systems, Anasazi area, 77; Chaco Canyon, 69-74, dating, 75
White Dog Phase: dating, 94; site locations, 95-97; types of sites, 98-103
Wijiji, 67

Zuni, 2, 4, 55, 204-05